George Cooper Lewis

The Soldier's Companion

Containing an abridgement of Hardee's infantry tactics; with the heavy infantry and rifle manuals, skirmish drill and bayonet exercise, field fortification, picket and outpost duty, with various regulations, forms, &c.

George Cooper Lewis

The Soldier's Companion
Containing an abridgement of Hardee's infantry tactics; with the heavy infantry and rifle manuals, skirmish drill and bayonet exercise, field fortification, picket and outpost duty, with various regulations, forms, &c.

ISBN/EAN: 9783337309329

Printed in Europe, USA, Canada, Australia, Japan

Cover: Foto ©ninafisch / pixelio.de

More available books at **www.hansebooks.com**

THE SOLDIER'S COMPANION:

CONTAINING

AN ABRIDGEMENT OF HARDEE'S INFANTRY TACTICS;

WITH THE

HEAVY INFANTRY AND RIFLE MANUALS,

SKIRMISH DRILL AND BAYONET EXERCISE, FIELD FORTIFICATION,

PICKET AND OUTPOST DUTY,

WITH VARIOUS REGULATIONS, FORMS, &C., THAT WILL BE FOUND USEFUL TO THE SOLDIER IN CAMP AND ON THE MARCH;

WITH AN APPENDIX CONTAINING

FANCY MOVEMENTS FOR VOLUNTEER COMPANIES,

UNIFORM AND DRESS OF THE ARMY, &C.

By Capt. GEO. C. LEWIS,

PROVISIONAL ARMY OF THE CONFEDERATE STATES.

RALEIGH, N. C.:
JOHN SPELMAN, PRINTER, OFFICE STATE JOURNAL.
1863.

TO THE
OFFICERS AND SOLDIERS
OF THE
NORTH CAROLINA TROOPS,

THIS LITTLE VOLUME IS AFFECTIONATELY AND RESPECTFULLY
INSCRIBED.

PREFACE.

The following pages of this little volume have been prepared and compiled by the undersigned, with the view of supplying what he believes to be an important want of the Officers and Soldiers, constituting the army of the Confederate States. It embraces an abridgment of HARDEE'S INFANTRY TACTICS, with the Heavy Infantry and Rifle Manuals, adapted to the use of either the Percussion Musket or the Enfield Rifle; also the Skirmish Drill and Bayonet Exercise, and a Synopsis of FIELD FORTIFICATION, PICKET and OUTPOST DUTY, and the Regulations as to Parades, Reviews, Inspections, Guard-mountings, &c.

It contains many suggestions that the practical soldier needs in camp and on the march, with various forms that are essentially necessary in a work of this kind, such as guard-reports, officers and soldiers, pay accounts, furloughs, leaves of absence, &c.

It has been the object of the compiler, in the preparation of this work, to embrace as much as possible in the smallest limit, as he knows from experience how inconvenient it is, in an active campaign, for an officer or soldier to be lugging around several works, when all that he needs might easily be combined in one.

PREFACE.

Under the head of FIELD FORTIFICATION, the author has introduced only so much as will enable the inexperienced soldier, in case of necessity, to throw up temporary breastworks for the protection of his men, or to enable them the better to hold some important point to which they may have been assigned. In a war like the one at present waged between the Confederate and United States, where there is such an extented frontier, it is very essential that every soldier, and especially every officer, should know something of field fortification.

During the winter campaign of 1861 and 1862, on the Potomac, and more recently when the City of Richmond was besciged by the enemy, the compiler saw many instances where young and inexperienced officers, were by force of circumstances, placed in positions that rendered it exceedingly necessary that they should have a knowledge of entrenching and erecting temporary breastworks.

In the appendix will be found the regulations as prescribed by the War Department for the dress and uniform of the army; also, some movements that are intended principally for volunteer companies in times of peace on their public parades. They were translated from a French work written by M. DuPre' and were used by the compiler previous to the war.

The undersigned presents this little volume to his fellow soldiers, with the knowledge that it contains many deficiencies, but assures them that none but official works and those most in repute have been consulted in the selection of its contents.

It was prepared during the long weary hours when the author was confined to his room from disease contracted in camp, and was written partially to relieve the monotony of the sick-room, and with the hope that though prevented at that time from being in active service, he still might do something to aid the glorious cause for which our brave people are so gallantly struggling; and should this work be the means of imparting to a brother soldier one item of information that he otherwise would not have known, the author will feel amply rewarded for his trouble.

GEO. C. LEWIS.

RALEIGH, N. C., January, 1863.

INTRODUCTION.

DIRECTIONS FOR CONDUCTING DRILLS.

A good method of instruction in military discipline, should exclude everything that is unnatural or not applicable to actual military service in action. If anything be admitted at any time in the parades of show, mounting guard, or the like, it should be taught separately, and after the principles of a rational discipline are well established.

It is too much the practice to commit the charge of the elementary drills to non-commissioned officers, by which many great evils are produced. No officer can expect to command a company, much less a regiment, (to which every officer should through merit aspire,) unless he has had practical experience; and in no circumstances can an officer so soon acquire the habit of command, or learn the mode of instruction and the effect of discipline, as by personally conducting the drill of his men. By devolving these first duties on non-commissioned officers, the commissioned officers remain ignorant and timid; and the chance of finding non-commissioned officers who can clearly comprehend and explain the principles of a good discipline, is not one in twenty; from which cause it is twenty to one that the recruits are imperfectly or erroneously taught.

He, therefore, who has the charge of a drill, or who teaches others, should not be himself ignorant; nor should he be offended at the ignorance of those who never had an opportunity to learn—he should be patient, but firm; generous, but without relaxing from the strictness of duty; he should command his own temper, in order to secure respect; and he should never be tired of rendering what he teaches intelligible. Every word should be explained, and a single explanation to those whom he is to teach, will not be sufficient—every man in the drill should understand every word that is used, and the use of every motion and movement he makes; and personal actions should be used as examples wherever practicable; so that whenever a word is used, or a movement commanded, not only the word shall be familiar to the ear by repeated use and illustration, but the movement itself, by frequent practice, familiar to the eye.

All drills should, therefore, be superintended or conducted by a commissioned officer, who should always keep in mind, that discipline is as necessary for him who teaches, as for those that are taught. He should, therefore, be careful that he acts personally according to the manner he teaches, and that his own motions conform to the principles he gives; he should keep in mind that the soldier very soon discovers the capacity of the officer; and that unless the officer possesses skill himself, he cannot expect the soldiers to confide in him, nor to respect him; they may be made to fear his power, but the confiidence which is most precious to a good officer, is that which arises out of the voluntary esteem and respect, produced by the generosity of his conduct and the skill which he manifests in the discharge of his duty; when he treats those over whom he is placed, as men, whose hapiness and credit he studies, rather than as slaves over whom he has the right to tyranise. The celebrated General Lloyd, speaking of the German discipline, reprobates its savage character by observing: "that blows may make a man a coward, but never made a hero."

The instructor of a drill should be of a cheerful, but firm disposition; he must have discernment and good sense to know that as the habits of persons newly entering upon military exercises have been formed differently, that they cannot be expected to change their habits suddenly, or embrace habits at once different from those they have been accustomed to.

It should be explained that the first lessons of the *position—the facings*—the *step* and *wheeling*, are only like the first lessons in reading and writing; that it is requisite to practice them often, and to perform them with the greatest exactness in the first beginnings, in order to carry the same correctness and exactness into more enlarged practice.

That the duties of a company are the same as the duties of a regiment and of a whole army---that the whole of the military art consists in *marching, facing* and *wheeling*, according to the rules which experience has proved to be the most effective; and that without perfection in these particulars, arms would be of little or no use, opposed to troops who are well disciplined,

INTRODUCTION.

These instructions should be introduced in familiar and persuasive language, as advice, rather than command; always with good temper and kindness---*abuse never !!*

The advantages and security of a good discipline should be constantly brought into view; and the necessity of marching correctly ever oqual spaces in equal times, should be hinted at as being the means by which the whole power and strength of a line or column is brought to bear at the same instant.

No opportunity should be lost, that is practicable, to present to the eye of the soldier the manner of any operation which he is to perform. A well disciplined man presented in front, whose actions may accord with the command, and who may be seen by the whole of the drill, will have an excellent effect in producing a ready understanding, It is much easier to imitate what is seen, than to execute what is barely described. The variety of habits, and the different signification of the same word in the understanding of different persons, render verbal descriptions generally imperfect. There can be no mistake by the eye, and every word should be explained which may not be otherwise understood.

The Compiler of this work, would particularly and earnestly suggest that officers be careful in their treatment of those under their command. In some armies, the mind and feelings of the man are never studied; his passions are never called forth, except to excite terror and hatred of his officers; and there have been men who have held, that the army should be more afraid of their own General than of the enemy! But we must reprobate such ignorance of human nature, "He who attempts to govern by the lash," said Timour "knows not how to govern."---There is no incompatibility in exciting the generous affections of the soldier, with the principles of discipline. Cruelty may make cowards and deserters, but in never made a good, faithful, honorable soldier.

Officers have only to convince soldiers that they understand their own duties, and the soldiers will respect them; officers have only to demonstrate that they are soldiers' friends, and they may lead them to the cannon's mouth, or in the face of the death dealing bullet, with an enthusiasm that never fails to triumph when regulated by discipline. The triumphs of the French armies, in which no man is ever beaten with a cane, and in which whipping never was known, clearly evince the futile barbarity of military punishments, by the lash, or by any species of degrading torture. The humblest bred man that fills the ranks of an army, is as susceptible of the sentiment of glory, and honor, and shame, as the proudest captain that ever carried a plume.

The principle of discipline most prevalent is terror, cruelty and degradation---the soldier is treated as an outcast of the earth, and however different he may be when he enters the ranks, the manner of his treatment too often transforms him into the miserable slave which he is presupposed to be.

This treatment is inconsistent with reason and humanity. Officers should remember that the great majority of the privates who constitute the Confederate army, and who are so gallantly exposing themselves to the rigors and hardships of a soldier's life---in the defence of our country, are not of the material that compose other armies, and that in thousands of cases, they are the cherished and loved idol of some household circle.

Besides, it is not necessary to discipline or subordination. A generous, affectionate, and cherishing courtesy, will overcome the most hardened villian, and where it fails, cruelty or barbarity will never succeed.

The line between familiarity and kind conduct, is easily drawn by men of sense, conscious of themselves. None but *incompetent men* will treat a soldier in the ranks with contempt or cruelty. On the parade, good temper and good manners should never be absent. Haughtiness is incompatible with true dignity; openness, generosity and firmness, constitute the true deportment which inspires respect without exciting fear; which commands with decision, and is obeyed implicitly, and which is inflexible only in the discharge of duty.

In the manner of command, much depends upon the clearness and distinctness of the utterance of him who teaches. At drill, he must not be sparing of explanation, but on parade he gives no instruction; he commands only, and sees that what he orders, be executed promptly and properly.

It is observed by the British General Dundas, with a degree of truth that cannot be too strongly impressed upon the mind of every man who holds a military commission— "That the complete instruction of an officer enlarges with his situation and at last takes in the whole circle of military science. But an officer who cannot thoroughly discipline and exercise the body entrusted to his command, large or small, is not fit, in time of service, to lead it against an enemy; he cannot be cool and collected in time of danger; he cannot profit by circumstances, from his inability to comprehend what is doing by the enemy, or what is necessary to be done against them, to direct it properly. The fate of many depend on his well or ill acquitting himself of his duty; for it is not sufficient to advance with bravery; it is requisite to possess that degree of intelligence, which should distinguish every officer, according to his station. Soldiers will not act with spirit or animation, when they have *no reliance on he capacity of those who conduct them.*"

The intention of all discipline is to supp.y a kind of artificial instinct, and to make this uniform throughout the whole mass of an army, so that whenever an operation is required to be performed by an army, no more is requisite than to assign stations to the several divisions, and appoint the time when the movements commence, or when the concert of operations should meet and produce the effect required.

To discipline men well, there must be a familiar, comprehensible, and rational method.

The more simple it is, the more easily it is understood, the better will it be executed.

To this end, the language must be that of the science, and it must be taught and explained with clearness.

There must be nothing unnecessary or unnatural in the system. Every operation and movement should be executed exactly as required, in the shortest period of time, and occupying the least possible space in which it can be accomplished.

As all discipline is intended for action, and not for parade, discipline should be directed to inculcate that which is adapted to action only, as fundamental, and to make all that appertains to parade, secondary—action must never be lost sight of in teaching discipline.

It may be proper to remark here, for the information of those who are not already conversant in the subject, that many of the words of instruction, direction, and precaution, employed in the drill, cease to be employed when the battalion is completed in its discipline. Numerous words and commands are used in the elementary instruction, which are no longer required to be employed, though their application and practical use are never to be omitted. These directions cannot be made too familiar.

Officers should remember that there are three kinds of *commands*, viz:

The command of *caution*, which is *attention*.

The *preparatory command*, which indicates the movement which is to be executed.

The command of *execution*, such as *march* or *halt*, or in the manual of arms, the part of command which causes an execution.

The tone of command should be animated, distinct, and of a loudness proportioned to the number of men under instruction.

The command *attention*, is pronounced at the top of the voice, dwelling on the last syllable.

The command of *execution* will be pronounced in a tone firm and brief.

THE SOLDIER'S COMPANION.

PART FIRST

Position of the Soldier and Squad Drill.

The correct position of the soldier, and the drill of the squad, being the ground work of proficiency in all military exercises, it is exceedingly necessary that the men should fix and keep their attention upon the instructor---who should be as clear and concise as possible in his instructions and explanations, and should endeavor to habituate himself and men, by precept and example, to that composure and presence of mind which is so essentially requisite in drilling and instructing recruits.

Great care should be taken in learning them the correct position at first, as considerable difficulty is sometimes experienced in their further progress when they have been incorrectly taught in the beginning,

In most cases it is impracticable to instruct recruits in squads of less than four or eight men at a time.

Position of the Soldier.

1. Heels on the same line and as close together as the conformation of the man will permit, the feet turned out equally and forming with each other something less than

a right angle; knees straight without stiffness; body erect on the hips, inclining a little forward; shoulders square and falling equally; arms hanging naturally; elbows near the body; palms of the hands turned a little to the front, the little fingers behind the seam of the pantaloons; head erect and square to the front, without constraint; chin a little drawn in and near the stock without covering it; eyes fixed straight to the front and striking the ground at about fifteen paces.

2. The instructor having given the recruit the position of the soldier without arms, will now teach him the turning of the head and eyes; he will command:

1. *Eyes*---Right. 2. Front.

3. At the word *right*, the recruit will turn the head gently to the right, so as to bring the inner corner of the left eye in a line with the centre of the body, the eye fixed on the line of the eyes of the men in, or supposed to be in the same rank. At the word *front*, resume the direct position.

4. The movement of *eyes*---Left will be executed by inverse means.

5. The instructor will take care that the movement of the head does not derange the squareness of the shoulders.

Rest.

6. At the command rest, stand at ease.

7. When the instructor wishes to cause a resumption of the habitual position, he will command:

POSITION OF THE SOLDIER.

1. *Attention.* 2. SQUAD.

8. At the first word, the recruit will fix his attention: at the second, he will resume the prescribed position and steadiness.

Facings.

1. *Squad.* 2. *Right* (or *left*)---FACE.

9. At the second command, raise the right foot slightly, turn to the right (or left,) on the left heel, raising the toe a little, and then replace the right heel, by the side of the left, and on the same line.

10. At the command *front*, turn on the left heel so as to regain the first position, and replace the right heel by the side of the left.

11. To full face to the rear (or front), the command will be given:

1. *Squad.* 2. *About*---FACE.

12. At the word *about*, turn on the left heel, bring the left toe to the front, carry the right foot to the rear, the hollow opposite to and full three inches from the left heel, the feet square to each other.

13. At the word *face*, turn on both heels, raise the toes a little, extend the thighs and face to the rear, bringing, at the same time, the right heel by the side of the left.

14. The instructor will take care that these motions do not derange the position of the body.

The Direct Step

15. The direct step, or pace, in common time, is *twenty eight inches*, reckoning from heel to heel and at the rate of ninety a minute.

16. The instructor wishing to instruct the recruit in the principles of this step, will place himself six or eight paces in front and facing him. He will then execute the step slowly, by way of illustration, and command:

1. *Squad forward.* 2. *Common time.* 3. MARCH.

17. At the first command, feel the weight of the body on the right leg, without bending the left knee.

18. At the command *march*, step off with the left foot, carrying it straight forward twenty-eight inches from the right, the sole near the ground, the ham extended, the toe a little depressed, and, as also the knee, slightly turned out; at the same time, throw the weight of the body forward, and plant flat the left foot, without shock, precisely at the distance where it finds itself from the right, when the weight of the body is brought forward, the whole of which will now rest on the advanced foot. Next, in like manner, advance the right foot and plant it as above, the heel twenty-eight inches from the heel of the left foot, and thus continue to march, without crossing the legs, or striking the one against the other, without turning the shoulders, and preserving always the face direct to the front.

19. The instructor wishing the squad to halt, will command: .

1. *Squad.* 2. HALT.

20. At the command *halt*, which will be given at the instant either foot is coming to the ground, the foot in the

rear will be brought up, and planted by the side of the other, without shock.

The Quick-Step.

21. The principles of the step in quick time are the same as for common time, but its swiftness is at the rate of one hundred and ten steps per minute. As soon as the recruit has the required steadiness, and has become established in the manual of arms, and in the mechanism of the step i common time, he will be practiced only in quick time, the double quick, and the run. When the time is not indicated in the preparatory command, the squad will always move in quick time.

22. The instructor wishing to march in quick time, will command:

1. *Squad, forward.* 2. MARCH.

23. At the command *march*, the squad will step off and continue to march in quick time.

The Double Quick-Step.

24. The length of the double quick-step is thirty-three inches, and its swiftness at the rate of one hundred and sixty-five steps per minute.

25. The instructor wishing to teach the recruit the principles of this step, will command:

1. *Double quick-step.* 2. MARCH.

26. At the first command, raise the hands to a level with the hips, the hands closed, the nails towards the body, the elbows to the rear.

27. At the second command, raise to the front the left leg bent to its greatest elevation, the part of the leg between the knee and instep vertical, the toe depressed; replace the foot in its former position; execute with the right leg what has just been prescribed for the left, and continue the alternate movement of the legs until the command:

1. *Squad.* 2. HALT.

28. At the command *halt*, bring the foot which is raised by the side of the other, drop the hands to the side, and resume the position of the soldier.

29. The instructor should place himself six or eight paces from, and facing the recruit, and indicate the cadence by the commands *one* and *two*, given alternately, as each foot is brought to the ground.

30. The recruit being sufficiently established in the principles of this step, the instructor will command:

1. *Squad, forward.* 2. *Double quick.* 3. MARCH.

31. At the first command, throw the weight of the body on the right leg.

32. At the second, place the arms as indicated in No. 26.

33. At the third, carry forward the left foot, the leg slightly bent, the knee raised, plant the left foot, toe first, thirty-three inches from the right, and with the right foot execute what has just been prescribed for the left. This alternate movement of the legs will take place by throwing the weight of the body on the foot that is planted, and by allowing a natural oscillatory motion of the arms.

24. The instructor should caution the recruit to breathe as much as possible through the nose, keeping the mouth closed, as it will enable him to go a much longer distance, without experiencing the fatigue that he otherwise would.

The Run.

35. The recruits will also be exercised in running.
36. The principles are the same as for the double quick step, the only difference consisting in a greater degree of swiftness.

Alignments.

37. The instructor will at first teach the recruits to align themselves man by man, in order the better to make them comprehend the principles of alignment; to this end he will command the two men on the right flank to march to the front, and having aligned them, he will cause the remainder of the squad to move up, as they may be successively called, each by his number, and align themselves successively on the line of the first two men.

38. Each recruit, as designated by his number, will turn the head and eyes to the right as prescribed in No. 3, and will march in *quick time two paces forward*, shortening the last so as to find himself about six inches behind the new alignment, which he ought never to pass; he will next move up steadily by steps of two or three inches, the thighs extended, to the side of the man next to him on the alignment, so that, without deranging the head, the

line of the eyes, or that of the shoulders, he may find himself in the exact line of his neighbor, whose elbow he will lightly touch without opening his own.

39. The instructor seeing the rank well aligned, will command:

FRONT.

40. At this, the recruits will turn their eyes to the front and remain firm.

41. Alignments to the left will be executed on the same principles.

42. When the recruits shall have learned to align themselves correctly, the instructor will cause the entire rank to align itself at once by the command:

Right (or *left*) DRESS.

43. At this, the rank, except the two men placed in advance as a basis of alignment, will move up in *quick time*, and place themselves on the new line as prescribed in No. 38.

44. The instructor will carefully observe that the principles are followed, and will place himself on the flank that has served as a basis, to see that the alignment is correct.

45. The instructor seeing the rank aligned, will command:

FRONT.

46. Alignments to the rear will be executed on the same principles, the recruits stepping back a little beyond the

line, and then dressing up according to the principles prescribed in No. 38, the instructor commanding:

1. *Right* (or *left*) *backward*—DRESS.

To March to the Front.

47. The rank being correctly aligned, when the instructor shall wish to cause it to march to the front, he will place a well instructed man on the right or left, according to the side on which he may wish the guide to be, and command:

1. *Squad, forward.* 2. *Guide right* (or *left.*) 3. MARCH.

48. At the command *march*, the rank will step off smartly with the left foot; the guide will take care to march straight to the front, keeping his shoulder in a square with that line.

49. The men should touch lightly the elbow towards the side of the guide, be careful not to open out the left elbow nor the right arm, yield to the pressure coming from the side of the guide, and resist that coming from the opposite side.

50. They should keep the head direct to the front, no matter on which side the guide may be, and if found before or behind the alignment, the man in fault must correct himself by shortening or lengthening the step, by degrees, almost insensible.

51. The instructor will labor to cause the recruits to

comprehend that the alignment can only be preserved, in marching, but by the regularity of the step, the touch of the elbow, and the maintainance of the shoulders in a square with the line of direction.

52. The squad being in march, the instructor wishing to march them obliquely, will command:

1. *Right* (or *left*) *oblique.* 2. MARCH.

53. At the second command, each man will make a half face to the right (or left) and will then march straight forward in the new direction. As the men no longer touch elbows, they should glance along the shoulders of the nearest files towards the side to which they are obliquing, and should regulate their steps so that the shoulders shall always be behind that of their next neighbor on that side, and that his head shall conceal the heads of the other men in the rank.

54. The men should preserve the same length of pace and the same degree of obliquity.

55. The instructor wishing to resume the primitive direction, will command:

1. *Forward.* 2. MARCH.

56. At the second command, each man will make a half face to the left (or right) and all will then march straight to the front, as in the direct march.

57. The squad being at a halt, if the instructor should wish to march it in the back step, he will command:

1. *Squad backward.* 2. *Guide right* (or *left.*) 3. MARCH.

58. At the command *march*, the recruit will step off

smartly with the left foot fourteen inches to the rear, reckoning from heel to heel, and so on with the feet in succession, till the command *halt*, which will always be preceded by the caution, *Squad*.

59. The men will halt promptly at this command and bring the foot in front by the side of the other.

60. This step will always be executed in quick time.

To Mark Time.

61. The squad marching in the direct step in common or quick time, the instructor will command:

1. *Mark time.* 2. MARCH.

62. At the command *march*, which will be given at the instant either foot is coming to the ground, make a semblance of marching, by advancing first one foot and then the other, always bringing back the advanced foot and placing its heel by the side of the heel of the other.

To Change Step.

63. The squad being in march, the instructor will command:

1. *Change step.* 2. MARCH.

64. At the second command, which will be given at the instant either foot is coming to the ground, bring up quickly the foot in the rear to the side of that just come to the ground, and step off with the latter.

65. The squad marching in common, quick or double quick time, and the instructor wishing to face it about, will command:

1. *Squad, right about.* 2. MARCH.

66. At the command *march*, which will be given the instant the left foot is coming to the ground, bring this foot to the ground, and turning on it, face to the rear, then place the right foot in the new direction, and step off with the left foot.

67. If the squad be marching and the instructor wishes to bring it to a halt and faced to the rear, he will command:

1. *Squad, right about.* 2. HALT.

68. At the command *halt*, which will be given as the left foot is coming to the ground, bring this foot to the ground, and turning on it face to the rear, then bring the right foot to the side of the left.

69. The squad being at a halt, the instructor wishing to move it to the right on the same line, will command:

1. *Side step to the right.* 2. MARCH.

70. At the second command, each man will glance his eyes to the right, and at the same time carry his right foot about ten inches to the right, and instantly bring up his left foot, and so on, the whole with perfect precision of time.

71. The shoulders must be kept square to the front, and

each man perceptibly halting, when he has closed on the fixed point, or on the man next to him.

72. When the instructor shall wish the squad to halt, he will command:

1. *Squad.* 2. HALT.

73. At the command *halt*, bring up the left foot to the side of the right, and stand firm.

74. To change the position by *side step to the left* it will be executed on the same principles by inverse means.

To March by the Flank.

75. The rank being at a halt and correctly alligned, the instructor will command:

Count twos.

6. At this command the men count from right to left, pronouncing in a loud and distinct voice, in the same tone, and without turning the head, *one, two*, according to the place which he occupies.

77. This being accomplished, the instructor will command:

1. *Squad, right*—FACE. 2. *Forward.* 3. MARCH.

78. At the command *face*, the squad will face to the right; the even numbered men after facing to the right, will step quickly to the side of the odd numbered men, the latter standing fast, so that when the movement is executed, the men will be formed into files of two abreast·

79. At the command march, the squad will step off smartly with the left foot; the files keeping aligned and preserving their intervals.

80. To march by the left flank, will be executed by the same command, substituting the word *left* for *right*, and by inverse means; in this case the even numbered men after facing to the left will stand fast, and the odd number will place themselves on their left.

81. The instructor should place himself five or six paces on the flank of the rank marching in file, to watch over the execution of the principles prescribed. He will also, sometimes place himself in its rear, halt and suffer it to pass fifteen or twenty paces, the better to see whether the men cover each other accurately.

82. When he wishes to halt the rank, marching by the flank, he will command:

1. *Squad.* 2. Halt. 3. Front.

83. At the second command, the rank will halt, and afterward no man will stir, although he may have lost his distance.

84. At the third command, each man will front by facing to the left, if marching by the right flank, and by a face to the right, if marching by the left flank.

85. The rear rank men will at the same time move quickly into their places, so as to form the squad again into one rank.

86. To change direction by file, the instructor will command:

1. *By file left* (or *right*) 2. March.

87. At the command *march*, the first file will change direction to the left (or right) in describing a small arc of a

circle, and will then march straight forward; the two men of this file in wheeling will keep up the touch of the elbows, and the man on the side to which the wheel is made, will shorten the first three or four steps. Each file will come successively to wheel on the same spot where that which preceded it wheeled.

88. To face by the right or left flank, in marching, the instructor will command:

1. *Squad, by the right* (or *left*) *flank.* 2. MARCH.

89. At the command *march*, which will be given a little before either foot comes to the ground, the recruit will turn the body, plant the foot that is raised in the new direction, and step off with the other foot, without altering the cadence of the step; the men will double or undouble rapidly.

90. If in facing by the right or left flank, the squad should face to the rear, the men will come into one rank agreeably to the principles as indicated in Nos. 84 and 85. Observe that the men who are in the rear always move up to form into single rank, and in such manner as never to invert the order of the numbers in the rank.

91. If, when the squad has been faced to the rear, the instructor should cause it to face by the left flank, it is the even numbers who will double by moving to the left of the odd numbers; but if by the right flank, it is the odd numbers who will double to the right of the even numbers.

92. Should the instructor wish the men to march in one rank, he will caution them not to double files.

Wheelings.

93. Wheelings are of two kinds; from halts or on fixed pivots, and in march or on movable pivots.

94. Wheeling on a fixed pivot takes place in passing a corps from the order in battle to the order in column, or from the latter to the former.

95. Wheels in marching, take place in changes of direction in column, as often as this movement is executed to the side opposite to the guide.

96. In wheels from a halt, the pivot-man only turns in his place without advancing or receding.

97. In the wheels in marching, the pivot-man takes steps of nine or eleven inches, according as the squad is marching in quick or double quick time, so as to clear the wheeling point before the next subdivision arrives on the same ground, which is necessary in order that the succeeding subdivisions may not lose their distances by being delayed.

98. The man on the wheeling flank will take the full step of twenty-eight inches, or thirty-three inches, according to the gait.

Wheeling from a Halt, or on a Fixed Pivot.

99. The rank being at a halt, the instructor will place a well instructed man on the wheeling flank to conduct it, and then command:

 1. *By squad, right wheel.* 2. MARCH.

100. At the command *march*, the rank will step off with the left foot, turning at the same time the head a little to

the left, the eyes fixed on the line of the eyes of the men to the left; the pivot man will merely mark time in gradually turning his body, in order to conform himself to the movement of the marching flank; the man who conducts this flank will take steps of twenty-eight inches, and from the first step, advance a little the left shoulder, cast his eyes from time to time along the rank, and feel constantly the elbow of the next man lightly, but never push him.

101. The other men will feel lightly the elbow of the next man, towards the pivot, resist pressure coming from the opposite side, and each will conform himself to the marching flank, shortening his step according to his approximation to the pivot.

102. The instructor will make the rank wheel round the circle once or twice before halting, in order to cause the principles to be better understood, and he will be watchful that the centre does not break.

103. The wheel to the left will be executed according to the same principles.

104. When the instructor shall wish to arrest the wheel, he will command:

1. *Squad.* 2. HALT.

105. At the second command the rank will halt and no man stir. The instructor going to the flank opposite the pivot, will place the two outer men of that flank in the direction he may wish to give to the rank, without, however, displacing the pivot, who will conform the line of his shoulders to this direction.

106. The instructor will take care to have between these two men and the pivot, only the space necessary to contain the other men. He will then command:

1. *Left* (or *right*)—Dress.

107. At this the rank will place itself on the allignment of the two men established as a basis in conformity with principles prescribed in No. 38.

108. The instructor will next command *Front*, which will be executed as prescribed in No. 39.

Wheeling in Marching, or on a Movable Pivot.

109. The rank being in march, and the instructor wishing to change the direction to the reverse flank, (to the side opposite to the guide or pivot flank) he will command:

1. *Right* (or *left*) *wheel*. 2. March.

110. The first command will be given when the rank is yet *four* paces from the wheeling point.

111. At the command *march*, the wheel will be executed in the same manner as from a halt, except that the touch of the elbow will remain towards the marching flank (or side of the guide) instead of the actual pivot; that the pivot man, instead of merely turning in his place, will conform himself to the movement of the marching flank, feel lightly the elbow of the next man, take steps of full nine inches, and thus gain ground forward in describing a small curve, to clear the point of wheel. The middle of the rank will bend slightly to the rear. As soon as the movement shall commence, the man who conducts the marching flank will cast his eyes on the ground over which he will have to pass.

112. The wheel being ended, the instructor will command :

1. *Forward.* 2. MARCH.

113. The first command will be pronounced when *four* paces are yet required to complete the change of direction.

114. At the command *march*, which will be given at the instant of completing the wheel, the man who conducts the marching flank will direct himself straight forward; the pivot man and all the rank will retake the step of twenty-eight inches, and bring the head direct to the front.

Turning.

115. The change of direction to the side of the guide, in marching, will be executed as follows: The instructor will command:

1. *Left (or right) turn.* 2. MARCH.

116. The first command will be given when the rank is yet *four* paces from the turning point.

117. At the command *march*, to be pronounced at the instant the rank ought to turn, the guide will face to the left (or right) in marching, and move forward in the new direction without slackening or quickening the cadence, and without shortening or lengthening the step. The whole rank will promptly conform itself to the new direction, to effect which, each man will advance the shoulder opposite the guide, take the double quick step, to carry himself in the new direction, turn the head and eyes to the side of the guide, and retake the touch of the elbow on that side in placing himself on the allignment of the guide, from

whom he will take the step, and then resume the direct position of the head. Each man will thus arrive successively on the allignment.

118. When the recruits comprehend and execute well, in quick-time, the wheels, at a halt and in marching, and the change of direction to the side of the guide, the instructor will cause the same movements to be executed in double quick time.

Manual of Arms for Heavy Infantry.

119. The manual of arms will be taught to four men, placed at first in one rank, elbow to elbow, and afterwards in two ranks.

120. Each command will be executed in one *time*, (or pause) and this time will be divided into motions.

121. The rate or swiftness of each motion, except the motions relative to the cartrige, to the rammer and to the fixing and unfixing of the bayonet, is fixed at the ninetieth part of a minute; but the motions here excepted should be executed with promptness and regularity.

122. As soon as the recruits shall well comprehend the positions of the several motions, they will be taught to execute the time without resting on the motions.

123. Recruits are frequently seen with natural defects in the conformation of the shoulders, breast, and hips.— These the instructor will endeavor to correct in the lessons without arms, and afterwards by steady endeavors, so that the appearances of the pieces in the same line may be uniform, and this without constraint to the men.

Principles of Shouldered Arms.

124. The recruit being placed in the position of the soldier, the instructor will cause him to seize the piece in the left hand, the arm but a very little bent, the elbow back, near the body, the palm of the hand passing on the outer edge of the butt on the upper joints of the fingers, (the inner edge on the lower joints, and the ends inside,) the heel of the butt between the middle and forefingers, the thumb on the front screws of the butt plate, the remaining fingers under the butt, the butt more or less kept back, according to the conformation of the man, so that the piece seen from the front (or side) shall appear perpendicular, and also that the movement of the thigh, in marching, may not raise it, or cause it waver; the stock below the tail band resting against the hollow of the shoulder, just within the joint, the right arm hanging naturally as in the position of the soldier.

125. The instructor, before proceeding to drill the recruit in the manual will cause to be repeated, the movements of *eyes right*, *left* and *front* and the *facings*.

126. The manual of arms will be taught in the following progression: The instructor will command:

Present---ARMS.

One time and two motions.

127. (*First motion.*) Turn the piece with the left hand, the lock out, seize the small of the stock at the same time with the right hand, the piece perpendicular and detached from the shoulder, the left hand remaining under the butt.

128. (*Second motion.*) Complete the turning inwards of the piece so as to bring it erect before the centre of the

body, the rammar to the front, the right hand under and against the guard; seize it smartly at the same time with the left hand above the lock, the thumb extended along the barrel and on the stock, the forearm resting on the body without constraint, and the hand at the hight of the elbow.

Shoulder---Arms.

One time and two motions.

129. (*First motion.*) Turn the piece with the right hand, the barrel out, (with the thumb on the S plate, and the forefinger against the cock,) raise and support it against the left shoulder with the right hand, drop the left hand under the butt, the right hand resting on, without grasping the small of the stock.

130. (*Second motion.*) Drop quickly the right hand into its position.

Order---Arms.

One time and two motions

131. (*First motion.*) Drop the piece smartly by extending the left arm, seize it at the same time with the right hand above and near the tail band; (without the least pause,) quit the hold of the left hand, and carry the piece opposite the right shoulder, the rammer in front, the little finger behind the barrel, the right hand supported against the hip, the butt three inches from the ground, the piece erect, the left hand hanging by the side.

132. (*Second motion.*) Let the piece slip through the right hand, without shock, to the ground and take the following position:

Position of Order Arms.

133. The hand low, the barrel between the thumb and forefinger, extended along the stock; the other fingers extended and joined; the muzzle about two inches from the right shoulder; the rammer in front: the toe (or beak) of the butt, against, and in a line with the toe of the right foot; the barrel perpendicular.

134. The instructor will see the recruit is well established in the position of *order arms*, and then command:

Shoulder—ARMS.

One time and two motions.

135. (*First motion.*) Raise the piece smartly with the right hand, carry it against the left shoulder, so as to bring the barrel to the front, place, at the same time, the left hand under the butt, and slip the right hand down to the hammer.

136. (*Second motion.*) Let fall smartly the right hand into position.

Support—ARMS.

One time and three motions.

137. (*First motion.*) With the right hand, seize the small of the stock four inches below the lock, raising a little but not turning the piece.

138. (*Second motion.*) Take the left hand from the butt, extend the left forearm upward, across the body, under the cock, the hand flat on the right breast.

139. (*Third motion.*) Drop the right hand smartly into its position.

Shoulder (or *carry*)—Arms.

One time and three motions.

140. (*First motion.*) Carry quickly the right hand to the small of the stock.

141. (*Second motion.*) Place quickly the left hand under the butt, and at the same time, without any pause, let the right hand, with the fingers extended slip up under the cock of the piece, the cock resting on the forefinger between the middle and third joints, and the thumb extended along the S plate.*

142. (*Third motion.*) Let fall smartly the right hand into its position, and drop with the left, at the same time, the piece into the position of *shoulder arms*.

Unfix—Bayonet.

One time and three motions.

143. (*First motion.*) Drop the piece by a full extension of the left arm, seize it at the same time with the right hand above and near the tail band.

144. (*Second motion.*) Drop the piece with the right hand along the left thigh, seize it with the left hand above the right, lengthen out the left arm, rest the butt on the ground without shock, and carry at the same time the right hand to the bayonet; with the thumb turn the clasp

---

*This movement is somewhat different from that prescribed in other works, but it will be found that it causes uniformity and precision, and adds much more ease and grace in its execution, especially from a front view. It was used entirely by the lamented Col. C. C. Tew, Sup't. of the North Carolina Military Academy, at Hillsboro', N. C.

against the stop, seize the bayonet at the socket and shank, so that the lower end of the socket may be about an inch below the heel of the palm, and that in wresting off the bayonet, the thumb may be extended on the blade.

115. (*Third motion.*) Wrest off the bayonet, return it to the scabbard, place immediately the right little finger on the butt of the rammer, lower the left hand along the barrel, extending the arm, without depressing the shoulder.

Shoulder---Arms.

One time and three motions.

146. (*First motion.*) Raise the piece with the left hand along the left side, the hand at the height of the chin, the forearm touching the piece, the barrel to the front; drop at the same time the right hand to seize the piece a little above the small of the stock, the forefinger touching the cock, and the thumb on the S plate.

147. (*Second motion.*) Raise the piece with the right hand, drop the left and place it under the butt, support the piece with the right hand against the shoulder in the position of *shoulder arms*, the right hand resting on without grasping the piece.

148. (*Third motion.*) Let fall smartly the right hand into its position.

149. The instructor should be careful that in all movements where the hand is under the cock, as in the second motion above, that the fingers are extended and perfectly straight, the cock resting on the forefinger between the middle and third joints, and the thumb on the S plate.

Secure---ARMS.

One time and two motions.

150. (*First motion.*) Seize quickly the piece with the right hand, the thumb on the S plate, and the forefinger against the cock; at the same instant, detach the piece from the shoulder, the barrel to the front, seize it at the tail band with the left hand, the thumb extended on the rammer, the piece erect, opposite the shoulder the left elbow on the piece.

151. (*Second motion.*) Reverse the piece, pass it under the left arm the left hand remaining at the tail band, the thumb on the rammer, the little finger resting against the hip, and the right hand falling at the same time into its position.

Shoulder---ARMS.

One time and two motions.

152. (*First motion.*) Raise the piece with the left hand, (but not too suddenly lest the rammer should fly out,) seize the small of the stock with the right hand to support it against the shoulder, allowing the hand to assume the position as indicated in No. 141, quit the hold of the left hand and pass it quickly under the butt.

153. (*Second motion.*) Let fall smartly the right hand into its position; drop at the same time the piece into the position of *shoulder arms.*

Fix---BAYONET.

One time and three motions.

154. (*First motion.*) As in *unfix bayonet*, No. 143.
155. (*Second motion.*) As in *unfix bayonet*, No. 144,

except that the right hand will go to the scabbard, to seize the bayonet by the socket and shank, so that the lower (now upper) end of the socket shall extend about an inch above the heel of the palm.

156. (*Third motion.*) Draw the bayonet from the scabbard, carry it and fix it on the muzzle, turning the clasp towards the body with the right thumb; place immediately the little finger on the head of the rammer, lower the left hand along the barrel, extending the arm without depressing the shoulder.

Shoulder---ARMS.

One time and three motions.

157. (*First, Second and Third motions.*) As in *shoulder arms* from *unfix bayonet.*

Charge---BAYONET.

One time and two motions.

158. (*First motion.*) Make a half face to the right on the left heel, bring the left toe to the front, place at the same time the right foot behind and at right angles with the left, the hollow of the right foot opposite to and about three inches from the left heel; turn the piece with the left hand, lock outwards, and seize the small of the stock at the same time with the right hand, the piece perpendicular and detached from the shoulder; leaving the left hand under the butt.

159. (*Second motion.*) Bring down the piece with the right hand into the left, the latter seizing it a little in advance of the tail band, the barrel up, the left elbow near the body

the right hand supported against the hip, the point of the bayonet at the height of the eye.

160. The men of the rear rank will take care and not touch their file leaders with the points of their bayonets.

Shoulder—Arms.

One time and two motions.

161. (*First motion.*) Face to the front by turning on the left heel, bring up the right foot by the side of the left heel, at the same time spring up the piece with the right hand, to the left shoulder, and place the left hand under the butt, allowing at the same time the right hand to assume the position as indicated in No. 141.

162. (*Second motion.*) Let fall smartly the right hand into its position.

Trail—Arms.

One time and two motions.

163. (*First motion.*) As first motion of *order arms* No. 131.

164. (*Second motion.*) Incline a little the muzzle to the front, the butt to the rear, and about three inches from the ground, the right hand grasping the piece and supported at the hip.

165. Should the instructor wish to relieve the men when marching with arms trailed, he will command: *Change—* Trail, which will be executed in one motion, by raising the muzzle to the shoulder, passing the piece across the front of the body, trailing it with the left. At the command *Rechange—*Trail, raise the muzzle to the shoulder, pass the piece to the right hand and retake the position of *trail arms.*

Shoulder—Arms.

166. At the command *shoulder* raise the piece perpendicular in the right hand; at the command *arms* execute the two motions in the *shoulder arms*, from the position of *order arms*.

167. The instructor wishing to give the men repose in the position of *order arms*, will command:

Rest.

168. At this command, the men will no longer be required to preserve silence, or to remain steady in position. Or he may command:

1. *In place.* 2. Rest.

169. At the second command, the men will not be required to preserve silence or steadiness of position, but they must always keep one of their heels and their pieces on the allignment.

[*Remarks.*] (The instructor will be careful that the men do not squat or lie down, as it is exceedingly unmilitary and apt to make them careless and inattentive. The compiler of this work has often seen recruits stretched at full length on the ground. Young officers particularly, should be cautioned against allowing it.)

If the instructor wishes, he will command:

1. *Parade.* 2. Rest.

170. At the second command, the men will carry the right foot six inches in rear of the left heel, the left knee slightly bent, the body upright upon the right leg, the piece resting against the hollow of the right shoulder, the

hands crossed in front, the back of them outwards, the left hand uppermost, the eyes directed to the front.

171. To cause a resumption of the original position, the instructor will command:

1. *Attention* 2. SQUAD.

172. At the second command, the men will resume their correct position of *order arms*.

173. If the squad should be at the position of *support arms*, when the command *in place* or *parade rest* is given, the men will be regulated by the directions indicated in No. 169, 170 except they will bring up the right hand smartly to the small of the stock and seize it.

174. At the command *attention* they will resume the correct position of *support arms*.

1. *To Right Shoulder Shift* 2. ARMS. (*From a Shoulder Arms.*)

One time and two motions.

175. (*First motion.*) Turn the piece with the left hand, lock to the front, seize it at the same time with the right hand at the small of the stock.

176. (*Second motion.*) Carry the piece to the right shoulder, the lock plate upwards, the left hand still holding the butt, the muzzle elevated; place the right hand on the butt, the beak between the two first fingers, the other two fingers under the butt plate, and let fall the left hand by the side.

*Shoulder—*ARMS.

One time and two motions.

177. (*First motion.*) Raise the piece and extend the right arm, seize it with the left hand above the lock, carry

the piece against the left shoulder, turning the barrel to the front, (in turning place the thumb of the right hand on the S plate, fingers extended, cock resting on the forefinger as indicated in No. 141,) the right hand being at the small of the stock, place the left hand under the butt.

178. (*Second motion.*) Let the right hand fall by the side.

Arms—AT WILL.

One motion.

179. Carry the piece at pleasure on either shoulder, with one or both hands, the muzzle elevated.

Shoulder—ARMS.

180. Retake the position of *shoulder arms*.

Arms—PORT.

181. Throw the piece diagonally across the body, the lock to the front, seize it smartly at the same time with both hands, the right at the small of the stock, the left at the tail band, the thumbs pointing towards the muzzle, the barrel sloping upwards and crossing opposite to the point of the left shoulder, the butt proportionately lowered; the palm of the right hand above, that of the left under the piece, and the nails of both hands next to the body, to which the elbows will be closed.

Shoulder—ARMS.

One time and two motions.

182. (*First motion.*) Bring the piece smartly to the left shoulder, place the left hand quickly under the butt, the fingers of the right hand under the cock and extended as in No. 141.

183. (*Second motion.*) Drop the right hand smartly by the side.

To Ground Arms.

184. The squad being at ordered arms, if the instructor wish the piece to be placed on the ground, he will command:

Ground—Arms.

One time and two motions.

185. (*First motion.*) Turn the piece with the right hand, the barrel to the left, at the same time seize the cartridge box with left hand, bend the body, advance the left foot, the heel opposite the lower band; lay the piece on the ground with the right hand, the toe of the butt on a line with the right toe, the knee slightly bent, the right heel raised.

186. (*Second motion.*) Rise up, bring the left foot by the side of the right, quit the cartridge box with the left hand, and drop the hands by the side.

Raise—Arms.

187. Seize the cartridge box with the left hand, bend the body, advance the left foot opposite the lower band, and seize the piece with the right hand.

188. Raise the piece, bringing the left foot by the side of the right; turn the piece with the right hand, the rammer to the front; at the same time quit the cartridge box with the left hand, and drop this hand by the side.

To Stack Arms,

189. The squad being in two ranks at order arms, the instructor will command:

Stack—Arms.

190. At this command, the front rank man of every even numbered file will pass his piece before him, seizing it with the left hand above the middle band, and place the butt outside and near the left foot, the barrel turned to the front, the muzzle opposite the right shoulder. At the same time the front rank man of every odd numbered file will pass his piece before him, seizing it with the left hand below the middle band, and hand it to the man next on the left; the latter will receive it with the right hand two inches above the middle band, throw the butt about thirty-two inches to the front, opposite to his right shoulder, inclining the muzzle towards the right shoulder, and lock the shanks of the two bayonets, the barrel remaining to the rear and its shank above that of the first piece. The rear rank man of every even file projects his bayonet forward, the barrel to the right, and introduces it (using both hands) between the muzzles and under the shanks of the two other bayonets. He will then abandon the piece to his file leader, who will receive it with the right hand under the middle band, bring the butt to the front, holding up his own piece and the stack with the left hand, and place the butt of this third piece between the feet of the man next on his right, the barrel to the right. The stack thus formed, the rear rank man of every odd file will pass his piece into his left hand, the barrel turned to the front, and, sloping the bayonet forward rest it on the stack.

191. When organized companies stack arms, the sergeants, (and also the corporals, if in the rank of file closers,) will rest their pieces against the stacks nearest them respectively, after ranks are broken and resume their pieces on the signal to reform ranks.

192. The men of both ranks having assumed the position of the soldier without arms, the instructor may give the command:

    1. *Break ranks.* 2. MARCH.

193. The instructor having reformed the ranks will command:

    Take—ARMS.

194. At this command the rear rank man of every odd file will withdraw his piece from the stack; the front rank man of every even file will seize his own piece with the left hand, and that of the man on his right with his right; the rear rank man of every even file will seize his piece with the right hand at the middle band, advancing for the purpose the hollow of the right foot as far as the right heel of the file leader; these two men will raise up the stack to loosen the shanks; the front rank man of every odd file receives his piece from the hand of the man next on the left, and the four men retake the position of the soldier at *order arms*.

195. The instructor having brought the men to the position of shoulder arms, will command:

    Reverse—ARMS.

    One time and two motions.

196. (*First motion.*) Grasp the piece with the right hand, the finger nail to the front, at the height of the shoulder, turn the piece to the right and front of the body, and bring it reversed under the left arm, the barrel sloping to the rear; at the same time, slip the left hand to the small of the stock grasping it with the finger nails up.

197. (*Second motion.*) Remove and carry briskly the right hand to the rear of the body, and with it grasp the piece between the middle and lower bands, the finger nails outwards.

Shoulder—Arms.

One time and two motions.

198. (*First motion.*) Bring the right hand briskly to the front and with it grasp the piece at the swell of the stock, the finger nails inward; at the same time slip the left hand to the butt and invert the piece with both hands bringing it in front of the body, to the shoulder, and slipping the right hand, let it fall to the hammer.

199. (*Second motion.*) Drop the right hand by the side.

Rest on—Arms.

One time and two motions.

200. (*First motion.*) Grasp the piece at the height o the shoulder with the right hand, the finger nails to the front, reverse it by turning it to the right in front of the body, let the muzzle rest on the left foot, the left hand resting on the butt.

201. (*Second motion.*) Remove quickly the right hand to the butt and let it rest there, the finger nails outward; at the same time bow the head and bend the right knee.

[*Remark.*] (This movement is rarely used except in funeral ceremonies, &c.)

Shoulder—Arms.

One time and two motions.

202. (*First motion.*) Drop the right hand, and with it seize the piece at the swell of the stock, with both hands,

(the left depressed and the right raised,) turn the piece in front of the body, bringing it against the shoulder, and slipping the right hand let it fall to the hammer.

203. (*Second motion.*) Drop the right hand by the side.

Inspection of Arms.

204. The men being at *ordered arms*, and having the bayonet in the scabbard, the instructor will command:

Inspection—ARMS.

One time and three motions.

205. (*First motion.*) Face to the right once and a half carrying the right foot perpendicular to the allignment, about six inches from, and at right angles with the left, foot; seize promptly the peice with the left hand a little above the middle band, incline the muzzle to the rear without displacing the heel of the butt, the rammer turned towards the body; carrying at the same time the right hand to the bayonet as indicated in *fix bayonet*.

206. (*Second motion.*) Draw the bayonet from the scabbard, carry and fix it on the muzzle; seize next the rammer, draw it as explained in the fifth time of *loading* (see *Draw*—RAMMER, Nos. 217, 218, 219.) and let it glide to the bottom of the bore.

207. (*Third motion.*) Face promptly to the front, seize the peice with the right hand and retake the position of *order arms*.

208. The instructor will then inspect, in succession, the piece of each man, in passing along the front of the rank. Each as the instructor reaches him will raise smartly his piece with his right hand, seize it with the left near the

POSITION OF THE SOLDIER.

lower band, the lock to the front, the left hand at the height of the chin, the piece opposite to the left eye; the instructor will take it with the right hand at the handle, and after inspecting it, will return it to the recruit, who will receive it back with the right hand and replace it in the position of *order arms*.

209. When the instructor shall have passed him, each man will take the position prescribed in No. 203, return the rammer as explained in the seventh time of loading, (see *Return--*RAMMER, Nos. 221, 222, 223.)

210. If, instead of *inspection of arms*, the instructor shall wish bayonets to be fixed, he will command:

Fix—BAYONET.

211. Take the position prescribed in the first motion of inspection arms, No. 203, fix bayonet and face to the front.

212. If the instructor should wish to ascertain if any of the pieces are loaded, he will command:

Spring---RAMMER.

213. Put the rammers in the barrel as above explained, and retake the position of *order arms*.

The instructor for the purpose stated, can take the rammer by the small end, and spring it in the barrel, or cause each man to make it ring in the barrel.

214. Each man after the instructor passes him will return rammer and resume the position of order arms.

Remark. [The compiler would caution officers against striking the butts of the pieces against the ground to make the rammer spring, as it is liable to injure the lock.]

Loading and Firing.

Load in ten times.

1. LOAD.

Two motions.

215. (*First motion.*) Drop the piece by a full extension of the left arm, seize it with the right hand above and near the tail band; at the same time carry the right foot forward, the heel against the hollow of the left foot.

216. (*Second motion.*) Drop the piece with the right hand along the left thigh, seize it with the left hand at the middle band, and with the left hand let it descend along to the ground, without shock, the piece touching the left thigh, and the muzzle opposite the centre of the body; carry the right hand quickly to the cartridge box and open it.

2. *Handle*—CARTRIDGE.

One time and one motion.

217. Seize the cartridge with the thumb and next two fingers and place it between the teeth.

3. *Tear*—CARTRIDGE.

One time and one motion.

218. Tear the paper down to the powder, hold the cartridge upright between the thumb and next two fingers, near the top; and in this position place it in front of and near the muzzle, the back of the hand to the front.

4. *Charge*—CARTRIDGE.

One time and one motion.

219. Fix the eye on the muzzle, turn quickly the back

of the right hand towards the body, in order to discharge the powder into the barrel, raise the elbow to the height of the wrist, shake the cartridge, force it into the muzzle and leave the hand reversed, the fingers extended, the thumb extended along the barrel.

5. *Draw*—RAMMER.

One time and three motions.

220. (*First motion.*) Drop smartly the right elbow and seize the rammer between the thumb and fore-finger bent, the other fingers shut; draw it smartly, extending the arm; seize the rammer again at the middle, between the thumb and fore-finger, the hand reversed, the palm to the front, the nails up, the eyes following the movement of the hand; clear the rammer from the pipes by again extending the arm.

221. (*Second motion.*) Turn rapidly the rammer between the bayonet and the face, closing the fingers, (the rammer of the rear rank man grazing the right shoulder of the man of the same file in front, respectively,) the rammer parallel to the bayonet, the arm extended, the butt of the rammer opposite to the muzzle, but not yet inserted, the eyes fixed on the muzzle.

222. (*Third motion.*) Insert the butt of the rammer and force it down as low as the hand.

6. *Ram*—CARTRIDGE.

One time and one motion.

223. Extend the arm to its full length to seize the rammer between the right thumb extended and the fore-finger bent, the other fingers closed; with force ram home twice, (the right elbow down and near the piece,) and

seize the rammer at the little end, between the thumb and fore-finger bent, the other fingers closed, the right elbow touching the body.

7. *Return*—RAMMER.

One time and three motions.

224. (*First motion.*) Draw briskly the rammer, re-seize the middle between the thumb and fore-finger, the hand reversed, the palm to the front, the nails up, the eyes following the movement of the hand, clear the rammer from the barrel by extending the arm.

225. (*Second motion.*) Turn rapidly the rammer between the bayonet and face, closing the fingers, (the rammer of the rear rank man grasing the right shoulder of the man of the same file in front,) the rammer parallel to the bayonet, the arm extended, the little end of the rammer opposite to the first pipe, but not yet inserted. The eyes fixed on that pipe.

226. (*Third motion.*) Insert the little end, and with the thumb, which will follow the movement, force it as low as the middle band; raise quickly the right hand a little bent, place the little finger on the butt of the rammer and force it down, at the same instant lower the left hand on the barrel to the extent of the arm, without depressing the shoulder.

8. *Cast*—ABOUT.

One time and two motions.

227. (*First motion.*) Raise the piece with the left hand along the left side, the hand at the height of the chin, the fore-arm touching the piece, the barrel to the front; drop at the same time the right hand to seize the piece a little

above the small of the stock, the fore-finger touching the lock, the thumb on the S plate, and bring the right heel to the side of the left.

228. (*Second motion.*) Make a half face to the right on the left heel, bring the left toe to the front, the right foot behind and at right angles with the left, the hollow of the right foot against the heel of the left. At the same time seize the small of the stock with the right hand, and bring down the piece with both hands to the position of *charge bayonet.*

9. PRIME.

One time and one motion.

229. Sustain the piece with the left hand, (half cock the piece,) brush off the old cap and with the thumb and first two fingers take a cap from the pouch, place it firmly on the cone, pushing it down with the thumb.

10. *Shoulder*—ARMS.

One time and two motions.

230. As from *Charge—Bayonet.* Nos. 161, 162.

To Load in Four Times.

231. The first time will be executed at the command *Load;* the three others at the words *two, three* and *four.*

Load in four times—LOAD.

222. Execute what is prescribed for *Load, Handle—Cartridge, Tear—Cartridge* and *Charge—Cartridge.*

TWO.

233. *Draw—Rammer* and *Ram—Cartridge.*

THREE.

234. *Return—Rammer* and *Cast—About.*

FOUR.

235. *Prime* and *Shoulder—Arms.*

To Load At Will.

236. The instructor wishing the men to execute the loading without pause, will command.

Load at Will—LOAD.

237. At the command *load*, the men will execute the loading as in four times, but without resting on the times.

READY.

One time and four motions.

238. (*First motion.*) Make a half face to the right on the left heel, bring the left toe to the front, place at the same time the right foot behind, and at right angles with the left, the hollow of the right foot against the left heel; turn the piece with the left hand, the lock outwards, and seize at the same time the small of the stock with the right hand, the piece perpendicular, and detached from the shoulder; leave the left hand under the butt.

239. (*Second motion.*) Bring the piece with the right hand to the middle of the body, place the left hand just above the lock, the thumb extended on the stock at the height of the chin, the S plate almost turned towards the body, the rammer obliquely to the left and front.

240. (*Third motion.*) Place the thumb on the hammer, the fore-finger under and on the guard, the other three fingers joined to the first, the elbow at the height of the wrist.

241. (*Fourth motion.*) Close the right elbow smartly to the body in cocking, seize the piece at the small of the stock, let it descend along the body in the left hand to the tail band, which will remain at the height of the shoulder, and opposite the centre of the body.

AIM.

One time and one motion.

242. Drop smartly the muzzle, the left hand remaining at the tail band, support the butt against the right shoulder, the left elbow a little down, shut the left eye, direct the right along the barrel, drop the head upon the butt to catch the object, and place the fore-finger on the trigger.

243. The rear rank will, at the same time, carry the right foot about eight inches towards the left heel of the man next on the right.

FIRE.

One time and one motion.

244. Apply the fore-finger with force to the trigger, without further lowering or turning the head, and remain in that position.

245. The instructor wishing the men to *load*, rom this position, will command:

LOAD.

One time and one motion.

246. (*First motion.*) Bring back the piece quickly with both hands, the rear rank man bringing the right foot beside the left; depress the butt strongly by extending the right arm, and carry it with the arm thus extended to the left side, the barrel turned to the front, and opposite the

left shoulder, open the left hand to let the piece slide through it to the middle band, the back of the hand to the front, the left fore-arm touching the stock; at the same time face to the front, and carry the right foot forward, the heel against the hollow of the left foot.

247. (*Second motion.*) Quit the hold of the right hand; with the left hand remaining at the middle band, let the piece descend to the ground, without shock, and take the position of the second motion of the first time of loading.

248. The men being in the position of *Fire*, and the instructor wishing them to come to the position of *Shoulder —Arms*, will command:

Shoulder—Arms.

One time and two motions.

249. (*First motion.*) Bring back the piece with both hands, face to the front, carry the piece to the left shoulder, the right hand under the cock in the position as prescribed in No. 141, the left hand under the butt.

250. (*Second motion.*) Let fall smartly the right hand into position.

251. The men being in the position of *Aim*, if the instructor wishes, he may command:

Recover—Arms.

One time and one motion.

252. At the word *recover*, withdraw the finger from the trigger; at the command *Arms*, throw up smartly the muzzle, and re-take the position of the fourth motion of ready.

253. The men being in the position of *ready;* the instructor will command;

Shoulder—Arms.
One time and one motion.

254. At the word *Shoulder*, face to the front, bring the piece to the middle of the body; the left thumb at the height of the chin, the piece supported by the left hand, holding it fast above the lock;. next place the right thumb, on the head of the cock, support the fore-finger on the trigger, sustain at the same time the cock in its descent till it nearly touches the cone, raise the cock to the half cock notch, (the reaching of which will be both felt and heard,) and seize the handle of the piece, (or small of the stock,) with the right hand. At the word *Arms*, carry the piece smartly to the shoulder, and re-take the position of shoulder—arms.

The Firing.

255. The firings are direct or oblique, and will be executed as follows:

The Direct Fire.

156. For the *direct fire* the instructor will command.

1. *Fire by Squad.* 2. *Squad.* 3. Ready. 4. Aim. 5. Fire. 6. Load.

257. These several commands will be executed as has been prescribed in the *Manual of Arms*.

258. At the fourth command they will aim according to the rank in which each man may find himself placed, the rear rank men inclining forward a little the upper part of the body, in order that their pieces may reach as much beyond the front rank as possible.

259. At the sixth command, they will load their pieces and return immediately to the position of ready.

260. The instructor will re-commence the firing by the commands;

    1. *Squad.*   2. AIM.   3. FIRE.   4. LOAD.

261. When the instructor wishes the firing to cease, he will command;

Cease—FIRING.

262. At this command the men will cease firing, but will load their pieces if unloaded, and afterwards bring them to a shoulder.

The Oblique Fire.

263. The oblique firings will be executed to the right and left, and by the same commands as the direct fire, with this single difference—the command *Aim*, will always be preceded by the caution, *right* or *left oblique.*

Position of the Ranks, in the Oblique Fire to the Right.

264. At the command *ready*, the two ranks will execute what has been prescribed for the direct fire.

265. At the cautionary command, *right oblique*, the two ranks will throw back the right shoulder and look steadily at the object to be hit.

266. At the command *Aim*, each front rank man will aim to the right without deranging his feet; each rear rank man will advance the left foot about eight inches towards the right heel of the man next on the right of his file leader, and aim to the right, inclining the upper par of the body forward, and bending a little the left knee.

267. At the command *load*, both ranks will resume the position of *load*, in the fire direct.

Position of the Ranks in the Oblique Fire to the Left

268. At the command *left oblique*, the two ranks wil throw back the left shoulder, and look steadily at the object to be hit

269. At the command *aim*, the front rank will take aim to the left without deranging the feet; each man in the rear rank will advance the right foot about eight inches towards the right heel of the man next on the right of his file leader, and aim to the left, inclining the upper part of the body forward, and bending a little the right knee.

270. At the command *load*, both ranks will come to the position of load as prescribed in the direct fire.

To Fire by File.

271. The fire by file, will be executed by the two ranks, the files of which will fire successively, and without waiting on each other, except for the first fire.

272. The instructor will command:

1. *Fire by file:* 2. *Squad.* 3. READY. 4. *Commence—* FIRING.

273. At the third command, the two ranks will take the position prescribed in the direct fire.

274. At the fourth command, the file on the right will aim and fire, the men together, the rear rank man, in taking aim, will carry the right foot about eight inches to the right.

275. The second file will aim at the instant the first brings down the pieces to re-load; and each file successively on to the left.

276. After the first fire, every man will load and fire without waiting for the others.

277. The instructor wishing the fire to cease, will command:

Cease—Firing.

278. At this command the men will cease firing. If they have fired, they will load their pieces and bring them to a shoulder; if at the position of *ready*, they will half cock and shoulder arms. It in the position of *Aim*, they will bring down their pieces, half cock and shoulder arms.

To Fire by Rank.

279. The fire by rank will be executed by each entire rank, alternately.

280. The instructor will command:

1. *Fire by rank.* 2. *Squad.* 3. Ready. 4. *Rear rank.* 5. Aim. 6. Fire. 7. Load.

281. At the third command, both ranks will take the position of *ready*.

282. At the seventh command, the rear rank will load and come to the position of *ready*.

283. As soon as the instructor shall see several men in the rear rank in the position of ready, he will command:

1. *Front rank.* 2. Aim. 3. Fire. 4. Load.

284. At these commands, the men in the front rank will execute what has been prescribed for the rear rank, but will not step off with the right foot.

285. The instructor will thus continue to alternate the fire from rank to rank, until he shall wish the firing to cease, when he will command *cease firing*, which will be executed as heretofore prescribed.

THE COMPANY.

PART SECOND
The Formation of the Company.

286. The company being assembled on its ground, will be formed in two ranks, by the first sergeant, who will command:

Fall In.

287. At which command the rank and file, (corporals and privates,) will form in two ranks faced to the right, the tallest corporal on the right, (or head of the company,) the two tallest men next, and so on down to the left or rear of the rank.

288. This having been accomplished, the first sergeant will command:

Front.

289. At this command the company will face to the front; the command Right—Dress, will then be given, which will be executed as has been prescribed; the men keeping their *eyes right* until the command *front.*

290. The company should fall in at a *support arms*, and if the roll is called, each man as he answers to his name, will first bring his piece to a *shoulder*, and then to an *order arms.*

291. This being done the first sergeant will bring the company to a shoulder, and command:

In each rank Count Twos.

292. At this command the men count in each rank from right to left, pronouncing in a loud and distinct voice, in the same tone, without hurry, and without turning the head, *one*, *two*, according to the place which each one occupies.

293. He will then divide the company into two equal platoons, and each platoon into two equal sections, place the corporals in position in the front rank, on the right and left of platoons, and report to the captain the formation of the company.

294. The officers and sergeants will now take their posts as follows:

295. The *captain* in the front rank on the right of the company, touching with the left elbow.

296. The *first lieutenant* two paces in rear of and opposite the centre of the fourth section.

297. The *second lieutenant* two paces in rear of and opposite the centre of the first platoon.

298. The *third lieutenant* two paces in rear of and opposite the centre of the second platoon.

299. The *first sergeant* in the rear rank and covering the captain. He is denominated the covering sergeant, or right guide of the company.

300. The *second sergeant* two paces in rear of and opposite the second file from the left of the company. He is designated as left guide of the company.

301. The *third sergeant* two paces in rear of and opposite the second file from the right of the second platoon.

302. The *fourth sergeant* two paces in rear of and opposite the second file from the left of the first platoon.

303. The *fifth sergeant* two paces in rear of and opposite the second file from the right of the first platoon.

304. Absent officers and sergeants will be re-placed—officers by sergeants, and sergeants by corporals.*

305. The officers and sergeants thus posted in the rear constitute the rank of closers. This rank is two paces in rear of the rear rank.

306. The pioneer is posted on the line of file closers on the right; and the music in a line with the front rank, four paces on its right, the drum on the right of the fifer or bugler.

To Open Ranks.

307. The company being at ordered arms, the ranks and file closers well aligned, to open ranks, the instructor will command:

1. *Attention.* 2. *Company.* 3. *Shoulder—*ARMS. 4. *Prepare to open ranks.* 5. *To the rear open order.*

308. At the fourth command the left guide will place himself on the left of the front rank.

309. At the fifth command the covering sergeant and the left guide will step off smartly to the rear, four paces from the front rank, in order to mark the alignment of the rear rank.

310. The instructor having observed that these two guides are on a line parallel to the front rank, will command:

G. MARCH.

311. At this command the front rank will stand fast.

---

*When the captain acts as instructor, or is in independent command of the company, the first lieutenant takes his post, and his post in turn is filled by the second lieutenant, and so on.

312. The rear rank will step to the rear without counting the step, and will place itself on the alignment marked out for it.

313. The covering sergeant will then align the rear rank on the left guide.

314. The file closers will step off at the same time with the rear rank, and place themselves two paces in the rear of it when it is aligned.

315. The instructor seeing the rank aligned, will command:

7. Front.

316. At this command the sergeant on the left of the rear rank, will return to his place as a file closer.

Alignments in Open Ranks.

317. The ranks being open, the instructor will, in the first exercises, align the ranks, man by man, the better to inculculate the principles.

318. To effect this he will cause two men on the right or left of each rank to march two or three paces forward, and after having aligned them, command:

By file right (or left)—Dress.

319. This command will be executed as has been prescribed. The instructor will also cause the men to align themselves backward, and he will be careful to observe that they dress correctly, and that their arms are in proper position.

Manual of Arms.

320. The ranks being open, the instructor will place

himself in a position to see the ranks, and will command the manual of arms in the following order :*

Present Arms.	*Shoulder Arms.*
Order Arms.	
Ground Arms.	
Raise Arms.	*Shoulder Arms.*
Support Arms.	*Shoulder Arms.*
Fix Bayonet.	*Shoulder Arms.*
Charge Bayonet.	*Shoulder Arms.*
Trail Arms.	*Shoulder Arms.*
Unfix Bayonet.	*Shoulder Arms.*
Secure Arms,	*Shoulder Arms.*

Load in ten times.

321. To close the ranks after the execution of the manual of arms, the instructor will command:

1. *Close order.* 2. MARCH.

322. At the command *march*, the rear rank will close up in quick time, each man directing himself on his file leader.

323. The company should be exercised in the *manual of arms, loading at will, firing by file, firing by rank, and direct and oblique firing, by company as* prescribed in the squad drill, the instructor substituting the word *company* for *squad* wherever it occurs.

324. At the preparatory command in firing, the captain will promptly place himself opposite the centre of his company, and four paces in rear of the line of file closers;

---

*The compiler would suggest to officers the practicability of causing the front rank to *about face*, and place themselves at one end, so that they can better see the execution of the movement by the whole company.

the covering sergeant will retire to that line, and place himself opposite to his interval. *This rule is general for both captain and covering sergeant in all the different firings.*

To Fire by the Rear Rank.

325. The instructor will cause the several fires to be executed to the rear, that is, by the rear rank. To effect this he will command:

1. *Face by the rear rank.* 2. *Company.* 3. *About*—FACE.

326. At the first command the captain will step out and place himself near to, and facing the right file of his company; the covering sergeant and file closers, will pass quickly through the captain's interval, and place themselves faced to the rear, the covering sergeant a pace behind the captain, and the file closers two paces from the front rank opposite their places in line, each passing behind the covering sergeant.

327. At the third command, which will be given at the instant the last file closer shall have passed through the interval, the company will face about; the captain will place himself in his interval in the rear rank, now become the front, and the covering sergeant will cover him in the front rank, now become the rear.

328. Faced by the rear rank, the different firings will be executed in the manner already prescribed.

329. The fire by file will commence on the left of the company, now become the right; and in the fire by rank, the firing will commence with the front rank, now become the rear.

330. To resume the proper front, the instructor will command:
1. *Face by the front rank.* 2. *Company.* 3. *About*—FACE.

331. At the first command the captain, covering sergeant and file closers will conform to what is prescribed in Nos. 326, 327.

332. At the third command the company having faced about, the captain and covering sergeant will resume their places in line.

To Advance in Line of Battle.

333. The company being in line and correctly aligned, to march it by the front the instructor will cause a sergeant to take position six paces in advance of the captain. This advanced sergeant, who is charged with the direction, will take two points on the ground in the straight line to the front to direct his course.

334. The instructor will then command:

1. *Company—Forward.* 2. MARCH.

335. At the command *march*, the company will step off with life. The directing sergeant will observe with the greatest precision, the length and cadence of the step, marching on the two points he has chosen; he will take in succession, and a little before arriving at the points nearest him, new points in advance, exactly in the same line with the first two, and at the distance of some fifteen or twenty paces from each other. The captain will march steadily in the trace of the directing sergeant, keeping always six paces from him. The men will march with the head direct to the front, touch lightly the elbow towards the captain, and resist pressure coming from the opposite

side. The file closers will march at the habitual distance of two paces behind the rear rank.

336. If the men lose the step, the instructor will command:

To the—STEP.

337. At this the men will glance towards the directing sergeant, re-take the step from him, and again direct the eyes to the front.

338. The instructor wishing to halt the company, will command:

1. *Company.* 2. HALT.

339. At the second command the company will halt; the directing sergeant will remain in advance, unless ordered to return to the line of file closers.

340. The captain will then rectify the alignment, by the commands and according to the principles prescribed in No. 9.

To March in Retreat.

341. The company being halted and correctly aligned, to cause it to march in retreat, the instructor will place the directing sergeant six paces in rear of the line of file closers, and in the same straight line with the covering sergeants, and will then command:

1. *Company.* 2. *About*—FACE.

342. The company and directing sergeant having faced to the rear, the instructor will command:

3. *Company*—FORWARD.

343. At this command the covering sergeant will step into the line of file closers, opposite to his interval, and

the captain will place himself in the rear rank now become the front.

344. This disposition being promptly made, the instructor will command:

4. MARCH.

345. At this the directing sergeant, the captain and the men will conform themselves to what has been prescribed in No. 335.

346. The instructor will cause to be executed, marching in retreat, all that has been prescribed for marching in advance; the commands and the means of execution will be the same.

Oblique March in Line of Battle.

347. The company being in the direct march, when the instructor shall wish to cause it to march obliquely, he will command:

1. *Right* (or *left*) *oblique*. 2. MARCH.

348. At the command march the company will take the oblique step, and execute the movement as prescribed in No. 53.

349. In the oblique march the men not having the touch of elbows, the guide will always be on the side to which the oblique is made, without any indication to that effect being given, and when the direct march is resumed, the guide will be, equally without indication, on the side where it was previous to the march.

350. When the instructor shall wish the direct march to be resumed, he will command.

1. *Forward*. 2. MARCH.

351. At the command *march* the company will resume the direct step.

352. The instructor should now exercise the company in the following commands, according to the principles prescribed in squad drill:

 1. *Mark Time.*   2. March.
 1. *Forward.*   2. March.
 1. *Common Time.*   2. March.
 1. *Double Quick.*   2. March.
 1. *Quick Time.*   2. March.
 1. *Change Step.*   2. March.
 1. *Right About.*   2. March.
 1. *Right About.*   2. Halt.

353. When the company is marching in the double quick, the pieces should be carried at a *right shoulder shift arms* or a *trail arms*, and the distance between the ranks should be twenty-six inches.

354. When the pieces are carried on the right shoulder, in quick time, the distance between the ranks should be sixteen inches.

355. Whenever the company is halted, the men will bring their pieces at once to a shoulder at the command *halt;* and the rear rank will close up to its proper distance of thirteen inches. *These rules are general.*

To March by the Flank.

356. The company being in line of battle, and at a halt, when the instructor shall wish to cause it to march by the right flank, he will command:

 1. *Company right*—Face.   2. *Forward*—March.

357. At the first command, the company will face to the

right, the covering sergeant will place himself at the head of the front rank, the captain having stepped out for the purpose, so far as to find himself by the side of the sergeant, and on his left; the front rank will double as is prescribed in No. 77; the rear rank will, at the same time, side step to the right one pace, and double in the same manner so that when the movement is completed, the files will be formed of four men aligned, and elbow to elbow. The intervals will be preserved.

358. The file closers will also move by side step to the right, so that when the ranks are formed, they will be two paces from the rearmost rank.

359. At the command *march*, the company will move off briskly in quick time; the covering sergeant at the head of the front rank, and the captain on his left, will march straight forward. The men of each file will march abreast of their respective front rank men, heads direct to the front; the file closers will march opposite their places in line of battle.

360. The instructor will cause the march by the left flank to be excuted by the same commands, substituting *left* for *right;* the ranks will double as has been prescribed in No. 83, the rear rank will side step to the left one pace before doubling.

361. At the instant the company faces to the left, the left guide will place himself at the head of the front rank; the captain will pass rapidly to the left, and place himself by the right side of this guide; the covering sergeant will replace the captain in the front rank, the moment the latter quits it to go to the left.

362. Should the instructor wish to face the company

to the right or left, without doubling files, he will command:

Company, in two ranks, right (or *left*)—FACE.

362. At which command, the company will face to the right or left, without doubling.

To Change Direction by File.

263. The company being faced by the flank, and either in march, or at a halt, when the instructor shall wish to cause it to wheel by file, he will command:

1. *By file left* (or *right.*) 2. MARCH.

365. At the command *march*, the first file will wheel; if to the side of the front rank man, the latter will take care not to turn at once, but to describe a short arc of a circle, shortening a little the first five or six steps in order to give time to the fourth man of this file to conform himself to this movement. If the wheel be to the side of the rear rank, the front rank man will wheel in the step of twenty-eight inches, and the fourth man will conform himself to the movement by describing a short arc of a circle, as has been explained.

366. Each file will come to wheel on the same ground when that which preceded it wheeled.

367. When the company is marching by the flank and the instructor wishes to halt it and face it to the front, he will command:

1. *Company.* 2. HALT. 3. FRONT.

368. The second and third commands will be executed as has been prescribed in No. 81, 82, 83. As soon as the files have undoubled, the rear rank will close to its proper distance.

369. The captain and covering sergeant, as well as the left guide, if the march be by the left flank, will return to their habitual places in line at the instant the company faces to the front.

370. The instructor may then rectify the alignment by the means prescribed.

371. The company being in march by the flank, to form it on the right (or left) by file into line of battle, the instructor will command:

1. *On the right, by file into line.* 2. MARCH.

372. At the command *march*, the rear rank men doubled, will mark time, the captain and covering sergeant will turn to the right, march straight forward, and be halted by the instructor, when they shall have passed at least six paces beyond the rank of file closers; the captain will place himself correctly on the line of battle, and will direct the alignment as the men of the front rank successively arrive; the covering sergeant will place himself behind the captain at the distance of the rear rank; the two men on the right of the front rank doubled, will continue to march, and passing beyond the covering sergeant and the captain, will turn to the right; after turning, they will continue to march elbow to elbow, and direct themselves toward the line of battle, but when they shall arrive at two paces from this line, the even number will shorten the step so that the odd number may precede him on the line, the odd number placing himself by the side and on the left of the captain; the even number will afterwards oblique to the left, and place himself on the left of the odd number; the next two men of the front rank doubled,

will pass in the same manner behind the two first, turn then to the right, and place themselves according to the means just explained, to the left and by the side of the two men already established on the line of battle; the remaining files of this rank will follow in succession, and be formed to the left in the same manner.

373. The rear rank doubled will execute the movement in the manner already explained for the front rank, taking care not to commence the movement until four men of the front rank are established on the line; the rear rank men as they arrive on the line, will cover accurately their file leaders.

374. If the company be marching by the left flank, and the instructor wishes to cause it to form by file on the left into line of battle, he will command:

    1. *On the left, by file into line.* 2. MARCH.

375. At the second command, the same movements will be made to the left; in this case the odd numbers will shorten the step, so that the even numbers may precede them on the line. The captain, placed on the left of the front rank, and the left guide, will return to their places in line of battle, by order of the instructor, after the company shall be formed and aligned.

376. The instructor should at first cause this movement to be executed separately by each rank doubled, and afterwards by the two ranks united and doubled. He should also place himself on the line of battle, and without the point where the right or left is to rest, in order to establish the base of alignment, and afterward will assure himself that each file conforms itself to what has just been prescribed.

377. If the company be marching by the right flank. and the instructor should wish to undouble the files, which might sometimes be found necessary, he will cause arms to be shouldered or supported, and command:

1. *In two ranks, undouble files.* 2. MARCH.

378. At the second command, the odd numbers will continue to march straight forward, the even numbers will shorten the step, and obliquing to the left will place themselves promptly behind the odd numbers; the rear rank will gain a step to the left so as to retake the touch of elbows on the side of the front rank.

379. If the company be marching by the left flank, it will be the even numbers who will continue to march forward, and the odd numbers who will undouble.

380. If the instructor should wish to double the files, he will command:

1. *In four ranks, double files.* 2. MARCH.

381. At the command *march*, the files will double in the manner as explained, when the company faces by the right or left flank.

382. The instructor should also cause these movements to be executed in double quick time.

Movements in Column.

383. The company being in march by the right flank, and the instructor wishing to form into line, will command,

1. *By company into line.* 2. MARCH.

384. At the command *march*, the covering-sergeant will continue to march straight forward ; the men will advance the right shoulder, take the double quick step, and move

into line by the shortest route, taking care to undouble the files, and to come on the line one after the other.

385. As the front rank men successively arrive into line with the covering sergeant, they will take from him the step, and then turn their eyes to the front.

386. The men of the rear rank will conform to the movements of their respective file leaders, but without endeavoring to arrive in line at the same time with the latter.

387. At the instant the movement begins, the instructor will face the company and observe the execution; and as soon as the company is formed, he will command, *guide left*.

388. At the command *guide left*, the second sergeant will promptly place himself in the front rank, on the left, to serve as guide, and the covering sergeant who is on the opposite flank, will remain there.

389. When the company is in march by the left flank, this movement will be executed according to the same principles and by the same commands. The company being formed, the captain will command, *guide right;* the covering sergeant, who is on right of the front rank, will serve as guide, and the second sergeant placed on the left flank will remain there.

390. Thus in column by company, right or left in front, the covering sergeant and the second sergeant of each company, will always be placed on the right and left, respectively, of the front rank, and they will be denominated *right guide* and *left guide*, and the one or the other charged with the direction.

391. The company being in march by the flank, and the instructor wishing to form platoons, he will command:

   1. *By platoon into line.* 2. MARCH.

392. This movement will be executed by each platoon according to the above principles. The captain will promptly place himself before the centre of the first platoon, and the first lieutenant before the centre of the second, and command, without waiting for each other—*guide left* (or *right*) as soon as the platoons are formed.

393. At the command, *guide left (or right)*, the guide of each platoon will pass rapidly to the flank indicated, if not already there.

394. The right guide of the company will always serve as the guide of the right or left of the first platoon, and the left guide of the company will serve, in like manner, as the guide of the second platoon.

395. Thus in a column, by platoon, there will be but one guide to each platoon, and he will always be placed on the left flank, if the right is in front, and on the right flank if the left is in front.

396. In these movements, the file closers will follow the platoons to which they are attached.

397. The instructor should exercise the company in passing, without a halt, from the march to the front to the march by the flank, and reciprocally, and in either case he will command.

1. *Company by the right* (or *left*) *flank.* 2. MARCH

398. At the command *march*, the company will face to the right or left, as is prescribed in No. 88, and the captain, file closers and guides will conform themselves to what has been prescribed for each, in the march by the flank, or the front.

399. If after facing to the right or left, in marching, the

company find itself faced by the rear rank, the captain will place himself two paces behind the centre of the front rank, now the rear, the guides will pass to the rear rank, now leading, and the file closers will march in front of this rank.

400. When the company is marching in column by platoon, right in front, and the instructor wishes to march it by the flank in the same direction, he will command:

1. *Column, by the right flank.* 2. *By file left.* 3. MARCH.

401. At the second command, each chief of platoon and its guide, will pass rapidly to the right flank, to conduct it.

402. At the command *march*, each platoon will face to the right in marching, wheel by file to the left, and then march straight forward; the leading file of the second platoon will unite with the rear file of the first, the chief and guide of the second will pass through the interval to their places as file closers.

403. When the left is in front, the movement will be executed by inverse means, substituting in the command, *left* for *right*, and *right* for *left*. The captain, (if a halt be will not immediately commanded), will replace the first lieutenant and conduct the left flank, and the covering sergeant will return to his place on the right flank now become the rear.

404. The company being at a halt, in line of battle, the instructor, wishing to break it into column, by platoon to the right, will command:

1. *By platoon, right wheel.* 2. MARCH.

405. At the first command, the chiefs of platoon will rapidly place themselves two paces before the centres of

their respective platoons, the lieutenant passing around the left of the company. They need not occupy themselves with dressing one upon the other. The covering sergeant will replace the captain in the front rank.

406. At the command *march*, the right front rank man of each platoon will face to the right, the covering sergeant standing fast; the chief of each platoon will move quickly by the shortest line, a little beyond the point at which the marching flank will rest when the wheel shall be completed, face to the late rear, and place himself so that the line which he forms with the man on the right (who had faced) shall be perpendicular to that occupied by the company in line of battle; each platoon will wheel according to the principles prescribed for the wheel on a fixed pivot, and when the man who conducts the marching flank shall approach near to the perpendicular, its chief will command:

1. *Platoon.* 2. HALT.

407. At the command *halt*, which will be given at the instant the man who conducts the marching flank shall have arrived at three paces from the perpendicular, the platoon will halt; the covering sergeant will move to the point where the left of the first platoon is to rest, passing by the front rank; the second sergeant will place himself in like manner, in regard to the second platoon. Each will take care to leave between himself and the man on the right of his platoon, a space equal to its front; the captain and first lieutenant will look to this, and each take care to align the sergeant between himself and the man of the platoon who had faced to the right.

408. The guide of each platoon, being thus established on the perpendicular, each chief will place himself two paces outside of his guide, and facing towards him, will command:

3. *Left*—Dress.

409. The alignment being ended, each chief of platoon will command Front, and place himself two paces before its centre.

410. The file closers will conform themselves to the movements of their respective platoons, preserving always the distance of two paces from the rear rank.

411. Should the instructor wish to break by platoon to the left, he will execute it according to the same principles and by inverse means, and will give the following commands:

1. *By platoon left wheel.* 2. March. 3. *Platoon.* 4. Halt. 5. *Right*—Dress. 6. Front.

Post of Officers in Column.

412. In *column by company* the captain is two paces in front of the centre of his company; the first sergeant on the right of the front rank, and is the right guide of the company; the second sergeant on the left of the front rank, and is the left guide of the company.

413. In *column by platoon* the captain commands the first platoon, the first lieutenant the second platoon; each two paces in front of the centre of his platoon; the first sergeant is the guide of the first platoon; the second sergeant is the guide of the second platoon; they will be, unless otherwise ordered, on the left of the front rank of their respective platoons, if the column is right in front, and on the right, if the left is in front.

414. In *column by section* the captain commands the first section; the first lieutenant the third; the second lieutenant the second; the third lieutenant the fourth; each two paces in front of his section; the first sergeant is guide of the first section, the second sergeant is guide of the fourth; the third is guide of the third; and the fourth is guide of the second; each on the left front rank of his section, if the column be right in front, and on the right if the left be in front.

415. In column by company, platoon or section, the file closers not otherwise provided for, are in their proper places behind the rear rank of their respective sub-divisions.

To March in Column.

316. The company having broken by platoon, right (or left) in front, the instructor wishing to cause the column to march, will command:

1. *Column forward.* 2. *Guide left* (or *right.*) 3. March.

417. At the command *march*, promptly repeated by the chiefs of platoon, the whole will step off together.

418. The men will each feel lightly the elbow of his neighbor toward the guide, and conform himself to the principles prescribed in the school of the squad.

419. The man next to the guide, in each platoon, will take care never to pass him, and also to march always about six inches to the right (or left) from him, in order not to push him out of the direction.

420. The leading guide will observe, with the greatest precision, the length and cadence of the step, and maintain the direction of his march by means prescribed in No. 335.

421. The following guide will march exactly in the trace of the leading one, preserving between the latter and himself a distance precisely equal to the front of his platoon, and marching in the same step with the leading guide.

422. If the following guide lose his distance from the one leading (which can only happen by his own fault,) he will correct himself by slightly lengthening or shortening a few steps, in order that there may not be sudden quickenings or slackenings in the march of his platoon.

423. The guide of each sub-division in column will be responsible for the direction, distance and step.

424. The chief of each sub-division, will be responsible for the order and conformity of his sub-division with the movements of the guide, accordingly the chief will frequently turn, in the march, to observe his sub-division.

425. In column the chiefs of sub-divisions will always repeat, with the greatest promptitude, the commands *march* and *halt;* they will give no other command given by the instructor, but may explain, if necessary, to their sub-divisions, in an under tone, what they will have to execute, as indicated by the commands of caution.

To Change Direction.

426. The changes of direction of a column while marching, will be executed according to the principles prescribed for wheeling on the march. Whenever, therefore, the direction of the column is to be changed, the instructor will change the guide, if not already there, to the flank opposite the side to which the change is to be made.

427. The column being in march right in front, if it be the wish of the instructor to change direction to the right,

he will give the order to the chief of the first platoon, and immediately go himself or send a marker to the point at which the change of direction is to be made; the instructor or marker will place himself on the direction of the guides, so as to present the breast to that flank of the column.

428. The leading guide will direct his march on that person, so that, in passing, his left arm may just graze his breast. When the leading guide shall have approached near the marker, the chief of the platoon will command:

1. *Right wheel.* 2. MARCH.

429. The first command will be given, when the platoon is at the distance of four paces from the marker.

430. At the command *march*, which will be pronounced at the instant the guide shall have arrived opposite the marker, the platoon will wheel to the right, conforming to what has been prescribed in the school of the squad.

431. The wheel being almost completed, the instructor will command:

3. *Forward.*

432. And when the wheel is finished, he will command:

4. MARCH.

433. At which the platoon will march straight forward in the new direction.

434. The second platoon will continue to march straight forward till up with the marker, when it will wheel to the right, and re-take the direct march by the same commands and the same means which governed the first platoon.

435. Should the instructor wish to change the direction to the left, he will command *guide right.* At this com-

mand the two guides will move rapidly to the right of their respective platoons, each passing in front of his subdivision; the men will take the touch of elbows to the right; the instructor conforming to what has been prescribed.

436. The change of direction to the left will then be executed according to the same principles as the change of direction to the right, but by inverse means.

437. When the change of direction is completed, the instructor will command, *guide left.*

438. The change of direction in a column left in front, will be executed according to the same principles.

439. Each chief will observe that his subdivision arrives at the point of change in a square with the line of direction; with this view, he will face to his subdivision when the one which precedes has commenced to turn or to wheel, and he will be watchful that it continues to march squarely until it arrives at the point where the change of direction is to commence.

To halt the column and to form to the right or left into line, either at a halt or on the march.

440. The column being in march, right in front, to halt it the instructor will command:

1 *Column*—2 Halt.

441. At the second command, promptly repeated by the chiefs of platoons, the column will halt; the guides also will stand fast, although they may have lost both distance and direction.

442. The instructor wishing to form it into line will place himself at platoon distance in front of the leading

guide, face to him and rectify, if necessary, the position of the guide beyond; which being executed he will command:

Left—Dress.

443. At this command, which will not be repeated by the chiefs of platoon, each of them will place himself briskly two paces outside of his guide and direct the alignment of the platoon perpendicularly to the direction of the column.

444. Each chief having aligned his platoon, will command Front, and return quickly to his place in the column.

445. The instructor having seen this disposition made, will command:

1. *Left into line, wheel.* 2. March.

446. At the command *march*, briskly repeated by the chiefs of p atoon, the front rank man on the left of each platoon will face to the left, and place his breast lightly against the arm of the guid- by his side, who stands fast; the platoons will then wheel to the left on the principles of wheels from a halt.

447. Each chief will turn to his platoon to observe its movements, and when the marching flank of his platoon is three paces from the line, he will command:

1. *Platoon.* 2. Halt.

448. The chief of the second platoon having halted it, will return to his place as file closer, passing around the left of his subdivision.

449. The captain having halted the first platoon, will move rapidly to the point at which the right of the company will rest in line of battle, and command:

Right. Dress.

450. At this command, the two platoons will dress up on the alignment.

451. The company being aligned, the captain will command:

Front.

452. The instructor seeing the company in line of battle, will command:

Guides. Posts.

453. At this command, the covering sergeant will cover the captain, and the left guide will return to his place as file closer.

453. If the column be left in front, and the instructor wishes to form it to the right into line of battle, it will be done upon the same principals and by inverse means.—The instructor will command:

1. *Right into line wheel.* 2. March.

454. At the command *march*, the front rank man on the right of each platoon will face to the right and place his breast lightly against the left arm of the guide by his side, who stands fast; each platoon will wheel to the right, and will be halted by its chief, when the marching flank has approached near the line of battle; for this purpose he will command:

1. *Platoon.* 2. Halt.

455. The platoon having halted, the chief of the second platoon will return to his place as file closer, and the captain will move briskly to the point at which the left of the company is to rest; and command:

Left. Dress.

456. At the command, the two platoons will dress up on the alignment; the man on the left of the second platoon, opposite the instructor, will place his breast lightly against the right arm of this officer, and the captain will direct the alignment from the left on the man on the opposite flank of the company.

457. The company being aligned the captain will command:

Front.

458. The instructor seeing the company in line of battle, will command:

Guides. Posts.

459. At the command, the captain will move to the right of his company, the covering sergeant will cover him, and the left guide will return to his place as file closer.

460. If the column be marching right in front, and the instructor should wish to form it into line without halting the column, he will give the command prescribed in No. 444, and move rapidly to platoon distance in front of the leading guides.

461. At the command *march*, briskly repeated by the chiefs of platoon, the left guides will halt short, the instructor, the chiefs of platoon, and the platoons will conform to what has been prescribed in No. 445.

462. If the column be in march left in front, the formation will be made, according to the same principles and by inverse means.

463. If the column be marching right in front, to form it into line without halting, and to march the company in line to the front, the command is:

1. *By platoons, left wheel.* 2. MARCH.

464. At the command *march*, briskly repeated by the chiefs of platoon, the left guides will halt; the man next to the left guide in each platoon will mark time; the platoons will wheel to the left; conforming to the principles of the wheel on a fixed pivot.

465. When the right of the platoons shall arrive near the line of battle, the instructor will command:

3. *Forward.* 4. MARCH. 5. *Guide right (or left.)*

466. At the fourth command, given the instant the wheel is completed, the company will move promptly together, the captain, the chief of the second platoon, the covering sergeant and the left guide will take their positions as in line of battle.

467 At the fifth command, to be given immediately after the fourth, the captain and covering sergeant, if not already there, will move briskly to the side on which the guide is designated.

468. The same principals are applicable to a column left in front.

To break the company into platoons.

469. The company marching right in front and supposed to make part of a column, to cause it to break by platoon, the instructor will command:

1. *Break into platoons.* 2. MARCH.

470. At the first command, the captain will place himself before the centre of the first platoon and give the caution: 1. *First platoon.* 2. *Forward*; the first lieutenant will pass quickly around the left to the centre of

his platoon and give the caution. 1. *Second platoon.* 2. *Mark time.*

471. At the command *march*, promptly repeated by the captain and first lieutenant, the first platoon will continue to march straight forward—the covering sergeant, as soon as the flank is disengaged will shift to the left flank of his platoon; the second platoon will begin to mark time and its chief will immediately add 1. *Right oblique.* 2. MARCH. The last command will be given so that this platoon may commence obliquing the instant the rear rank of the first platoon shall have passed.

472. The men will shorten the step in obliqing, so that when the command *forward march* is given, the platoon may have its exact distance.

473. The guide of the second platoon being near the direction of the guide of the first, the chief of the second will command *Forward*, and add MARCH the instant that the guide of his platoon shall cover the guide of the first.

474. In a column, left in front, the company will break into platoons by inverse means, applying to the first platoon all that has been prescribed for the second and reciprocally.

475. In this case, the left guide of the company will shift to the right flank of the second platoon, and the covering sergeant will remain on the right of the first.

To reform the company.

476. The column, by platoon, being in march, right in front and the instructor wishing to form it into company will command:

1. *Form company.* 2. MARCH.

477. At the first command, the captain will give the caution, 1. *First platoon;* 2. *Right oblique;* the first lieutenant will give the caution. 1. *Second platoon.* 2. *Forward.*

478. At the command *march*, promptly repeated by the captain and first lieutenant, the first platoon will obligue to the right in order to unmask the second—the covering sergeant will return to the right of the company, and the second will continue to march straight forward.

479. When the first platoon shall have nearly unmasked the second, the captain will command : *Mark time,* and at the instant the unmasking shall be complete, he will add : 2. March. The first platoon will then cease to oblique, and will mark time.

480. In the meantime the second platoon will have continued to march straight forward, and when it shall be nearly up with the first, the captain will command, *forward,* and at the instant the two platoons unite, he will add, March; the first platoon will then cease to mark time, the whole company stepping off together.

481. In a column left in front, the same movements will be executed by inverse means, the chief of the second platoon giving the command, *forward,* and the captain adding the command March, when the platoons are united.

482. The guide of the second platoon, on its right, will pass to its left flank the moment the platoon begins to oblique, the guide of the first, on its right, remaining on that flank of the platoon.

Being in column, to break files to the rear, and to cause them to re-enter into line.

483. The company being in march, and constituting part of a column, right in front, the instructor will command:

  1. *Two files from left to rear.* 2. MARCH.

484. At the command *march*, the first two files on the left of the company will mark time, the others will continue to march straitforward; the two rear rank men of the files will, as soon as the rear rank of the company shall clear them, move to the right by advancing the outer shoulder; the odd number will place himself behind the third file from that flank, the even number behind the fourth, passing for this purpose behind the odd number, the two front rank men will, in like manner, move to the right when the rear rank of the company shall clear them, the odd number will place himself behind the first file, the even number behind the second file, passing for this purpose behind the odd number.

485. At the command *march*, the files already broken, advancing a little the outer shoulder, will gain the space of two files to the right, shortening at the same time, the step, in order to make room between themselves and the rear rank of the company for the files last ordered to the rear; the latter will break by the same commands and in the same manner as the first. The men who double should increase the length of the step in order to prevent distances being lost.

486. Should the instructor wish to break files from the right, he will command:

  1. *Two files from right to rear.* MARCH.

487. At the command *march*, the files will now move to the left, advancing the outer shoulder, the even number of

the rear rank will place himself behind the third file, the odd number of the same rank behind the fourth; the even number of the front rank behind the second, the odd number for this purpose passing behind the even numbers.

489. When the front of the company is thus diminished by breaking off successive groups of two files, the rear files must always be broken from the same side.

490. If the instructor wish the files broken off to return into line, he will command:

   1. *Two files into line.* MARCH.

490. At the command *march*, the first ten files of those marching by the flank, will return briskly into line, as the others will gain the space of two files by advancing the inner shoulder towards the flank to which they belong.

491. On the same principals any number of files may be broken off togher, in which case the command will be:

1. *Four or six files from left (or right) to rear.* 2. MARCH.

On the same principals any number of files may be broken off together, in which case the command will be:

   1. *Four or six files into line.* 2. MARCH.

493. As often as files shall break off to rear, the guide on that flank will gradually close on the nearest front rank man remaining in line, and he will also open out to make room for files ordered into line.

494. Whenever there is on the right or left of a subdivision, a file which does not belong to a group, it will be broken off and brought into line singly.

The Coulumn in Route.

495. The company being in march, and supposed to

constitute a part of a column, if the instructor wish to march it in the route step, he will command:

1. *Route step.* 2. MARCH.

496. At the command *march*, repeated by the captain, the front rank will continue the step of twenty-eight inches, the rear rank will take, by gradually shortening the step, the distance of twenty-eight inches from the front rank, which distance will be computed from the breast of the man in the rear rank to the knapsack of the man in the front rank.

497. The men without further command, will immediately carry their arms *at will*, as has been prescribed in the school of the squad. They will no longer be required to march in the cadence step, or with the same foot, or remain silent.

498. The company marching in the route step, its front may be diminished by breaking into platoons or sections, by the same commands, and by the same means as if the company were marching in the cadence step.

499. When the company breaks into platoons, the chief of each will move to the flank of his platoon, and will take the place of the guide, who will step back into the rear rank.

500. As soon as the platoons shall be broken, each chief of section will place himself on its directing flank in the front rank, and the file closer will close up to within one pace of this rank. The moment the platoons are re-formed, the chiefs of the left sections will return to their places as file closers.

501. The company marching in the route step, to cause

it to pass to the cadenced step, the instructor will order the pieces to be brought to the right shoulder, and command:

1. *Quick time.* 2. MARCH.

502. At the command *march*, the men will resume the cadence step, and will close so as to leave a distance of sixteen inches between the rear rank and the front.

503. The company marching in the route step, the instructor will cause it to change direction, which will be executed without formal commands, on a simple caution from the captain; the rear rank will come up to change direction in the same manner as the front rank.

504. Each rank will conform itself to the principles prescribed for the change in close ranks with this difference only; that in wheeling the pivot man will take steps of fourteen inches, instead of nine, to close the wheeling point.

505. When the company marching in the route step shall halt, the rear rank will close up at the command *halt*, and the whole will shoulder arms.

Countermarch.

506. The company being at a halt, and supposed to constitute part of a column, right in front, when the instructor shall wish to cause it to countermarch, he will command:

1. *Countermarch.* 2. *Company, right* FACE. 3. *By file left.* 4. MARCH.

507. At the second command, the company will face to the right, the two guides to the right-about; the captain will go to the right of his company and cause two files to

break to the rear, and then place himself by the side of the front rank man row to conduct him.

508. At the command *march*, both guides will stand fast; the company will step off smartly; the first file conducted by the captain will wheel around the right guide, and direct its march along the front rank so as to arrive behind, and two paces from the left guide; each file will come in succession to wheel on the same ground around the right guide; the leading file having arrived at a point opposite the left guide, the captain will command:

1. *Company.* 2. HALT. 3. FRONT. 4. *Right*-DRESS.

509. The first command will be given at *four* paces from the point where the leading file is to halt.

510. At the second command, the company will halt.

511. At the third, it will face to the front.

512. At the fourth, the captain will step two paces outside of the left guide, now on the right, and direct the alignment, so that the front rank may be enclosed between the guides; the company being aligned he will command, FRONT, and place himself before the centre of the company as if in column; the guides passing along the front rank, will shift to their proper places, on the right and left of that rank.

513. In a column by platoon, or section, the countermarch will be executed by the same commands, and according to the same principles; the guide of each platoon, or section, will face about, and its chief will place himself by the side of the file on the right to conduct it.

514. In a column left in front, the countermarch will be executed by inverse commands and means but according to the same principles. Thus the movement will be made

by the right flank of subdivisions, if the right be in front, and by the left flank if the left be in front; in both cases the subdivisions will wheel by file to the side of the front rank.

Being in column by platoon, to form on the right (or left) into line of battle.

515. The column by platoon, right in front, being in march, the instructor wishing to form it on the right into line of battle, will command:

1. *On the right into line.* 2. *Guide right*

516. At the second command, the guide of each platoon will shift quickly to its right flank; the column will continue to march straight forward; the instructor will move briskly to the point at which the right of the company ought to rest in line, and place himself facing the point of direction to the left which he will choose.

517. The head of the column being nearly opposite the instructor the chief of the first platoon will command: 1. *Right turn;* and when exactly opposite to that point he will add: 2. MARCH.

518. At this command the first platoon will turn to the right occording to the principles prescribed in No. 114, its guide will so direct his march as to bring the front rank man next on his left, opposite to the instructor; the chief of the platoon will march before its centre, and when the guide shall be near the line of battle, he will command:

1. *Platoon.* 2. HALT.

519. At this command, which will be given at the instant the right of the platoon shall arrive at the distance of

three paces from the line of battle, the platoon will *halt*; the files not yet in line will come up promptly.

520. The guide will throw himself on the line of battle opposite to one of the three left files of his platoon, and face to the instructor, who will align him on the point of direction to the left.

521. The chief of the platoon having at the same time, gone to the point where the right of the company is to rest, will, as soon as he sees all the files of the platoon in line command:

Right—DRESS.

522. The second platoon will continue to march straight forward, until its guide shall arrive opposite to the left file of the first; it will then turn to the right at the command of its chief, and march towards the line of battle, its guide directing himself on the left file of the first platoon.

523. The guide having arrived at the distance of three paces from the line of battle, this platoon will be halted, as prescribed for the first; at the instant it halts its guide will spring on the line of battle, opposite to one of the three left files of his platoon, and will be assured in his position by the instructor.

524. The chief of the second platoon, seeing all his files in line, and its guide established on the direction, will command:

Right—DRESS.

525. Having given this the command, he will return to his place as file-closer, passing around the left; the second platoon will dress up on the alignment of the first, and when established, the captain will command:

SCHOOL OF THE COMPANY.

FRONT.

526. The movement ended, the instructor will command:

Guides—POSTS.

527. At this command the guides will return to their places in line of battle.

528. A column by platoon, left in front, will form on the left into line of battle according to the same principles, and by inverse means, applying to the second platoon what is prescribed for the first, and reciprocally.

529. The chief of the second platoon having aligned it from the left, will return to his place as file closer.

530. The captain having halted the first platoon three paces behind the line of battle, will go to the same point to align this platoon, and then command: FRONT. At the command, *guides-posts*, given by the instructor, the captain will shift to his proper flank, and the guides take their places in line of battle.

Formation of a company from two ranks into single rank, and reciprocally.

531. The company being in two ranks, and supposed to make a part of a column, right or left in front, when the instructor shall wish to form it into single rank, he will command:

1. *In one rank form company.* 2. MARCH.

532. At the first command the right guide will face to the right.

533. At the command *march*, the right guide will step off and march in the prolongation of the front rank.

534. The first file will step off at the same time with the

guide; the front rank man will turn to the right at the first step, follow the guide, and be himself followed by the rear rank man of his file, who will turn on the same spot where he turned.

535. The second file, and all other files successively, will step off as has been prescribed for the first, the front rank man of each file following immediately the rear rank man of the file next on his right. The captain will superintend he movement, and when the last man shall have stepped off, he will halt the company, and face it to the front.

536. The file-closers will take their places in line of battle, two paces in rear of the rank.

537. The company being in single rank, where the instructor wishes to form it into two ranks, he will command:

1. *In two ranks, form company.* 2. MARCH.

538. At the second command, the company will face to the right; the right guide and the man on the right will remain faced to the front.

539. At the command *march*, the men who have faced to the right will step off and form files in the following manner; the second man in the rank will place himself behind the first to form the first file; the third will place himself by the side of the first in the front rank; the fourth behind the third in the rear rank. All the others *will* in like manner place themselves, alternately, in the front and rear rank, and will thus form files of two men, on the left of those already formed.

Formation of a company from two ranks into four, and reciprocally, at a halt and in march.

540. The company being in two ranks, at a halt, and

supposed to form part of a column right in front, when the instructor shall wish to form it into four ranks, he will command:

1. *In four ranks, form company.* 2. *Company, left*—FACE.
3. MARCH, (*or double-quick*—MARCH.)

541. At the second command, the left guide will remain faced to the front, the company will face to the left, the rear rank will gain the distance of one pace from the front by a side step to the left and rear, and the men will form into four ranks as prescribed in the school of the squad.

542. At the command *march*, the first file of four men will reface to the front without undoubling. All the other files of four will step off, and closing successively to about five inches of the preceding file, will halt, and immediately face to the front, the men remaining doubled.

543. The file closers will take their new places in line of battle at two paces in rear of the front rank.

544. The captain will superintend the movement.

545. The company being in four ranks, when the instructor shall wish to form it into two ranks, he will command:

1. *In two ranks form company.* 2. *Company right*—FACE.
3. MARCH, (*or double-quick*—MARCH.)

546. At the second command, the left guide will stand fast, the company will face to the right.

547. At the command *march*, the right guide will step off and march in the prolongation of the front rank. The leading file of four men will step off at the same time, the other files standing fast; the second file will step off when there shall be between it and the first space sufficient to form two ranks.

548. The following files will execute successively what has been prescribed for the second. As soon as the last file shall have its distance, the instructor will command:

  1. *Company.* 2. HALT. 3. FRONT.

549. At the command *front*, the company will face to the front, and the files will undouble.

550. The company being in two ranks and marching to the front, when the instructor shall wish to form it into four ranks, he will command:

  1. *In four ranks form company.* 2. *By the left, double files.* 3. MARCH, (*or double-quick*—MARCH.)

551. At the command *march*, the left guide and the left file of the company will continue to march straight to the front; the company will make a half face to the left, the odd numbers placing themselves behind the even numbers. The even numbers of the rear rank will shorten their steps a little, to permit the odd numbers of the front rank to get between them and the even numbers of that rank.

552. The files thus formed of fours, except the left file, will continue to march obliquely, lengthening their steps slightly, so as to keep constantly abreast of the guide; each file will close successively on the file next on its left, and when at the proper distance from that file, will face to the front by a half face to the right, and take the touch of elbows to the left.

553. The company being in march to the front in four ranks, when the instructor shall wish to form it into two ranks, he will command:

  1. *In two ranks form company.* 2. *By the right undouble files.* MARCH, (*or double-quick*—MARCH.)

554. At the command *march*, the left guide and the left file of the company will march straight to the front; the company will make a half face to the right and march obliquely, lengthening the step a little, in order to keep as near as possible abreast of the guide.

555. As soon as the second file from the left shall have gained to the right the interval necessary for the left file to form into two ranks, the second file will face to the front by a half face to the left and march straight forward; the left file will immediately form into two ranks, and take the touch of elbows to the left.

556. Each file will execute successively, what has just been prescribed for the file next to the left, and each file will form into two ranks, when the file next on its right has obliqued the required distance and faced to the front.

557. If the company be supposed to make part of a column, left in front, these different movements will be executed according to the same principles and by inverse means, substituting the indication *left* for *right*.

RIFLE AND LIGHT INFANTRY MANUAL.

PART THIRD.

Manual of Arms for Riflemen or Light Infantry.

Position of Shouldered Arms.

1. The recruit being placed as explained in the first part of squal drill, the instructor will cause him to bend the right arm slightly, and to place the piece in it in the following manner.

2. The piece in the right hand—the barrel nearly vertical and resting in the hollow of the shoulder—the guard to the front, the arm hanging nearly at its full length, near the body; the thumb and forefinger embracing the guard, the remaining fingers closed together, grasping the swell of the stock just under the cock, which rests on the little finger.

3. In learning the recruits the manual of arms, the last syllable of the command will decide the brisk execution of the first motion of each time or pause, and the commands *two, three* and *four*, will decide the brisk execution of the other motions.

4. The manual of arms will be taught in the following progression. The recruit having the piece at the shoulder, the instructor will command:

Support—Arms.
One time and three motions.

5. (First motion.) Bring the piece, with the right hand, perpendicularly to the front and between the eyes, the barrel to the rear; seize the piece with the left hand at the lower band, raise this hand as high as the chin, and seize the piece at the same time with the right hand four inches below the cock.

6. (Second motion.) Turn the piece with the right hand, the barrel to the front; carry the piece to the left shoulder, and pass the forearm extended on the breast between the right hand and the cock; support the cock against the left forearm, the left hand resting on the right breast.

7. (Third motion.) Drop the right hand by the side.

Shoulder—Arms.
One time and three motions.

8. (First motion.) Grasp the piece with the right hand under and against the left forearm; seize it with the left hand at the lower band, the thumb extended; detach the piece slightly from the shoulder, the left forearm along the stock.

9. (Second motion.) Carry the piece vertically with both hands, to the right shoulder, the rammer to the front, change the position of the right hand so as to embrace the guard with the thumb and forefinger, slip the left hand to the height of the shoulder, the fingers extended and joined, the right arm nearly straight.

10. (Third motion.) Drop the left hand quickly by the side.

Present—Arms.

One time and two motions.

11. (First motion.) With the right hand, bring the piece erect before the centre of the body, the rammer to the front; at the same time seize the piece with the left hand half way between the guide sight and lower band, the thumb extended along the barrel and against the stock, the forearm horizontal and resting against the body, the hand as high as the elbow.

12. (Second motion.) Grasp the small of the stock with the right hand below and against the guard.

Shoulder—Arms.

One time and two motions.

13. (First motion.) Bring the piece to the right shoulder, at the same time change the position of the right hand so as to embrace the guard with the thumb and forefinger, slip up the left hand to the height of the shoulder, the fingers extended and joined, the right arm nearly straight.

14. (Second motion.) Drop the left hand quickly to the side.

Order—Arms.

One time and two motions.

15. (First motion.) Seize the piece briskly with the left hand near the upper band, and detach it slightly from the shoulder with the right hand; loosen the grasp of the right hand, lower the piece with the left, re-seize the piece with the right hand above the lower band, the little finger to the rear of the barrel, the butt about four inches from

the ground, the right hand supported against the hip, drop the left hand by the side.

16. (Second position.) Let the piece slip through the right hand to the ground by opening slightly the fingers, and take

The position of Order Arms.

17. The hand low, the barrel between the thumb and forefinger extended along the stock; the other fingers extended and joined; the muzzle about two inches from the right shoulder; the rammer in front; the toe (or beak of the butt against and in a line with the toe of the right foot, the barrel perpendicular.

Shoulder—ARMS.

One time and two motions.

18. (First motion.) Raise the peace vertically with the right hand to the height of the right breast, and opposite the shoulder, the elbow close to the body; seize the piece with the left hand below the right, and drop quickly the right hand to grasp the piece at the small of the stock, the thumb and forefinger embracing the guard; press the piece against the shoulder with the left hand, the right arm nearly straight.

19. (Second motion.) Drop the left hand quickly by the side.

Load in nine times.

I. LOAD.*

20. Grasp the piece with the left hand as high as the

---

*(NOTE.) Whenever the loadings and firings are to be executed, the instructor will cause the cartridge boxes to be brought to the front.

right elbow, and bring it vertically opposite the middle of the body, slip the right hand to the upper band, place the butt between the feet, barrel to the front; seize it with the left hand near the muzzle, which should be three inches from the body; carry the right hand to the cartridge box.

2. *Handle*—CARTRIDGE.

One time and one motion.

21. Seize the cartridge with the thumb and next two fingers, and place it between the teeth.

3. *Tear*—CARTRIDGE.

One time and one motion.

22. Tear the paper to the powder, hold the cartridge upright between the thumb and first two fingers, near the top; in this position place it in front of and near the muzzle—the back of the hand to the front.

4. *Charge*—CARTRIDGE.

One time and one motion.

23. Empty the powder into the barrel; disengage the ball from the paper with the right hand and the thumb and first two fingers of the left; insert it into the bore, the pointed end uppermost, and press it down with the right thumb; seize the head of the rammer with the thumb and forefinger of the right hand, the other fingers closed, the elbow near the body.

5. *Draw*—RAMMER.

One time and three motions.

24. (First motion.) Half draw the rammer by extending the right arm; steady it in this position with left

thumb; grasp the rammer near the muzzle with the right hand, the little finger uppermost, the nails to the front, the thumb extended along the rammer.

25. (Second motion.) Clear the rammer from the pipes by again extending the arm; the rammer in the prolongation of the pipes.

26. (Third motion.) Turn the rammer, the little end of the rammer passing near the left shoulder; place the head of the rammer on the ball, the back of the hand to the front.

6. *Ram*—CARTRIDGE.
One time and one motion.

27. Insert the rammer as far as the right, and steady it in this position with the thumb of the left hand; seize the rammer at the small end with the thumb and forefinger of the right hand, the back of the hand to the front; press the ball home, the elbows near the body.

7. *Return*—RAMMER.
One time and three motions.

28. (First motion.) Draw the rammer half way out, and steady it in this position with the left thumb; grasp it near the muzzle with the right hand, the little forefinger uppermost, the nails to the front, the thumb along the rammer; clear the rammer from the bore by extending the arm, the nails to the front, the rammer in the prolongation of the bore.

29. (Second motion.) Turn the rammer, the head of the rammer passing near the left shoulder, and insert it in the pipes until the right hand reaches the muzzle, the nails to the front.

30. (Third motion.) Force the rammer home by placing the little finger of the right hand on the head of the rammer; pass the left hand down the barrel to the extent of the arm, without depressing the shoulder.

8. PRIME.
One time and two motions.

31. (First motion.) With the left hand raise the piece until the hand is as high as the eye, grasp the small of the stock with the right hand; half face the right; place at same time, the right foot behind and at right angles with the left, the hollow of the right foot against the left heel. Slip the left hand down to the lower band, the thumb along the stock, the left elbow against the body; bring the piece to the right side, the butt below the right forearm—the small of the stock against the body and two inches below the right breast, the barrel upward, the muzzle on a level with the eye.

32. (Second motion.) Half cock with the thumb of the right hand, the fingers supported against the guard and small of the stock—remove the old cap with one of the fingers of the right hand, and with the thumb and forefinger of the same hand, take a cap from the pouch, place it on the nipple, and press it down with the thumb; seize the small of the stock with the right hand.

9. *Shoulder*—ARMS.
One time and two motions.

33. (First motion.) Bring the piece to the right shoulder and support it there with the left hand, face to the front; bring the right hand to the side of and on a line with the left; grasp the piece with the right hand as indicated in the position of *shoulder arms*.

34. (Second motion.) Drop the left hand quickly to the side.

READY.
One time and three motions.

35. (First motion.) Raise the piece slightly with the right hand, making a half face to the right on the left heel; carry the righ foot to the rear, and place it at right angles to the left, the hollow of it opposite to and against the left heel; grasp the piece with the left hand at the lower band and detach it slightly from the shoulder.

36. (Second motion.) Bring down the piece with both hands, the barrel upward, the left thumb extended along the stock, the butt along the right forearm, the small of the stock against the body and two inches below the right breast, the muzzle as high as the eye, the left elbow against the side; place at the same time, the right thumb on the head of the cock, the other fingers under and against the guard.

37. (Third motion.) Cock and seize the piece at the small of the stock, without deranging the position of the butt.

AIM.
One time and one motion.

38. Raise the piece with both hands, and support the butt against the right shoulder; the left elbow down, the right nearly as high as the shoulder, incline the head upon the butt so that the right eye may perceive quickly the object aimed at; the left eye closed, the right thumb extended along the stock, the forefinger on the trigger.

39. The rear rank men, in aiming, will each carry the

right foot about eight inches to the right, and towards the left heel of the man next on the right, inclining the upper part of the body forward.

FIRE.

40. Press the forefinger against the trigger, fire, without lowering or turning the head, and remain in this position.

LOAD.

One time and one motion.

41. Bring down the piece with both hands, at the same time face to the front, and take the position of *load.* Each rear rank man will bring his right foot by the side of the left.

43. If, after firing, the instructor should not wish the recruits to re-load, he will command :

Shoulder—ARMS.

One time and one motion.

43. Throw up the piece briskly with the left hand, and resume the position of *shoulder arms,* at the same time face to the front, turning on the left heel, and bringing the right heel on a line with the left.

44. To accustom the recruits to wait for the command, *fire,* the instructor, when they are in the position of *aim,* will command :

Recover—ARMS.

One time and one motion.

45. At the first part of the command, withdraw the finger from the trigger; at the command, *arms,* retake the position of the third motion of *ready.*

46. The recruits being in the position of the third motion of *ready ;* if the instructor should wish to bring them to a shoulder, he will command :

Shoulder—ARMS.
One time and one motion.

47. At the command *shoulder*, place the thumb upon the cock, the forefinger on the trigger, half cock, and seize the small of the stock with the right hand. At the command *arms*, bring up the piece briskly to the right shoulder and re-take the position of *shoulder arms*.

Fix—BAYONET.
One time and three motions.

48. (First motion.) Grasp the piece with the left hand at the height of the shoulder, and detach it slightly from the shoulder with the right hand.

49. (Second motion.) Quit the piece with the right hand, lower it with the left hand, opposite the middle of the body, and place the butt between the feet without shock, the rammer to the rear, the barrel vertical, the muzzle three inches from the body; seize it with the right hand at the upper band, and carry the left hand reversed to the handle of the sabre bayonet.

50. (Third motion.) Draw the sabre bayonet from the scabbard and fix it on the barrel; seize the piece with the left hand, the arm extended, the right hand at the upper band.

Shoulder—ARMS.
One time and two motions.

51. (First motion.) Raise the piece with the left hand,

and place it against the right shoulder, the rammer to the front; seize the piece at the same time with the right hand, at the small of the stock, the thumb and forefiger, embracing the guard, the right arm nearly extended.

52. (Second motion.) Drop the piece briskly, the left hand by the side.

Charge—BAYONET.

One time and two motions.

53. (First motion.) Raise the piece slightly with the right hand, and make a half face to the right on the left heel; place the hollow of the right foot opposite to, and three inches from the left heel, the feet square; seize the piece at the same time, with the left hand a little above the lower band.

54. (Second motion.) Bring down the piece with both hands, the barrel uppermost, the left elbow against the body; seize the small of the stock at the same time, with the right hand, which will be supported against the hip; the point of the sabre bayonet as high as the eye.

Shoulder—ARMS.

One time and two motions.

55. (First motion.) Throw up the piece briskly with the left hand, in facing to the front, place it against the right shoulder, the rammer to the front; turn the right hand so as to embrace the guard, slide the left hand to the height of the shoulder, the right hand nearly extended.

56. (Second motion.) Drop the left hand smartly by the side.

Trail—ARMS.

One time and two motions.

57. (First motion.) The same as the first motion of *Order arms*.

58. (Second motion.) Incline the muzzle slightly to the front, the butt to the rear and about four inches from the ground. The right hand supported at the hip, will so hold the piece that the rear-rank men may not touch with their bayonet, the men in the front rank.

Shoulder—Arms.

59. At the command *shoulder*, raise the piece perpendicularly in the right hand, the little finger in rear of the barrel. At the command *arms*, execute the two motions prescribed for the *shoulder*, from the position of *order arms*.

Unfix—Bayonet.

One time and three motions.

60. (First motion.) The same as first motion of *fix bayonet*.

61. (Second motion.) The same as second motion of *fix bayonet*, except that the thumb of the right hand will be placed on the spring of the sabre bayonet, and the left hand will embrace the handle of the sabre bayonet and the barrel, the thumb extended along the blade.

62. (Third motion.) Press the thumb of the right hand on the spring, wrest off the sabre bayonet, turn it to the right, the edge to the front, lower the guard until it touches the right hand, which will seize the back and the edge of the blade between the thumb and first two fingers, the other fingers holding the piece; change the position of the hand without quitting the handle, return the sabre bayonet to the scabbard, and seize the piece with the left hand, the arm extended.

Shoulder—Arms.

One time and two motions.

63. (First motion.) The same as the first motion, from *fix bayonet*.

64. (Second motion.) The same as the second motion in *fix bayonet*.

Secure—Arms.

One time and three motions.

65. (First motion.) The same as the first motion of *support arms*, except, with the right hand seize the piece at the small of the stock.

66. (Second motion.) Turn the piece with both hands, the barrel to the front; bring it opposite the left shoulder the butt against the hip, the left hand at the lower band, the thumb as high as the chin and extended on the rammer; the piece erect and detached from the shoulder, the left forearm against the piece.

67. (Third motion.) Raise the piece, pass it under the left arm, the left hand remaining at the lower band, the thumb on the rammer to prevent it from falling out, the little finger resting on the hip, the right hand falling at the same time by the side.

Shoulder—Arms.

One time and three motions.

68. (First motion.) Raise the piece with the left hand, and seize it with the right hand at the small of the stock, the piece erect and detached from the shoulder, the butt against the hip, left foream along the piece.

69. (Second motion.) The same as the second motion of *shoulder arms from a support*.

70. (Third motion.) The same as the third motion of *shoulder arms from a support*.

Right Shoulder Shift—Arms.

One time and two motions.

71. (First motion.) Detach the piece perpendicularly from the shoulder with the right hand, and raise it with the left between the lower band and guide sight, raise the piece, the left hand at the height of the shoulder and four inches from it; place, at the same time, the right hand on the butt, the back between the first two fingers, the other two fingers under the butt plate.

72. (Second motion.) Quit the piece with the left hand, raise and place the piece on the right shoulder with the right hand, the lock plate upwards; let fall, at the same time, the left hand by the side.

Shoulder—Arms.

One time and two motions.

73. (First motion.) Raise the piece perpendicularly by extending the right arm to its full length, the rammer to the front, at the same time, seize the piece with the left hand between the lower band and guide sight.

74. (Second motion.) Quit the butt with the right hand, which will immediately embrace the guard, lower the piece to the position of shoulder arms, slide up the left hand to the height of the shoulder, the fingers extended and closed. Drop the left hand by the side.

75. The men being at *support arms*, the instructor will sometimes cause the pieces to be brought to the right shoulder. To effect this, he will command:

Right Shoulder Shift—ARMS.
One time and two motions.

76. (First motion.) Seize the piece with the right hand, below and near the left forearm, place the left hand under the butt, the heel of the butt between the first two fingers.

77. (Second motion.) Turn the piece with the left hand, the lock plate upward, carry it to the right shoulder, the left hand still holding the butt, the muzzle elevated; hold the piece in this position and place the right hand upon the butt as is prescribed in No. 71, and let fall the hand by the side.

Support—ARMS.
One time and two motions.

78. (First motion.) The same as the first motion of *shoulder arms*, No. 73.

79. (Second motion.) Turn the piece with both hands, the barrel to the front, carry it opposite the left shoulder, slip the right hand to the small of the stock, place the left forearm, extended, on the breast and let fall the right hand to the side.

Arms—AT WILL.
One time and one motion.

80. Carry the piece at pleasure on either shoulder, with one or both hands, the muzzle elevated.

Shoulder—ARMS.
One time and one motion.

81. Retake quickly the position of *shoulder arms*.

Ground—ARMS.
One time and two motions.

82. (First motion.) As prescribed in *heavy infantry manual,* (squad drill.)

83. (Second motion.) As prescribed in *heavy infantry manual,* (squad drill.)

Raise—Arms.

One time and two motions.

84. (First motion.) As prescribed in *heavy infantry manual,* (squad drill.)

85. (Second motion.) As prescribed in *heavy infantry manual,* (squad drill.)

86. The recruits being at *order arms,* and having the sabre bayonet in the scabbard, if the instructor wishes to cause an inspection of arms, he will command,

Inspection—Arms.

One time and two motions.

87. (First motion.) Seize the piece with the left hand below and near the upper band, carry it with both hands opposite the middle of the body, the butt between the feet, the rammer to the rear, the barrel vertical, the muzzle about three inches from the body; carry the left hand reversed to the sabre-bayonet, draw it from the scabbard and fix it on the barrel; grasp the piece with the left hand below and near the upper band, seize the rammer with the thumb and forefinger of the right hand, bent, the other fingers closed.

88. (Second motion.) Draw the rammer, as has been explained in *loading,* and let it glide to the bottom of the bore, replace the piece with the left hand, opposite the right shoulder, and take the position of order arms.

89. The instructor will then inspect in succession, the

piece of each recruit, in passing along the front of the rank, in conformity with the principles prescribed in *squad drill* for the inspection of arms

90. When the instructor shall have passed him, each recruit will retake the position prescribed at the command *inspection arms.*

91. The men being at order arms, the instructor will command,

Stack—ARMS.

92. At this command, the front rank man of every even numbered file will pass his piece before him, seizing it with the left land near the upper band; will place the butt a little in advance of the left toe, the barrel turned toward the body, and draw the rammer slightly from its place, the front rank man of every odd numbered file will also draw the rammer slightly, and pass his piece to the man next on his left, who will seize it with the right hand near the upper band, and place the butt a little in advance of the right toe of the man next on his right, the barrel turned to the front; he will then cross the rammer of the two pieces, the rammer of the piece of the odd numbered man being inside; the rear rank man of evry even file will also draw his rammer, lean the piece forward, the lock plate downward, advance the right foot about six inches, and insert the rammer between the rammer and the barrel of the piece of his front rank man; with his left hand he will place the butt of his piece on the ground, thirty-two inches in rear of and perpendicular to the front rank, bring back his right foot by the side of the left; the front rank man of every even file, will at the same time lean the stock to the rear, quit it with the right hand and force all the rammers

down. The stack being thus formed, the rear rank man of every odd file will pass his piece into his left hand, the barrel to the front, and inclining it forward, will rest it on the stack.

93. The men of both ranks having taken the position of the soldier without arms, the instructor will command

1. *Break ranks*—2. MARCH.

To Resume Arms.

94. Both ranks being reformed in rear of their stacks, the instructor will command:

Take—ARMS.

95. At this command, the rear rank man of every odd numbered piece, will withdraw his piece from the stack; the front rank man of every even file, will seize his own piece with the left hand, and that of the man on his right, with his right hand, both above the lower band; the rear rank man of the even file will seize his piece with the right hand below the lower band; these two men will raise up the stack to loosen the rammers; the front rank man of every odd file, will facilitate the disengagement of the rammers, if necessary, by drawing them out slightly with the left hand, and will receive his piece from the hand of the man next on the left; the four men will retake the position of the soldier at order arms.

Formation of a Regiment in line of Battle or in line.

96. A Regiment is composed of ten companies, which will habitually be posted from right to left, in the following order: first, sixth, fourth, ninth, third, eighth, fifth,

tenth, seventh, second, according to the rank of captains.

97. With a less number of companies the same principle will be observed, viz: the first captain will command the right company, the second captain the left company, the third captain the right centre company, and so on.

98. The companies thus posted will be designated from right to left, *first* company, *second* company, etc. This designation will be observed in the manœuvres.

99. The first two companies on the right, whatever their denomination, will form the *first division;* the next two companies the *second division;* and so on, to the left.

100. Each company will be divided into two equal parts which will be designated as the first and second platoon, counting from the right; and each platoon, in like manner, will be subdivided into two sections.

101. In all exercises and manœvres, every regiment, or part of a regiment, composed of two or more companies, will be designated as a battalion.

102. The color, with a guard to be hereinafter designated, will be posted on the left of the right centre battalion company. That company and all on its right, will be denominated the *right wing* of the battalion; the remaining companies the *left wing*.

103. The farmation of a regiment is in two ranks; and each company will be formed into two ranks, in the following manner: the corporals will be posted in the front rank, and on the right and left of platoons, according to height; the tallest corporal and the tallest man will form the first file, the next two tallest men will form the second file, and so on to the last file, which will be composed of the shortest corporal and the shortest man.

104. The odd and even files, numbered as one, two, in the company, from right to left, will form groups of four men, who will be designated *comrades in battle.*

105. The distance from one rank to another will be thirteen inches, measured from the breasts of the rear rank men to the backs or knapsacks of the front rank men.

106. For manœuvring, the companies of a battalion will always be equalized, by transferring men from the strongest to the weakest companies.

Posts of Field Officers and Regimental Staff.

107. The field officers, colonel, lieutenant-colonel and major, are supposed to be mounted, and on active service shall be on horseback. The adjutant, when the battalion is manœuvring, will be on foot.

108. The colonel will take post thirty paces in rear of the file closer, and opposite the centre of the battalion. This distance will be reduced whenever there is a reduction in the front of the battalion.

109. The lieutentant-colonel and the major will be opposite the centres of the right and left wings respectively, and twelve paces in rear of the file closers.

110. The adjutant and sergeant major will be opposite the right and left of the battalion, respectively, and eight paces in the rear of the file closers.

111. The adjutant and sergeant-major will aid the lieutenant-colonel and major, respectively, in the manœuvres.

112. The colonel, if absent, will be replaced by the lieutenant-colonel, and the latter by the major. If all the field officers be absent, the senior captains will command the battalion; but if either be present, he will not call the

senior captain to act as field officer, except in case of evident necessity.

113. The quarter-master, surgeon, and other staff officers, in one rank, on the left of the colonel, and three paces in his rear.

114. The quarter-master sergeant on a line with the front rank of the field music, and two paces on the right.

Posts of Field Music and Band.

115. The buglars will be drawn up in four ranks, and posted twelve paces in rear of the file closers, the left opposite the centre of the left centre company. The senior principle musician will be two paces in front of the field music, and the other two paces in the rear.

116. The regimental band, if there be one, will be drawn up in two or four ranks, according to its numbers, and posted five paces in rear of the field music, having one of the principal musicians at its head.

Color-Guard.

117. In each battalion the color-guard will be composed of eight corporals, and posted on the left of the right centre company, of which company, for the time being, the guard will make a part.

118. The front rank will be composed of a sergeant, to be selected by the colonel, who will be called, for the time, *color-barer*, with the two ranking corporals, respectively, on his right and left; the rear rank will be composed of the three corporals next in rank; and the three remaining corporals will be posted in their rear, and on the line of file closers. The left guide of the color company, when

these three last named corporals are in the rank of file closers, will be immediately on their left.

119. In battalions with less than five companies present, there will be no color-guard, and no display of colors, except it may be at reviews.

120. The corporals for the color-guard will be selected from those most distinguished for regularity and percision, as well in their positions under arms as in their marching. The latter advantage, and a just carriage of the person, are to be more particularly sought for in the selection of the color-bearer.

General Guides.

121. There will be two *general* guides in each battalion, selected, for the time, by the colonel, from among the sergeants (other than first sergeants) the most distinguished for carriage under arms and accuracy in marching.

122. These sergeants will be respectively denominated, in the manœuvres, *right general guide* and *left general guide*, and be posted in the line of file closers; the first in rear of the right and the second in rear of the left flank of the battalion.

SKIRMISH DRILL AND BAYONET EXERCISE.

PART FOURTH.

INSTRUCTION FOR SKIRMISHERS.

General principles and division of the instruction.

1. The movements of skirmishers should be subjected to such rules as will give to the commander the means of moving them in any direction with the greatest promptitude.

2. It is not expected that these movements should be executed with the same precision as in closed ranks, nor is it desirable, as such exactness would materially interfere with their prompt execution.

3. When skirmishers are thrown out to clear the way for, and to protect the advance of the main corps, their movements should be so regulated by this corps as to keep it constantly covered.

4. Every body of skirmishers should have a reserve, the strength and composition of which will vary according to circumstances.

5. If the body thrown out be within sustaining distance

of the main corps, a very small reserve will be sufficient for each company, whose duty it shall be to fill vacant places, furnish the line with cartridges, relieve the fatigued, and serve as a rallying point for the skirmishers.

6. If the main corps be at a considerable distance, besides the company reserves, another reserve will be required, composed of entire companies, which will be employed to sustain and reinforce such parts of the line as may be warmly attacked; this reserve should be strong enough to relieve at least half the companies deployed as skirmishers.

7. The reserve should be placed behind the centre of the line of skirmishers, the company reserves at one hundred and fifty, and the principal reserve at four hundred paces. This rule however, is not invariable. The reserves, while holding themselves within sustaining distance of the line, should be, as much as possible, in a position to afford each other mutual protection, and must carefully profit by any accidents of the ground to conceal themselves from the view of the enemy, and to shelter themselves from his fire.

8. The movements of skirmishers will be executed in quick, or double quick time. The run will be resorted to only in cases of urgeant necessity.

9. Skirmishers will be permitted to carry their pieces in the manner most convenient to them.

10. The movements will be habitually indicated by the sounds of the bugle.

11. The officers, and, if necessary, the non-commissioned officers, will repeat, and cause the commands to be executed, as soon as they are given; but to avoid mistakes, when the signals are employed, they will wait until the

last bugle note is sounded before commencing the movement.

12. When skirmishers are ordered to move rapidly, the officers and non-commissioned officers will see that the men economize their strength, keep cool, and profit by all the advantages which the ground may offer for cover. It is only by this continual watchfulness on the part of all grades, that a line of skirmishers can attain success.

13. This instruction will be divded into five articles, and subdivided as follows:

ARTICLE FIRST.

1. To deploy forward.
2. To deploy by the flank.
3. To extend intervals.
4. To close intervals.
5. To relieve skirmishers.

ARTICLE SECOND.

1. To advance in line.
2. To reteat in line.
3. To change direction.
4. To march by the flank.

ARTICLE THIRD.

1. To fire at a halt.
2. To fire marching.

Article Fourth.

1. The rally.
2. To form column to march in any direction.
3. The assembly.

Article Fifth.

1. To deploy a battallion as skirmishers.
2. To rally the battalion deployed as skirmishers.

14. In the first four articles, it is supposed that the movements are executed by a company deployed as skirmishers, on a front equal to that of the battalion in order of battle. In the fifth article, it is supposed that each company of the battalion, being deployed as skirmishers, occupies a front of one hundred paces. From these two examples, rules may be numerically deduced for all cases, whatever may be the strength of the skirmishers, and the extent of ground they ought to occupy.

Article First.

Deployments.

15. A company may be deployed as skirmishers in two ways: forward and by the flank.
16. The deployment forward will be adopted when the company is behind the line on which it is to be established as skirmishers: it will be deployed by the flank, when it finds itself already on that line.

17. Whenever a company is to be deployed as skirmishers, it will be divided into two platoons, and each platoon will be subdivided into two sections; the comrades in battle, forming groups of four men, will be careful to know and to sustain each other. The captain will assure himself that the files in the centre of each platoon and section are designated.

18. A company may be deployed as skirmishers on its right, left, or centre file, or on any other named file whatsoever. In this manner, skirmishers may be thrown forward with the greatest possible rapidity on any ground they may be required to occupy.

19. A chain of skirmishers ought generally to preserve their alignment, but no advantage which the ground may present should be sacrificed to attain this regularity.

20. The interval between skirmishers depends on the extent of ground to be covered; but in general, it is not proper that the groups of four men should be removed more than forty paces from each other. The habitual distance between men of the same group in open grounds will be five paces; in no case will they lose sight of each other.

21. The front to be occupied to cover a battalion comprehends its front and the half of each interval which separates it from the battalion on its right and left. If a line, whose wings are not supported, should be covered by skirmishers, it will be necessary either to protect the flanks with skirmishers, or to extend them in front of the line so far beyond the wings as effectually to oppose any attempt which might be made by the enemy's skirmishers to disturb the flanks.

To deploy forward.

22. A company being at a halt or in march, when the captain shall wish to deploy it forward on the left file of the first platoon, holding the second platoon in reserve, he will command:

1. *First platoon—as skirmishers.*
2. *On the left file—take intervals.*
3. MARCH (*or double quick—March.*)

23. At the first command, the second and third lieutenants will place themselves rapidly two paces behind the centres of the right and left sections of the first platoon; the fifth sergeant will move one pace in front of the centre of the first platoon, and will place himself between the two sections in the front rank as soon as the movement begins; the fourth sergeant will place himself on the left of the front rank of the same platoon, as soon as he can pass.— The captain will indicate to this sergeant the point on which he wishes him to direct his march. The first lieutenant, placing himself before the centre of the second platoon, will command:

Second platoon backward—MARCH.

24. At this command, the second platoon will step three paces to the rear, so as to unmask the flank on the first platoon. It will then be halted by its chief, and the second sergeant will place himself on the left, and the third sergeant on the right flank of this platoon.

25. At the command *march*, the left group of four men,

conducted by the fourth sergeant, will direct itself on the point indicated; all the other groups of fours throwing forward briskly the left shoulder, will move diagonally to the front in double quick time, so as to gain to the right the space of twenty paces, which shall be the distance between each group and that immediately on its left. When the second group from the left shall arrive on a line with and twenty paces from the first, it will march straight to the front, conforming to the gait and direction of the first, keeping constantly on the same alignment and at twenty paces from it. The third group, and all the others, will conform to what has just been prescribed for the second; they will arrive successively on the line. The right guide will arrive with the last group.

26. The left guide having reached the point where the left of the line should rest, the captain will command the skirmishers to halt; the men composing each group of fours will then immediately deploy at five paces from each other, and to the right and left of the front rank man of the even file in each group, the rear rank men placing themselves on the left of their file leaders. If any groups be not in line at the command *halt*, they will move up rapidly, conforming to what has just been prescribed.

27. If, during the deployment, the line should be fired upon by the enemy, the captain may cause the groups of fours to deploy, as they gain their proper distances.

28. The line being formed the non-commissioned officers on the right, left and centre of the platoon will place themselves ten paces in rear of the line, and opposite the position they respectively occupied. The chiefs of sections will promptly rectify any irregularities, and then place

themselves twenty-five or thirty paces in rear of the centre of their sections, each having with him four men taken from the reserve, and also a bugler, who will repeat, if necessary, the signals sounded by the captain.

29. Skirmishers should be particularly instructed to take advantage of any cover which the ground may offer, and should lie flat on the ground whenever such a movement is necessary to protect them from the fire of the enemy. Regularity in the alignment should yield to this important advantage.

30. When the movement begins, the first lieutenant, will face the second platoon *about*, and march it promptly, and by the shortest line, to about one hundred and fifty paces in rear of the centre of the line. He will hold it always at this distance, unless ordered to the contrary.

31. The reserve will conform itself to all the movements of the line. *This rule is general.*

32. Light troops will carry their bayonets habitually in the scabbard, and this rule applies equally to the skirmishers and the reserve; whenever bayonets are required to be fixed, a particular signal will be given. The captain will give a general superintendence to the whole deployment, and then promptly place himself about eighty paces in the rear of the centre of the line. He will have with him a bugler and four men taken from the reserve.

33. The deployment may be made on the right or the centre of the platoon, by the same commands, substituting the indication *right* or *centre*, for that of *left* file.

34. The deployment on the right or the centre will be made according to the principles prescribed above; in this latter case, the centre of the platoon will be marked by

the right group of fours in the second section; the fifth sergeant will place himself on the right of this group, and serve as the guide of the platoon during the deployment.

35. In whatever manner the deployment be made, on the right, left or centre, the men in each group of fours will always deploy at five paces from each other, and upon the front rank man of the even numbered file. The deployments will habitually be made at twenty paces interval; but if a greater interval be required, it will be indicated in the command.

36. If a company be thrown out as skirmishers, so near the main body as to render a reserve unnecessary, the entire company will be extended in the same manner, and according to the same principles, as for the deployment of a platoon. In this case, the third lieutenant will command the fourth section, and a non-commissioned officer designated for that purpose, the second section; the fifth sergeants will act as centre guard; the file closers will place themselves ten paces in the rear of the line, and opposite their places in line of battle. The first and second lieutenant will each have a bugler near him.

To deploy by the flank.

37. The company being at a halt, when the captain shall wish to deploy it by the flank, holding the first platoon in reserve, he will command:

1. *Second platoon—as skirmishers.* 2. *By the right flank —take intervals.* 3. MARCH, (*or double quick*—MARCH.)

38. At the first command, the first and third lieutenants

will place themselves, respectively, two paces behind the centres of the first and second sections of the second platoon; the fifth sergeant will place himself one pace in front of the centre of the second platoon; the third sergeant, as soon as he can pass, will place himself on the right of the front rank of the same platoon. The captain will indicate to him the point on which he wishes him to direct his march. The chief of the first platoon will execute what has been prescribed for the chief of the second platoon, Nos. 23 and 24. The fourth sergeant will place himself on the left flank of the reserve, the first sergeant will remain on the right flank.

39. At the second command, the first and third lieutenants will place themselves two paces behind the left group of their respective sections.

40. At the command *march*, the second platoon will face to the right, and commence the movement; the left group of fours will stand fast, but will deploy as soon as there is room on its right, comforming to what has been prescribed, No. 26; the third sergeant will place himself on the left of the right group, to conduct it; the second group will halt at twenty paces from the one on its left, the third group at twenty paces from the second, and so on to the right. As the groups halt, they will face to the enemy, and deploy as has been explained for the left group.

41. The chiefs of sections will pay particular attention to the successive deployments of the groups, keeping near the group about to halt, so as to rectify any errors which may be committed. When the deployment is completed, they will place themselves thirty paces in rear of the centre of their sections, as has been heretofore prescribed.

The non-commissioned officers will also place themselves as previously indicated.

42. As soon as the movement commences, the chief of the first platoon, causing it to face about, will move it as indicated, No. 30.

43. The deployment may be made by the left flank according to the same principles, substituting *left flank* for *right flank*.

44. If the captain should wish to deploy the company upon the centre of the platoons, he will command:

1. *Second platoon—as skirmishers.* 2. *By the right and left flank—take intervals.* 3. MARCH (or *double quick—* MARCH.)

45. At the first command, the officers and non-commissioned officers will conform to what has been prescribed, No. 38.

46. At the second command, the first lieutenant will place himself behind the left group of the right section of the second platoon, the third lieutenant behind the right group of the left section of the same platoon.

47. At the command *march*, the right section will face to the right, the left section will face to the left, the group on the right of this latter section will stand fast. The two sections will move off in opposite directions; the third sergeant will place himself on the left of the right file to conduct it, the second sergeant on the right of the left file. The two groups nearest that which stands fast, will each halt at twenty paces from this group, and each of the other groups will halt at twenty paces from the group which

is in rear of it. Each group will deploy as heretofore prescribed, No. 40.

48. The first and third lieutenants, will direct the movement, holding themselves always abreast of the group which is about to halt.

49. The captain can cause the deployment to be made on any named group whatsoever; in this case, the fifth sergeant will place himself before the group indicated, and the deployment will be made according to the principles heretofore prescribed.

50. The entire company may be also deployed, according to the same principles.

To extend intervals.

51. This movement, which is employed to extend a line of skirmishers, will be executed according to the principles prescribed for deployments.

52. If it be supposed that the line of skirmishers is at a halt, and that the captain wishes to extend it to the left, he will command:

1. *By the left flank, (so many paces), extend intervals.*
2. MARCH (or *double quick*—MARCH.)

53. At the command *march*, the group on the right will stand fast, all the other groups will face to the left, and each group will extend its interval to the prescribed distance by the means indicated, No. 40.

54. The men of the same group will continue to preserve between each other the distance of five paces, unless the nature of the ground should render it necessary that they

should close nearer, in order to keep in sight of each other. The intervals refer to the spaces between the groups, and not to the distances between the men in each group. The intervals will be taken from the right or left man of the neighboring group.

55. If the line of skirmishers be marching to the front, and the captain should wish to extend it to the right, he will command:

1. *On the left group* (*so many paces*), *extend intervals.*
   2. MARCH (or *double quick*—March.)

56. The left group, conducted by the guide, will continue to march to the point of direction; the other groups throwing forward the left shoulder, and taking the double quick step, will open their intervals to the prescribed distance, by the means indicated, No. 25, conforming also to what is prescribed, No. 54.

57. Intervals may be extended on the centre of the line, according to the same principles.

58. If in extending intervals, it be intended that one company or platoon should occupy a line which had been previously occupied by two, the men of the company or platoon which is to retire will fall successively to the rear as they are relieved by the extension of the intervals.

To close intervals.

59. This movement, like that of opening intervals, will be executed according to the principles prescribed for the deployments.

60. If the line of skirmishers be halted, and the cap-

tain should wish to close intervals to the left, he will command:

1. *By the left flank (so many paces) close intervals.*
2. MARCH (or *double quick*—MARCH.)

61. At the command *march*, the left group will stand fast, the other groups will face to the left and close to the prescribed distance, each group facing to the enemy as it attains its proper distance.

62. If the line be marching to the front, the captain will command:

1. *On the left group (so many paces) close intervals.*
2. MARCH (or *double quick*—March.)

63. The left group, conducted by the guide, will continue to move on in the direction previously indicated; the other groups, advancing the right shoulder, will close to the left, until the intervals are reduced to the prescribed distance.

64. Intervals may be closed on the right, or on the centre, according to the same principles.

65. When intervals are to be closed up, in order to reinforce a line of skirmishers, so as to cause two companies to cover the ground which had been previously occupied by one, the new company will deploy so as to finish its movement at twenty paces in rear of the line it is to occupy, and the men will successively move upon that line, as they shall be unmasked by the men of the old company. The reserves of the two companies will unite behind the centre of the line.

To relieve a company deployed as skirmishers.

66. When a company of skirmishers is to be relieved, the captain will be advised of the intention, which he will immediately communicate to his first and second lieutenants.

67. The new company will execute its deployment forward, so as to finish the movement at about twenty paces in rear of the line.

68. Arrived at this distance, the men of the new company, by command of their captain, will advance rapidly a few paces beyond the old line at halt; the new line being established, the old company will assemble on its reserve, taking care not to get into groups of fours until they are beyond the fire of the enemy.

69. If the skirmishers to be relieved, are marching in retreat, the company thrown out to relieve them will deploy by the flank, as prescribed, No. 38, and following. The old skirmishers will continue to retire with order, and having passed the new line, they will form upon the reserve.

ARTICLE SECOND.

To advance.

To advance in line, and to retreat in line.

70. When a platoon or a company, deployed as skirmishers, is marching by the front, the guide will be habitually in the centre. No particular indication to this effect need be given in the commands, but if on the contrary it be in-

tended that the directing guide should be on the right, or left, the command *guide right*, or *guide left*, will be given immediately after that of forward.

71. The captain, wishing the line of skirmishers to advance, will command:

1. *Forward.* 2. MARCH (or *double quick*—MARCH.)

72. This command will be repeated with the greatest rapidity by the chief of sections, and in case of need, by the sergeants. This rule is general, whether the skirmishers march by the front or by the flank.

73. At the first command, three sergeants will move briskly on the line, the first on the right, the second on the left, and the third in the centre.

74. At the command *march*, the line will move to the front, the guide charged with the direction, will move on to the point indicated to him, the skirmishers will hold themselves aligned on this guide, and preserve their intervals toward him.

75. The chiefs of sections will march immediately behind their sections, so as to direct their movements.

76. The captain will give a general superintendence to the movement.

77. When he shall wish to halt the skirmishers, he will commmand :

HALT.

78. At this command, briskly repeated, the line will halt. The chiefs of sections will promptly rectify any irregularity in the alignment and intervals, and after taking every

possible advantage which the ground may offer for protecting the men, they, with the three sergeants in the line, will retire to their proper places in rear.

79. The captain, wishing to march the skirmishers in retreat, will command:

1. *In retreat.* 2. MARCH (or *double quick*—MARCH.

80. At the first command, the three sergeants will move on the line as prescribed, No. 73.

81. At the command *march*, the skirmishers will face about individually, and march to the rear, conforming to the principles prescribed, No. 74.

82. The officers and sergeants will use every exertion to preserve order.

83. To halt the skirmishers, marching in retreat, the captain will command:

HALT.

84. At this command, the skirmishers will halt, and immediately face to the front.

85. The chiefs of sections and the three guides, will each conform himself to what is prescribed, No. 78.

To change direction.

86. If the commander of a line of skirmishers shall wish to cause it to change direction to the right, he will command:

1. *Right wheel.* 2. MARCH (or *double quick*—MARCH.)

87. At the command *march*, the right guide will mark time in his place; the left guide will move in a circle to the right, and that he may properly regulate his movements, will occasionally cast his eyes to the right, so as to observe the direction of the line, and the nature of the ground to be passed over. The centre guide will also march in a circle to the right, and in order to conform his movements to the general direction, will take care that his steps are only half the length of the steps of the guide on the left.

88. The skirmishers will regulate the length of their steps by their distance from the marching flank, being less as they approach the pivot, and greater as they are removed from it; they will often look to the marching flank, so as to preserve the direction and their intervals.

89. When the commander of the line shall wish to resume the direct march, he will command:

1. *Forward.* 2. March.

90. At the command *march*, the line will cease to wheel, and the skirmishers will move direct to the front; the centre guide will march on the point which will be indicated to him.

91. If the captain should wish to halt the line, in place of moving it to the front, he will command:

Halt.

92. At this command, the line will halt.

93. A change of direction to the left will be made according to the same principles, and by inverse means.

94. A line of skirmishers marching in retreat, will change direction by the same means, and by the same commands, as a line marching in advance; for example, if the captain should wish to refuse his left, now become the right, he will command: 1. *Left wheel.* 2. MARCH. At the command *halt*, the skirmishers will face to the enemy.

95. But if, instead of halting the line, the captain should wish to continue to march it in retreat, he will, when he judges the line has wheeled sufficiently, command:

1. *In retreat.* 2. MARCH.

To march by the flank.

96. The captain, wishing the skirmishers to march by the right flank, will command:

1. *By the righ flank.* 2. MARCH (or *double quick*—MARCH.)

97. At the first command, the three sergeants will place themselves on the line.

98. At the command *march*, the skirmishers will face to the right, and move off; the right guide will place himself by the side of the leading man on the right to conduct him, and will march on the point indicated; each skirmisher will take care to follow exactly in the direction of the one immediately preceding him, and preserve his distance.

99. The skirmishers may be marched by the left flank, according to the same principles, and by the same commands, substituting *left* for *right*; the left guide will

place himself by the side of the leading man to conduct him.

100. If the skirmishers be marching by the flank, and the captain should wish to halt them, he will command:

HALT.

101. At this command, the skirmishers will halt and face to the enemy. The officers and sergeants will conform to what has been prescribed, No. 78.

102. The reserve should execute all the movements of the line, and be held always about one hundred and fifty paces from it, so as to be in position to second its operations.

103. When the chief of the reserve shall wish to march it in advance, he will command : 1. *Platoon, forward.* 2. *Guide left.* 3. MARCH. If he should wish to march it in retreat, he will command: 1. *In retreat.* 2. MARCH. 3. *Guide right.* At the command *halt*, it will re-face to the enemy.

104. The men should be made to understand that the signals or commands, such as *forward*, mean that the skirmishers shall march on the enemy ; *in retreat*, that they shall retire, and to *the right or left flank*, that the men must face to the right or left, whatever may be their position.

105. If the skirmishers be marching by the flank, and the captain should wish to change direction to the right (or left) he will command: 1. *By file right* (or *left*) 2. MARCH. These movements will be executed by the signals Nos. 14 and 15.

Article Third.

The firings.

106. Skirmishers will fire either at a halt or marching.

To fire at a halt.

107. To cause this fire to be executed, the captain will command:

Commence—Firing.

108. At this command, briskly repeated, the men of the front rank will commence firing; they will reload rapidly, and hold themselves in readiness to fire again. During this time the men of the rear rank will come to a ready, and as soon as their respective file leaders have loaded, they will also fire and reload. The men of each fire will thus continue the firing, conforming to this principle, that the one or the other shall always have his piece loaded.

109. Light troops should be always calm, so as to aim with accuracy; they should, moreover, endeavor to estimate correctly the distances between themselves and the enemy to be hit, and thus be enabled to deliver their fire with the greater certainty of success.

110. Skirmishers will not remain in the same place whilst reloading, unless protected by accidents in the ground.

To fire marching.

111. This fire will be executed by the same commands as the fire at a halt.

112. At the command *commence firing*, if the line be advancing, the front rank man of every file will halt, fire, and reload before throwing himself forward. The rear rank man of the same file will continue to march, and after passing ten or twelve paces beyond his front rank man, will halt, come to a ready, select his object, and fire when his front rank man has loaded ; the fire will thus continue to be executed by each file ; the skirmishers will keep united, and endeavor as much as possible to preserve the general direction of the alignment.

113. If the line be marching in retreat, at the command *commence firing*, the front rank man of every file will halt, face to the enemy, fire, and then reload whilst moving to the rear ; the rear rank man of the same file will continue to march, and halt ten or twelve paces beyond his front rank man, face about, come to a ready, and fire when his front rank man has passed him in retreat and loaded ; after which he will move to the rear and reload ; the front rank man in his turn, after marching briskly to the rear, will halt ten or twenty paces from the rear rank, face to the enemy, load his piece and fire, conforming to what has just been prescribed , the firing will thus be continued.

114. If the company be marching by the right flank, at the command, *commence firing*, the front rank man of every file will face to the enemy, step one pace forward, halt, and fire; the rear rank man will continue to move forward. As soon as the front rank man has fired, he will place himself briskly behind his rear rank man and reload whilst marching. When he has loaded, the rear rank man will, in his turn, step one pace forward, halt, and fire ; and returning to the ranks, will place himself behind

his front rank man; the latter, in his turn, will act in the same manner, observing the same principles. At the command, *cease firing*, the men of the rear rank will retake their original positions, if not already there.

115. If the company be marching by the left flank, the fire will be executed according to the same principles, but in this case, it will be the rear rank men who will fire first.

116. The following rules will be observed in the cases to which they apply.

117. If the line be firing at a halt, or whilst marching by the flank, at the command, *Forward*—MARCH, it will be the men whose pieces are loaded, without regard to the particular rank to which they belong, who will move to the front. Those men whose pieces have been discharged, will remain in their places to load them before moving forward, and the firing will be continued agreeably to the principles prescribed, No. 112.

118. If the line be firing either at a halt, advancing, or whilst marching by the flank, at the command, *In retreat*—MARCH, the men whose pieces are loaded will remain faced to the enemy, and will fire in this position; the men whose pieces are discharged will retreat loading them, and the fire will be continued agreeably to the principles prescribed, No. 113.

119. If the line of skirmishers be firing either at a halt, advancing, or in retreat, at the command, *By the right* (or *left*) *flank*—MARCH, the men, whose pieces are loaded, will step one pace out of the general alignment, face to the enemy, and fire in this position; the men whose pieces are unloaded will face to the right (or left) and march in the direction indicated. The men who stepped out of

the ranks will place themselves, immediately after firing, upon the general direction, and in rear of their front or rear rank men, as the case may be. The fire will be continued according to the principles prescribed, No 114.

120. Skirmishers will be habituated to load their pieces whilst marching; but they will be enjoined to halt always an instant, when in the act of charging cartridge and priming.

121. They should be practised to fire and load kneeling, lying down and sitting, and much liberty should be allowed in these exercises, in order that they may be executed in the manner found to be most convenient. Skirmishers should be cautioned not to forget that, in whatever position they may load, it is important that the piece should be placed upright before ramming, in order that the entire charge of powder may reach the bottom of the bore.

122. In commencing the fire, the men of the same rank should not all fire at once, and the men of the same file should be particular that one or the other of them be always loaded.

123. In retreating, the officer commanding the skirmishers should seize on every advantage which the ground may present for arresting the enemy as long as possible.

124. At the signal to *cease firing*, the captain will see that the order is promptly obeyed; but the men who may not be loaded, will load. If the line be marching, it will continue the movement; but the man of each file who happens to be in front, will wait until the man in rear shall be abreast with him.

125. If a line of skirmishers be firing advancing, at the command *halt*, the line will re-form upon the skirmishers

who are in front; when the line is retreating, upon the skirmishers who are in rear.

126. Officers should watch with the greatest possible vigilance over a line of skirmishers; in battle they should neither carry a rifle or fowling piece. In all the firings, they, as well as the sergeants, should see that order and silence are preserved, and that the skirmishers do not wander imprudently; they should especially caution them to be calm and collected; not to fire until they distinctly perceive the objects at which they aim, and are sure that those objects are within proper range. Skirmishers should take advantage promptly, and with intelligence, of all shelter, and of all accidents of the ground, to conceal themselves from the view of the enemy, and to protect themselves from his fire. It may often happen that intervals are momentarily lost when several men near each other find a common shelter; but when they quit this position, they should immediately resume their intervals and their places in line, so that they may not, by crowding, needlessly expose themselves to the fire of the enemy.

ARTICLE FOURTH.

THE RALLY.

To form column.

127. A company deployed as skirmishers, is rallied in order to oppose the enemy with better success; the rallies are made at a run, and with bayonets fixed; when ordered to rally, the skirmishers fix bayonets without command.

128. There are several ways of rallying, which the chief of the line will adopt according to circumstances.

129. If the line, marching or at a halt, be merely disturbed by scattered horsemen, it will not be necessary to fall back on the reserve, but the captain will cause bayonets to be fixed. If the horsemen should, however, advance to charge the skirmishers, the captain will command, *rally by fours.* The line will halt, if marching, and the four men of each group will execute this rally in the following manner: the front rank man of the even numbered file will take the position of *guard against cavalry*; the rear rank man of the odd numbered file will also take the position of *guard against cavalry*, turning his back to him, his right foot thirteen inches from the right foot of the former, and parallel to it; the front rank man of the odd file, and the rear rank man of the even file, will also place themselves back to back, taking a like position, and between the two men already established, facing to the right and left; the right feet of the four men will be brought together, forming a square and serving for mutual support. The four men in each group will come to a ready, fire as occasion may offer, and load without moving their feet.

130. The captains and chiefs of sections will each cause the four men who constitute his guard to form square, the men separating so as to enable him and the bugler to place themselves in the centre. The three sergeants will each promptly place himself in the group nearest him in the line of skirmishers.

131. Whenever the captain shall judge these squares too weak, but should wish to hold his position by strengthening his line, he will command:

Rally by sections.

132. At this command, the chiefs of sections will move rapidly on the centre group of their respective sections, or on any other interior group whose position might offer a shelter, or other particular advantage; the skirmishers will collect rapidly at a run on this group, and without distinction of numbers. The men composing the group on which the formation is made, will immediately form square, as heretofore explained, and elevate their pieces, the bayonets uppermost, in order to indicate the point on which the rally is to be made. The other skirmishers, as they arrive, will occupy and fill the open angular spaces between these four men, and successively rally around this first nucleus, and in such manner as to form rapidly a complete circle. The skirmishers will take, as they arrive, the position of charge bayonet, the point of the bayonet more elevated, and will cock their pieces in this position. The movement concluded, the two exterior ranks will fire as occasion may offer, and load without moving their feet.

133. The captain will move rapidly with his guard, wherever he may judge his presence most necessary.

134. The officers and sergeants will be particular to observe that the rally is made in silence, and with promptitude and order; that some pieces in each of their subdivisions be at all times loaded, and that the fire is directed on those points only where it will be most effective.

135. If the reserve should be threatened, it will form into a circle around its chief.

136. If the captain, or commander of a line of skirmishers formed of many platoons, should judge that the rally

by sections does not offer sufficient resistance, he will cause the rally by platoons to be executed, and for this purpose, will command:

Rally by platoons.

137. This movement will be executed according to the same principles, and by the same means, as the rally by sections. The chiefs of platoons will conform to what has been prescribed for the chiefs of sections.

138. The captain wishing to rally the skirmishers on the reserve, will command:

Rally on the reserve.

139. At this command, the captain will move briskly on the reserve; the officer who commands it will take immediate steps to form square; for this purpose, he will cause the half sections on the flanks to be thrown perpendicularly to the rear; he will order the men to come to a ready.

140. The skirmishers of each section, taking the run, will form rapidly into groups, and upon that man of each group who is nearest the centre of the section. These groups will direct themselves diagonally toward each other, and in such manner as to form into sections with the greatest possible rapidity while moving to the rear; the officers and sergeants will see that this formation is made in proper order, and the chiefs will direct their sections upon the reserve, taking care to unmask it to the right and left. As the skirmishers arrive, they will continue and complete the formation of the square begun by the reserve, closing in rapidly upon the latter, without regard to their places in line; they will come to a ready without

command, and fire upon the enemy; which will also be done by the reserve as soon as it is unmasked by the skirmishers.

141. If a section should be closely pressed by cavaly while retreating, its chief will command *halt;* at this command, the men will form rapidly into a compact circle around the officer, who will re-form his section and resume the march, the moment he can do so with safety.

142. The formation of the square in a prompt and efficient manner, requires coolness and activity on the part of both officers and sergeants.

143. The captain will also profit by every moment of respite which the enemy's cavalry may leave him; as soon as he can, he will endeavor to place himself beyond the reach of their charges, either by gaining a position where he may defend himsef with advantage, or by returning to the corps to which he belongs. For this purpose, being in square, he will cause the company to break into column by platoons at half-distance; to this effect, he will command:

1. *Form column.* 2. March.

144. At the command *march*, each platoon will dress on its centre, and the platoon which was facing to the rear will face about without command. The guides will place themselves on the right and left of their respective platoons, those of the second platoon will place themselves at half distance from those of the first, counting from the rear rank. These dispositions being made, the captain can move the column in whatever direction he may judge proper.

145. If he wishes to march it in retreat, he will command:

1. *In retreat.* 2. March (or *double quick*—March.)

146. At the command *march*, the column will immediately face by the rear rank, and move off in the opposite direction. As soon as the column is in motion, the captain will command:

3. *Guide right* (or *left.*)

147. He will indicate the direction to the leading guide, the guides will march at their proper distances, and the men will keep aligned.

148. If again threatened by cavaly, the captain will command:

1. *Form square.* 2. March.

149. At the command *march*, the column will halt; the first plotoon will face about briskly, and the outer half sections of each platoon will be thrown perpendicularly to the rear, so as to form the second and third fronts of the square. The officers and sergeants will promptly rectify any irregularities which may be committed.

150. If he should wish to march the column in advance, the captain will command:

1. *Form column.* 2. March.

151. Which will be executed as prescribed, No. 174.

152. The column being formed, the captain will command:

1. *Forward.* 2. March (or *double quick*—March.)
Guide *left* (or *right.*)

153. At the second command, the column will move forward, and at the third command, the men will take the touch of elbows to the side of the guide.

154. If the captain should wish the column to gain ground to the right or left, he will do so by rapid wheels to the side opposite the guide, and for this purpose, will change the guide whenever it may be necessary.

155. If a company be in column by platoon, at half distance, right in front, the captain can deploy the first platoon as skirmishers by the means already explained; but if it should be the wish to deploy the second platoon forward on the centre file, leaving the first platoon in reserve, he will command:

1. *Second platoon—as skirmishers.* 2. *On the centre file—take intervals.* 3. March (or *double quick*—March.)

156. At the first command, the chief of the first platoon will caution his platoon to stand fast; the chiefs of sections of the second platoon will place themselves before the centre of their sections; the fifth sergeant will place himself one pace in front of the centre of the second platoon.

157. At the second command, the chief of the right section, second platoon, will command: *Section, right face;* the chief of the left section: *Section, left face.*

158. At the command *march,* these sections will move off briskly in opposite directions, and having unmasked the the first platoon, the chief of sections will respectively

command: *By the left flank*—MARCH, and *By the right flank*—MARCH; and as soon as the sections arrive on the alignment of the first platoon, they will command: *As skirmishers*—MARCH. The group will then deploy according to prescribed principles, on the right group of the left section, which will be directed by the fifth sergeant on the point indicated.

159. If the captain should wish the deployment made by the flank, the second platoon will be moved to the front by the means above stated, and halted after passing some steps beyon the alignment of the first platoon; the deployment will then be made by the flank according to the principles prescribed.

160. When one or more platoons are deployed as skirmishers, and the captain should wish to rally them on the battalion, he will command:

Rally on the battalion.

161. At this command, the skirmishers and the reserve no matter what position the company to which they belong may occupy in order of battle, will rapidly unmask the front of the battalion, directing themselves in a run toward its nearest flank, and then form in its rear.

162. As soon as the skirmishers have passed beyond the line of file closers, the men will take the quick step, and the chief of each platoon or section will re-form his subdivision, and place it in column behind the wing on which it is rallied, and at ten paces from the rank of file closers. These subdivisions will not be moved except by order of the commander of the battalion, who may, if he thinks

proper, throw them into line of battle at the extremities of the line, or in the intervals between the battalions.

163. If many platoons should be united behind the same wing of a battalion, or behind any shelter whatsoever, they should be formed always into close column, or into column at half distance.

164. When a battalion, covered by a company of skirmishers, shall be formed into square, the platoons and sections of the covering company will be directed by their chiefs to the rear of the square, which will be opened at the angles to receive the skirmishers, who will be then formed into close column by platoons in rear of the first front of the square.

165. If circumstances should prevent the angles of the square from being opened, the skirmishers will throw themselves at the feet of the front rank men, the right knee on the ground, the butt of the piece resting on the thigh, the bayonet in a threatening position. A part may also place themselves about the angles, where they can render good service by defending the sections without fire.

166. If the battalion on which the skirmishers are rallied be in column ready to form square, the skirmishers will be formed into close column by platoon, in rear of the centre of the third division, and at the command, *Form square*—March, they will move forward and close on the buglers.

167. When skirmishers have been rallied by platoon or section behind the wings of a battalion, and it be wished to deploy them again to the front, they will be marched by the flank toward the intervals on the wings, and be then deployed so as to cover the front of the battalion.

168. When platoons or sections, placed in the interior of squares and columns, are to be deployed, they will be marched out by the flanks, and then thrown forward, as is prescribed, No. 157; as soon as they shall have unmasked the column or square, they will be deployed, the one on the right, the other on the left file.

The assembly.

169. A company deployed as skirmishers will be assembled when there is no longer danger of being disturbed; the assembly will be made habitually in quick time.

170. The captain wishing to assemble the skirmishers on the reserve, will command:

Assemble on the reserve.

171. At this command, the skirmishers will assemble by groups of fours; the front rank men will place themselves behind their rear rank men; and each group of fours will direct itself on the reserve, where each will take its proper place in the ranks. When the company is re-formed, it will rejoin the battalion to which it belongs.

172. It may be also proper to assemble the skismishers on the centre, or on the right or left of the line, either marching or at a halt.

173. If the captain should wish to assemble them on the centre while marching, he will command:

Assemble on the centre.

174. At this command, the centre guide will continue to march directly to the front on the point indicated; the front rank man of the directing file will follow the guide,

and be covered by his rear rank man; the other two comrades of this group, and likewise those on their left, will march diagonally, advancing the left shoulder and accelerating the gait, so as to re-form the groups while drawing nearer and nearer the directing file; the men of the right section will unite in the same manner into groups, and then upon the directing file, throwing forward the right shoulder. As they successively unite on the centre, the men will bring their pieces to the right shoulder.

175. To assemble on the right or left will be executed according to the same principles.

176. The assembly of a line marching in retreat will also be executed according to the same principles, the front rank men marching behind their rear rank men.

177. To assemble the line of skirmishers at a halt, and on the line they occupy, the captain will give the same commands; the skirmishers will face to the right or left, according as they should march by the right or left flank, re-form the groups while marching, and thus arrive on the file which served as the point of formation. As they successively arrive, the skirmishers will support arms.

Article Fifth.

To deploy a battalion as skirmishers, and to rally this battalion.

To deploy the battalion as skirmishers.

178. A battalion being in line of battle, if the commander should wish to deploy it on the right of the sixth com-

pany, holding the three right companies in reserve, will signify his intention to the lieutenant-colonel and adjutant, and also to the major, who will be directed to take charge of the reserve. He will point out to the lieutenant-colonel the direction he wishes to give the line, as well as the point where he wishes the right of the sixth company to rest, and to the commander of the reserve the place he may wish it established.

179. The lieutenant-colonel will move rapidly in front of the right of the sixth company, and the adjutant in front of the left of the same company. The commander of the reserve will dispose of it in the manner to be hereinafter indicated.

180. The colonel will command :

1. *First* (or *second*) *platoons—as skirmishers.*
2. *On the right of the sixth company—take intervals.*
3. MARCH (or *double quick*)—MARCH.

181. At the second command, the captains of the fifth and sixth companies will prepare to deploy the first platoons of their respective companies, the sixth on its right, the fifth on its left file.

182. The captain of the fourth company will face it to the right, and the captains of the seventh and eight companies will face their respective companies to the left.

183. At the command *march*, the movement will commence. The platoons of the fifth and sixth companies will deploy forward; the right guide of the sixth will march on the point which will be indicated to him by the lieutenant colonel.

184. The company which has faced to the right, and

also the companies which have faced to the left will march straight forward. The fourth company will take an interval of one hundred paces counting from the left of the fifth, and its chief will deploy its first platoon on its left file. The seventh and eighth companies will each take an interval of one hundred paces, counting from the first file of the company, which is immediately on its right; and the chiefs of these companies will afterward deploy their first platoons on the right file.

185. The guides who conduct the files on which the deployment is made, should be careful to direct themselves toward the outer man of the neighboring company, already deployed as skirmishers; or if the company has not finished its deployment, they will judge carefully the distance which may still be required to place all these files in line, and will then march on the point thus marked out. The companies, as they arrive on the line, will align themselves on those already deployed.

186. The lieutenant-colonel and adjutant will follow the deployment, the one on the right, the other on the left; the movement concluded, they will place themselves near the colonel.

187. The reserves of the companies will be established in echellon in the following manner: the reserve of the sixth company will be placed one hundred and fifty paces in rear of the right of this company; the reserves of the fourth and fifth companies, united, opposite the centre of their line of skirmishers, and thirty paces in advance of the reserve of the sixth company; the reserves of the seventh and eighth companies, also united, opposite the centre of their line of skirmishers, and thirty paces far-

ther to the rear than the reserve of the sixth company.

188. The major commanding the companies composing the reserve, on receiving an order from the colonel to that effect, will march these companies thirty paces to the rear, and will then deploy them into column by company, at half distance; after which, he will conduct the column to the point which shall have been indicated to him.

189. The colonel will have a general superintendence of the movement; and when it is finished, will move to a point in rear of the line, whence his view may best embrace all the parts, in order to direct their movements.

190. If, instead of deploying forward, it be desired to deploy by the flank, the sixth and fifth companies will be moved to the front ten or twelve paces, halted, and deployed by the flank, the one on the right the other on the left file, by the means already indicated. Each of the other companies will be marched by the flank; and as soon as the last file of the company, next toward the direction, shall have taken its interval, it will be moved upon the line established by the fifth and sixth companies, halted and deployed.

191. In the preceeding example, it has been supposed that the battalion was in order of battle; but if in column, it would be deployed as skirmishers by the same commands and according to the same principles.

192. If the deployment is to be made *forward*, the directing company, as soon as it is unmasked, will be moved ten or twelve paces in front of the head of the column, and will be then deployed on the file indicated. Each of the other companies will take its interval to the right or left, and deploy as soon as it is taken.

193. If the deployment is to be made by the flank, the directing company will be moved in the same manner to the front, as soon as it is unmasked, and will then be halted and deployed by the flank on the file indicated. Each of the other companies will be marched by the flank, and when its interval is taken, will be moved on the line, halted, and deployed as soon as the company next towards the direction shall have finished its deployment.

194. It has been prescribed to place the reserves in echellon, in order that they may, in the event of a rally, be able to protect themselves without injuring each other; and the reserves of two contiguous companies have been united, in order to diminish the number of the echellons, and to increase their capacity for resisting cavalry.

195. The echellons, in the example given, descend from right to left, but they may, on an indication from the colonel to the effect, be posted on the same principle, so as to descend from left to right.

196. When the color-company is to be deployed as skirmishers, the color, without its guard, will be detached, and remain with the battalion reserve.

The rally.

197. The colonel may cause all the various movements prescribed for a company, to be executed by the battalion, and by the same commands and the same signals. When he wishes to rally the battalion, he will cause the *rally on the battalion* to be sounded, and will so dispose his reserve as to protect this movement.

198. The companies deployed as skirmishers will be rallied in squares on their respective reserves; each reserve

of two contiguous companies will form the first front of the square, throwing to the rear the sections on the flanks; the skirmishers who arrive first will complete the lateral fronts, and the last the fourth front. The officers and sergeants will superintend the rally; as fast as the men arrive, they will form them into two ranks, without regard to height, and cause them to face outward.

199. The rally being effected, the commanders of square will profit by any interval of time the cavalry may allow for putting them in safety, either by marching upon the battalion reserve, or by seizing an advantageous position; to this end each of the squares will be formed into column, and march in this order; and if threatened anew, it will halt, and again form itself into square.

200. As the captains successively arrive near the battalion-reserve, each will re-form as promptly as possible, and without regard to designation or number, take place in the column next in rear of the companies already in it.

201. The battalion reserve will also form square, if itself threatened by cavalry. In this case, the companies in marching toward it will place themselves promptly in the sectors without fire, and thus march on the squares.

BAYONET EXERCISE.

1. In teaching the men these exercises, the instructor should cause them to form in one rank, with an interval of four paces between each man, so that in the execution of the movements, they may not come in conflict with each other.

2. The instructor seeing the recruits in the proper position, and at a light infantry shoulder, will command:

Take— GUARD. (*Fig.* 1.)
One time and two motions.

3. (First motion.) Make a half face to the right, keeping the heels together; turn the left toe square to the front, the feet forming a right angle, and at the same time raise a little the piece with the right hand.

4. (Second motion.) Carry the right foot about eighteen inches backward, the right heel on the prolongation of the left, the body erect and perpendicular on both legs, so that the weight of the body is divided equally between them, the knees bent, and take the position of charge bayonet.

5. The instructor wishing to allow the recruits a rest when on guard, will first command:

Shoulder—ARMS.

6. At this command, spring the musket up smartly into the hollow of the right shoulder, and retake the position of the soldier.

7. The instructor will then command REST, at which command the piece will be brought to the position of *order arms*, and the men are no longer required to remain immovable or to preserve silence.

Fig. 1.

Position of the Guard.

8. The instructor wishing to resume the position of guard, will first bring the squad to *attention*, and command, *Shoulder* — ARMS, which being done, he will command:

Take—GUARD.

9. At this command, raise the piece quickly with the right hand, seizing it with the left, at the height of the right breast, and at the same time grasp the small of the stock with the right hand, taking the guard, as before explained.

DEVELOP AND VOLTS.

10. The recruit being in the position of *guard*, the instructor will command:

Develop—MARCH. (*Fig. 2.*)

One time and one motion.

11. At the command *march*, advance quickly the left foot about twelve inches, the left leg vertical and the knee perpendicular with the ankle; the right foot flat on the ground, the right leg extended and straight, the body remaining erect.

12. At the command GUARD, re-take the position of guard by bringing back the left foot to its former position.

13. The instructor will then command:

Advance—MARCH.

One time and two motions.

14. (First motion.) At the command *march*, carry the right foot against the left heel.

15. (Second motion.) Advance the left foot about eighteen inches, preserving the position of the piece and the body.

Retreat—MARCH.

One time and two motions.

16. (First motion.) Bring back the left foot against the right.

17. (Second motion.) Carry the right foot eighteen inches to the rear.

Develop.

One pace to right—MARCH.

One time and two motions.

18. (First motion.) Carry the right foot about eighteen inches to the right in the same direction.

19. (Second motion.) Bring immediately the left foot the same distance, and to the same relative position to the right, that it before occupied.

One pace to the left—MARCH.

One time and two motions.

20. (First motion.) Carry the left foot about eighteen inches to the left.

21. (Second motion.) Bring back immediately the right foot to its distance, and in its position.

Right—VOLT.

One time and one motion.

22. Turn to the right on the toe of the left foot, (the right foot describing the quarter of an arc of a circle ; plant the right foot in its proper place and distance, keeping the piece in the position of *guard*.

Left—VOLT.

23. Turn to the left on the toe of the left foot, (the right foot describing the quarter of an arc of a circle), plant the right foot in its proper place and distance, keeping the piece in the position of *guard*.

24. The instructor should explain to the men that these movements are the same as *right* or *left* face in squad drill, except that the position of guard is always maintained.

Right rear—VOLT.

25. At this command, turn on the toe of the left foot, (the right foot describing the half on an arc of a circle,

plant the foot in its proper place and distance, keeping the piece in the position of *guard.*

Left rear—VOLT.

26. Turn on the toe of the left foot, (the right foot describing the half of an arc of a circle,) plant the foot in its proper place and distance, keeping the piece in the position of *guard.*

27. In all the volts, the instructor shall be careful to explain to the men, that when the word *right,* is used, they must carry the right foot, in turning, in the direction of their rear, and when *left* is used, in the direction of their front. In the *right* or *left rear volt,* the recruit faces quickly to the full rear, as in *about face.*

1. *Passade*—2. MARCH.

One time and two motions.

28. (First motion.) Throw the right foot eighteen inches in front of the left, the inside of it kept to the front.

29. (Second motion.) Carry quickly the left foot eighteen inches in front of the right, preserving the guard.

1. *Leap to the rear*—2. MARCH.

One time and two motions.

30. Throw the weight of the body on the left leg, and spring backward as far as possible, lighting on the toes and preserving the guard.

COMBINATION OF THE MOVEMENTS.

31. When the men are perfectly acquainted with the above movements, the instructor will cause them to execute the various movements put together, at the command MARCH. Example:

1. *Right rear volt and develop*—2. MARCH.

32. At this command the men will execute what has been prescribed in *right rear*—VOLT No. 25, and after facing to the rear they will extend the left foot as has been prescribed in DEVELOP No. 11.

1. *Left rear volt and develop*—2. MARCH.

33. At the command *march*, first execute as has been prescribed in No. 26, then execute what is prescribed in No. 11, preserving the guard in both cases.

1. *Passade and develop*—2. MARCH.

34. At the command *march*, first execute what has been prescribed in PASSADE No. 28, and then what is prescribed in No 11.

1. *Right rear volt, passade, and develop*—2. MARCH.

One time and three motions.

35. (First motion.) Execute what has been prescribed for *right rear volt*, No. 27.

36. (Second motion.) Execute what has been prescribed for PASSADE No. 28.

37. (Third motion.) Execute what has been prescribed for DEVELOP No. 11.

38. The instructor may vary these movements as he sees proper, but should see that the men understand them and can execute them promptly at the word of command.

39. When the men understand these movements thoroughly they will be taught the use of their weapon for attack and defence.

PARRIES AND THRUSTS.

40. The men being well-established in the principles and mechanism of the *guard*, and being in that position, the instructor will command:

    1. *In carte parry.* 2. ARMS.

41. At the second command, raise the muzzle of the piece twelve inches with the left hand, without moving the right; at the same time move the piece about six inches to the left, and remain in that position.

42. The men will, after the execution of each of the following movements, resume the position of *guard;* to effect this the instructor will, after each motion, command:

    Take.—GUARD.

43. At which the men will resume quickly the position of the guard.

    1. *In tierce parry.* 2. ARMS.

44. Raise quickly the muzzle of the piece twelve inches with the left hand, without moving the right; at the same time move the piece with the left hand six inches to the right, and remain in that position until the command *resume guard:*

    1. *In prime parry.* 2. ARMS.

45. Raise the piece with both hands, the arms fully ex-

tended, the piece covering the head, the lock plate turned towards the body, the barrel grasped by the thumb and fore-finger of the left hand, the bayonet menacing, although slightly inclined to the left, the tail band at the top of the bat.

   1. *In prime right (or left) parry.* 2. ARMS.

46. Advance the left shoulder (or the right shoulder) and parry (as explained in 45) to the right or the left.

   1. *In carte thrust.* 2. ARMS.

47. At the second command, throw the weight of the body forward; bend the left knee and straighten the right; extend the left arm in full, the fingers of the left hand being open and maintaining the piece; bringing the butt before the left breast, the lock-plate turned downward; and remain in that position until the command, *take guard:*

   1. *In tierce thrust.* 2. ARMS.

48. Bring the upper part of the body forward; straighten the right knee and bend the left; fully extend the left arm, the fingers of the left hand being open and maintaining the piece, the lock-plate turned upward, the butt before the right breast :

   1. *In prime thrust.* 2. ARMS.

49. Elevate the piece with both hands, the arms being extended, the trigger guard upward, the barrel between

the thumb and fingers of the left hand; bend the left knee and straighten the right, thurst at the same time the piece at the adversary, directing the blow at the height of a man on horseback.

1. *In prime to the right* (or *left*) *thrust.* 2. ARMS.

50. Advance the left shoulder (or the right shoulder,) advance to the right (or left) as explained in No. 49.

1. *Lunge.* 2. ARMS.

51. At the second command, throw the upper part of the body forward, by bending the left knee and straightening the right; thrust rapidly the piece at the adversary, fully extending the right arm, leaving off with the left hand when thrusting, which is kept extended to receive the piece, and resume guard.

52. When the men are on guard against infantry, they will thrust at the height of the breast of a man; when on guard against cavalry, they will aim the blow at the height of the horses head, or of the sides of the horseman.

53. When the instructor shall wish to bring the men to the position of *guard against infantry,* or *cavalry,* from shoulder arms, he will command:

1. *Guard against Infantry*—2. GUARD. (*Fig.* 3.)

One time and two motions.

54. (First motion.) Make a half face to the right on both heels, the feet square; raise at the same time the piece a little, and seize it with the left hand below and near the middle band.

55. (Second motion.) Bring the right leg to the rear perpendicularly, about eighteen inches, the right heel on the same line with the left; the knees a little bent, the weight of the body bearing equally on both legs; lower the piece with both hands, the barrel upward, the left el-

Fig. 2.

Guard against Infantry.

bow pressing against the body; sieze at the same time the piece below the trigger guard with the right hand; the arms hanging naturally, the point of the bayonet slightly elevated.

Shoulder—Arms.

One time and one motion.

56. Raise the piece with the left hand; bring at the same time the right heel on the alignment of the left, and face to the front.

1. *Guard against Cavalry*—2. Guard. (*Fig.* 4.)

One time and two motions.

57. The first and second motions as in guard against infantry, with the exception that the right hand will be fix-

(*Fig.* 4.)

Guard against Cavalry.

ed at the hip, and the bayonet as high as the eye, as in the position of charge bayonet.

58. When the men are perfectly acquainted with the divers paces, parries and thrusts, the instructor will cause them to execute these motions put together, at the command *march*. Example:

1. *Passade forward, in prime parry and thrust.*—2. MARCH.

59. At the second command the men will execute what has been prescribed for passade, parry in prime, and thrust in prime.

60. These movements and combinations may be varied as the instructor may think proper, but he should always execute some movement that will be useful to the men in either attack or defense, and should explain to them its object.

MANUAL OF THE SWORD OR SABRE, FOR OFFICERS.

POSITION OF THE SWORD OR SABRE, UNDER ARMS.

The carry. The gripe is in the right hand, which will be supported against the right hip, the back of the blade against the shoulder.

TO SALUTE WITH THE SWORD OR SABRE.

Three times (or *pauses.*)

One. At the distance of six paces from the person to be saluted, raise the sword or sabre perpendicularly, the point up, the flat of the blade opposite to the right eye, the guard at the height of the shoulder, the elbow supported on the body.

Two. Drop the point of the sword or sabre by extending the arm, so that the right hand may be brought to the side of the right thigh, and remain in that position until the person to whom the salute is rendered shall be passed or shall have passed, six paces.

Three. Raise the sword or sabre smartly, and place the back of the blade against the right shoulder.

COLOR-SALUTE.

In the ranks, the color-bearer, whether at a halt or in march, will always carry the heel of the color-lance supported at the right hip, the right hand generally placed on the lance at the height of the shoulder, to hold it steady. When the color has to render honors, the color-bearer will salute as follows:

At the distance of six paces slip the right hand along the lance to the height of the eye; lower the lance by straightening the arm to its full extent, the heel of the lance remaining at the hip, and bring back the lance to the habitual position when the person saluted shall be passed, or shall have passed, six paces.

MANUAL

FOR RELIEVING SENTINELS.

Arms—PORT.

One time and one motion.

Throw the piece diagonally across the body, the lock to the front, seize it smartly at the same instant with both hands, the right at the handle, the left at the lower band, the two thumbs pointing toward the muzzle, the barrel sloping upward and crossing opposite the point of the left shoulder, the butt proportionally lowered. The palm of the right hand will be above, and that of the left under the piece, the nails of both hands next to the body, to which the elbows will be closed.

Shoulder—ARMS.

One time and two motions.

(*First motion.*) Bring the piece smartly to the right

shoulder, placing the right hand as in the position of shoulder arms, slip the left hand to the height of the shoulder, the fingers extended.

(*Second motion.*) Drop the left had smartly by the side.

Being on parade and at order arms, if it be wished to give the men rest, the command will be:

Parade—R<small>EST</small>.

At the command *rest*, turn the piece on the heel of the butt, the barrel to the left, the muzzle in front of the centre of the body; seize it at the same time with the left hand just above, and with the right at the upper band; carry the right foot six inches to the rear, the left knee slightly bent.

INSTRUCTION

FOR THE CHIEF BUGLER AND DRUM-MAJOR.

The posts of the field music and band have been given, T<small>ITLE</small> I, for the order in battle.

In column in manœuvre, the field music and band will march abreast with the left centre company, and on the side opposite the guide.

In column in route, as well as in passage of defiles, to the front or in retreat, they will march at the head of their respective battalions.

GENERAL CALLS.

1. *Attention.*
2. *The general.*
3. *The assembly.*
4. *To the color.*
5. *The recall.*
6. *Quick time.*
7. *Double quick time.*
8. *The charge.*
9. *The reveille.*
10. *Retreat.*
11. *Tattoo.*
12. *To extinguish lights.*
13. *Assembly of the buglers.*
14. *Assembly of the guard.*
15. *Orders for orderly sergeants.*
16. *For officers to take their places in line after firing.*
17. *The disperse.*
18. *Officers' call.*
19. *Breakfast call.*
20. *Dinner call.*
21. *Sick call.*
22. *Fatigue call.*
23. *Church call.*
24. *Drill call.*
25. *School call.*

CALLS FOR SKIRMISHERS.

1. *Fix bayonet.*
2. *Unfix bayonet.*
3. *Quick time.*
4. *Double quick time.*
5. *The run.*
6. *Deploy as skirmishers.*
7. *Forward.*
8. *In retreat.*
9. *Halt.*
10. *By the right flank.*
11. *By the left flank.*
12. *Commence firing,*
13. *Cease firing.*
14. *Change direction to the right.*
15. *Change direction to the left.*
16. *Lie down.*
17. *Rise up.*
18. *Rally by fours.*
19. *Rally by sections.*
20. *Rally by platoons.*
21. *Rally on the reserve.*
22. *Rally on the battalion.*
23. *Assemble on the battalion.*

NOTE.—When the whole of the troops, in the same camp or garrison, are to depart, *the general, the assembly* and *to the color,* will be beaten or sounded, at the proper intervals, in the order herein mentioned. At the first, the troops will prepare for the movement; at the second, they will form by company, and at the third unite by battalion.

FIELD FORTIFICATION.

PART FIFTH.

1. FIELD WORKS are any constructions which have for their object to impede the advance of an enemy, or to enable an inferior force to maintain their position against the attack of a superior number.

2. The name of *Field Fortification* is applied to a work which is composed of an embankment of earth called a "parapet," and an excavation called a "ditch," on the exterior side, which last furnishes the earth for the embankment.

3. The general appellation of *Intrenchments* is applied to all field works, and a position strengthened by them, is said to be *Intrenched*.

4. The outline or form of the work varies with the character of the ground, the circumstances under which it is constructed, the strength of the force, and particular character of the defence. The profile or shape of the embankment or parapet is usually the same in all cases.

5. When the ground about a work within effective range of the firearms of the attacking party is quite flat, the height called the "command" of the work, must be at least 7 feet, 6 inches, in order that the defenders may be covered from the fire of men on horseback—that class of men being able to discharge their arms at 7 feet 6 inches above ground.

6. Unimportant works, or such as are situated on higher ground than that within effective artillery range, may have their parapets as low as 6 feet or even 5 feet.

7. Sometimes the parapet is formed of earth taken from an excavation or trench inside of it; in this case the parapet may be as low as 3 feet, because then, the defenders standing in the trench of equal depth, and close behind the parapet, are sufficiently covered by it.

[*Remarks.*] In this manner cover for troops may be very quickly obtained, with the advantage of having the power to advance over the parapet in order of battle when occasion offers.

8. The general form of a parapet and ditch may be understood by the following explanations: (*Fig.* 1.)

A B C D E F is the profile of the Parapet.
G H I K the profile of the Ditch.
L M N the profile of the Glacis.
A B the Banquette Slopes.
B C Tread of the Banquette.
C D the Interior Slope.
D E the Superior Slope.
E F the Exterior Slope.
F G the Berm.
G H the Scarp.
H I the Bottom of the Ditch.
I K the Counterscarp.
A the Foot of the Banquette Slope.
B the Crest of the Banquette.
C the Foot of the Interior Slope.
D the Interior Crest.

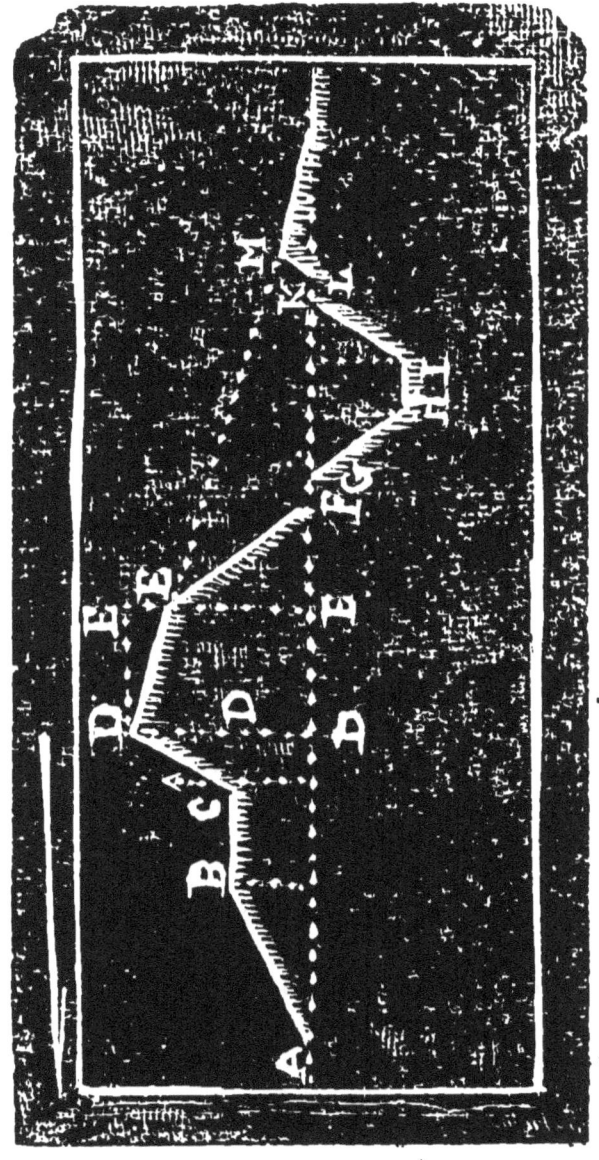

Fig. 1.

Profile of an Embankment.

E the Exterior Crest.
F the Foot of the Exterior Slope.
G the Crest of the Scarp.
H the Foot of the Scarp.
I the Foot of the Counterscarp.
K the Crest of the Counterscrp.
M the Crest of the Glacis.
N Foot of the Glacis.

9. The *interior slope* is the part of the parapet towards the enemy; it is usually made with the same slope that the earth, when first thrown up, naturally takes.

10. The top of the parapet, denominated the *superior slope*, is the line along which the assailed fire on the enemy.

11. The *interior slope*, sometimes denominated the *breast height*, is the part against which the assailed naturally lean in the act of firing.

12. The *banquette* is a small terrace on which the soldier stands to deliver his fire; the top of it is denominated the *tread*, and the inclined plane by which it is ascended, the *slope*.

13. The term *crest* is applied to those points of the profile, where a salient angle is formed; and when a re-entering angle is formed by two lines, the term *foot* is applied to the point, in connexion with the name of the superior line; thus, *foot of the exterior slope; foot of the interior slope*, &c.

14. The berm is a horizontal space left between the parapet and ditch, to prevent the earth from yielding.

15. The slope of the ditch next to the parapet is the scarp: the opposite the counterscarp.

16. The glacis is a small mound of earth raised in front of the ditch; it is seldom used in field works, therefore is not a constituent part of their profile.

17. Should there be ground near the position to be fortified, higher than that on which the parapet stands, the latter must have a greater command than 7 feet 6 inches, but in the more simple kind of field works the command does not exceed 12 feet: for as soldiers cannot easily throw dirt with a shovel to a greater height than 6 feet, and as other means are generally wanting in the field, it is evident that the height of a parapet for such a work, must be limited by the capability of executing it with shovels and pick axes by two parties of men, one standing on a level 6 feet above the other. The same reason determines the greatest depth of ditch to be 12 feet, a scaffolding being necessary at 6 feet above the bottom of the ditch to receive the earth which is thrown from thence; the earth is then thrown up to the level of the ground, by other laborers placed on the scaffolding.

18. In the construction of field works it should always be recollected that a great command of parapet not only requires additional means, trouble, and time to throw up the earth, but also renders necessary an increased mass of earth for the banquette, which may thus encumber the interior of the work.

19. To obviate as much as possible, the latter evil, it is usual to mount the banquette, by steps, when the parapet has a greater command than 8 feet.

20 The thickness of the parapets of field works must be regulated by the description of arms likely to be employed against them; in order, therefore, that they may af-

ford a reasonable degree of resistance to repeated firing, the thickness of parapets must somewhat exceed the penetration of the shot which may be used against them in the attack.

Penetration of shot.	Thickness of parapet.
Musket ball, 10 to 18 inches,	3 feet.
6-pounder, 3½ to 4 feet,	6 feet.
9-pounder, 6½ to 7 feet,	8 or 9 feet.
12-pounder, 8½ to 10 feet,	10 or 12 feet.

21. It is found by experiment that loose earth resists the penetration of shot just as well as that which has been rammed together.

22. Although a musket ball penetrates, at most, only 18 inches into earth, musketry parapets require to be made 3 feet thick, in order that they may be sufficiently substantial to preserve the requisite height, notwithstanding the action of the weather.

23. Heavier guns than 12-pounders are rarely brought into the field, consequently 12 feet may be considered as the greatest thickness of a parapet; and it has been shown that, for the simpler works, 12 feet is the greatest command of a parapet, and likewise the greatest depth of a ditch.

24. The exterior side of a parapet is formed with a slope which has a base equal to its height, that being the inclination which ordinary earth assumes when thrown up loosely; and, therefore, it is the most advantageous form for a mass of earth whose sides are supported.

25. The interior slope of a parapet has a base not greater than one-third or one-fourth of its height, in order to allow the men to approach near the crest, and fire over the parapet with ease.

MANNER OF THROWING UP A WORK.

26. The following will describe the manner of laying the work out on the field, which is called *profiling*; the distribution of the workmen to excavate the ditch, and form the parapet; and the precautions to be observed in the construction.

27. Poles having been planted at the angles of the work, and the height of the interior crest marked on them, a line is traced on the ground with a picks, showing the direction of the interior crests. At suitable distances, say from twenty to thirty yards apart, cords are stretched between two stout pickets, in a direction perpendicular to the line marked out by the pick; these cords should be exactly horizontal. The thickness of the parapet is measured on the cord, and a picket driven into the ground to mark the point. The base of the interior slope, and the tread of the banquette, are set off in a similar manner; and a slip of deal is nailed to each of the pickets.

28. The height of the interior crest, and the tread of the banquette, are easily ascertained, from the position of the cord, and the interior crest; these points having been marked on their respective slips, the outline of the parapet is shown by connecting them by other slips, which are nailed to the uprights; the banquette slope and the exterior slope, will be determined by a similar process.

29. From the profiles thus formed perpendicular to the interior crests, the oblique profiles at the angles can be readily set up, by a process which will suggest itself without explanation.

30. Having completed the profiling, the foot of the banquette, and that of the exterior slope, are marked out with a pick, and also the crests of the scarp and counterscarp. All the arrangements preparatory to commencing the excavation are now complete.

DISTRIBUTION OF THE WORKING PARTY.

31. Divide the men into 6 equal parts, 3 of which are to be provided with pick axes and shovels, 2 are to have shovels only, and the remainder are to be furnished with rammers only.

32. The party is then marched to the ground, and the men, having both pick-axes and shovels (viz: the diggers,) are to be stationed from $4\frac{1}{2}$ to 6 feet apart, (so as to not be in each others way,) on the ground when the ditch is to be dug along the berme line, and facing the work.

33. The excavation of the ditch is now begun, the men first loosening the earth with their pick-axes, and then shoveling it to the place where the parapet is to stand; here the rest of the party are posted, and as the earth is thrown up to them, the men with shovels spread it in layers, while the remainder, with their rammers, beat it down to a firm mass; and as the work is raised, they give it the form indicated by the profiles.

34. In making the parapet, care should be taken to form a drain, at some suitable point, to carry off the water from the interior into the ditch. It can be done by digging a trench across the ground where the parapet is to be raised, and plank the sides so as to form a gutter. A gutter of boards should also be made to prevent the water from running down the scarp, as it would soon destroy it.

35. For the facility of entering the ditch, whilst working, the offset at the scarp and counterscarp, may be formed into steps, with a rise of eighteen inches each; and if the ditch is deeper than six feet, an offset about four feet broad should be left at the scarp, about mid-depth of the ditch, to place a relay of shovels to throw the earth on the berme. In some cases, a scaffold of plank is raised in the ditch for the same purpose.

36. When the ditch has been excavated to the bottom, the offsets are cut way, and the proper slopes given to the sides. The earth furnished by the offsets, if not required to complete the parapet, may be formed into a small glacis.

37. When near the surface, in soil requiring but little use of the pick-axe, an excavation of six cubic yards in a day of eight hours, would be a fair task for a soldier, who, in general, is little accustomed to the use of the pick-axe and shovel.

38. In calculating the time required to throw up a field work, the following data may be assumed; in light, dry, sandy soil, that can be easily dug without the aid of a pick-axe, a man can, in a day of eight hours, load from nineteen to twenty cubic yards of earth on barrows. If a pick-axe be required, two men can do the same quantity of work.

39. If the whole mass must be first moved with the pick-axe, three or four men should be allowed.

40. A man can wheel 20 cubic yards of earth per day to a distance of 30 yards on level ground, or 20 yards on a ramp.

41. Twenty cubic yards of earth will fill 600 wheelbarrows.

42. A horse can do as much work as 7 men; he can car-

ry 300 lbs. 20 miles per day, or 200 lbs. 30 miles; he can draw 1,600 lbs. on a plain, and from 1,200, to 1,300 lbs. on irregular ground, when the roads are in good order.

43. Newly moved earth will not remain very well at such a steep slope as the "interior slope" of the parapet assumes, consequently artificial means have to be resorted to, to retain it in that state; these are called *revetments*.

REVETMENTS.

44. A *revetment* consists of a facing of stone, wood, sods of turf, or any other material, to sustain an embankment, when it receives a slope steeper than the natural slope.

45. In field works revetments are used only for the interior slope of the parapet and for the scarp; for the first, sods, hurdles, fascines, gabions, and plank are used; and for the last, timber.

46. *Revetment of sods.* Sod work forms a strong and durable revetment, and as they are generally procurable on the spot, they are much used in field works. The sods should be cut from a well clothed sward, with the grass of a fine, short blade, and thickly matted roots. If the grass be long, it should be mowed before the sod is cut.

47. Sods are of two sizes, one termed *stretchers*, are twelve inches square and four and a half inches thick; the other termed *headers*, are eighteen inches long, twelve inches broad, and four and a-half inches thick.

48. The sod revetment is commenced as soon as the parapet is raised to the level of the head of the banquette; the course consists of two stretchers and one header alternating, the end of the header laid to the front. The grass side is laid downward; and the sods should protrude a little beyond

the line of the interior slope, for the purpose of trimming the course even at the top, before laying another, and to make the interior slope regular. The course is firmly settled, by tapping each sod as it is laid with a spade or a wooden mallet; and the earth of the parapet is packed closely behind the course.

49. A second course is laid on the first, so as to cover the joints, or, as it is termed, to *break joints* with it, using otherwise the same precautions as with the first. The top course is laid with the grass up; and in some cases pegs are driven through the sods of two courses, to connect the whole more firmly, which is, however, by no means necessary to form a strong sodding.

50. When cut from a wet soil, the sods should not be lain until they are partially dried, otherwise they will shrink, and the revetment will crack in drying. In hot weather the revetment should be watered frequently, until the grass puts forth. The sods are cut rather larger than required for use; and are trimmed to a proper size from a model sod.

51. *Fascine revetment.* A *Fascine*, is a bundle of twigs closely bound up. There are two sizes of fascines; one size nine inches in diameter, and about ten feet long; the other which is generally termed a *soucisson*, is twelve inches in diameter and twenty feet long; it is chiefly used for the revetments of batteries.

52. To make a fascine, straight twigs are selected, between the thickness of the little finger and thumb, the longer the btter; they should be stripped of the smaller twigs. A machine, termed a *fascine horse*, is put up, by driving two stout poles into the ground obliquely, about

two feet, so as to cross each other about two feet above the ground, where they are firmly tied together; as many of these supports as may be required, are put up in a straight line, about eighteen inches apart; this forms the horse, on which the twigs are laid to be bound together.

53. Another machine termed a *fascine choker*, is formed of two stout levers, about five feet long, connected near their extremities by a chain or strong cord, which would be long enough to pass once around the fascine, and be drawn tight by means of the levers.

54 The twigs are laid on the horse, with their large and small ends alternating; the choker is applied to bring them together; and they are bound by *withs* or *gads*, made of tough twigs, properly prepared by untwisting the fibres over a blaze, so as to render them pliant, or else stout rope yarn may be substituted for them. The gads are placed twelve inches apart, and every third or fourth one should be made with an end three or four feet long, having a loop at the extremity to receive a picket through it; this picket is termed an *anchoring picket*, its object being to secure the fascine firmly to the parapet.

55. To form the revetment, the first row of fascines is imbedded about half its thickness below the tread of the banquette, and is secured by means of the anchoring pickets, and also by several pickets driven through the fascine itself about twelve inches into the earth. The knots of the wythes are laid inside, and the earth of the parapet is well packed behind the fascine. A second row is laid on the first, so as to give the requisite interior slope; it should break joints with the first row, and be connected with it

by several pickets driven through them both. The other rows are laid with similar precautions; and the parapet is usually finished at the top by a course of sods.

56. *Hurdle revetment.* This revetment is made by driving poles in the same direction as the interior slope, into the banquette, about eighteen inches below the tread, and then forming a wicker-work, by interlacing the twigs between them in a similar manner to basket work.

57. The poles should be nine inches apart, their diameter about one and a half inches. They should be secured to the parapet by long withes and anchoring pickets. The top twigs should be bound together by withes.

58. *Gabion revetment.* Gabions are strong cylindrical baskets without top or bottom, two feet in diameter, and two feet nine inches high. These are placed in rows along the line of work at an inclination corresponding to the required slope, and then filled with earth. To make a gabion, from eight to fourteen pickets, three feet six inches long, are fixed upright in the ground, at equal distances, in the circumference of a circle, one foot eleven inches in diameter; flexible twigs (or rods) are then interwoven with the upright pickets, commencing with three rods at the bottom, and weaving each in succession outside of two pickets and inside of one; as the twigs (or rods) are expended, others are added, and the basket work continued to the height of two feet nine inches; this work, which is called the web, is sewn in three or four parts, from top to bottom; withes, (called gads,) or spun yarn being used for that purpose, in order to keep it from coming off the pickets; the ends of these are then cut off about an inch from the web. A gabion, thus made, stands three feet

high in the revetment, and weighs from thirty-six to forty pounds. The best wood for the web, and particularly for the gads, is willow and hazel.

59. The gabion revetment is seldom used except for the trenches in the attack of permanent works, where it is desirable to place troops speedily under cover from the enemy's case shot and musketry.

60. *Plank revetment.* This revetment may be made by driving pieces of four-inch scantling about three feet apart, two feet below the tread of the banquette, giving them the same slope as the interior slope. Behind these pieces, boards are nailed to sustain the earth.

61. *Sand-bags* are bags of coarse canvass, measuring, when laid flat, two feet eight inches by one foot four inches; they contain, when quite full, a bushel of earth; but when tied and placed in revetment, only three-quarters of a bushel. In building a revetment with them, they are arranged with their ends and sides presented alternately to the front in each course, and with the joints in the successive courses broken, like brick-work. Sixteen sand-bags build ten square feet of revetment; they ought to be tarred, if the revetments are to last a considerable time; if not tarred, they rot in two months. An empty sand-bag weighs 1 lb. 2 oz., and when tarred, 1 lb. 12 oz.

62. Filled sand-bags are musket-shot proof, and are frequently placed on a parapet one across two others, the latter being a short distance asunder, in order that the intervals may serve as loop-holes.

63. When sand-bags or gabions are made use of to revet the cheeks of embrasures, they should be covered with raw hides, to prevent them from being damaged by the flash and the concussion caused by the discharge of the gun.

OBSTACLES.

64. The means employed as accessory, usually consists of artificial obstacles, so arranged as to detain the enemy in a position where he will be greatly cut up by the fire of the work. The proper disposition, therefore, of obstacles, is in advance of the ditch within short musket range.

65. In placing the ground around a work in a defensive attitude, every means should be taken to reduce to the smallest possible number, the points by which the enemy may approach; so that by accumulating the troops on the weak points, a more vigorous defense may be made. In making this arrangement, equal care should be given to everything that, affording a shelter to the enemy, would enable him to approach the work unexposed to its fires. To prevent this, all hollow roads, or dry ditches, which are not enfiladed by the principal works, should be filled up or else be watched by a detachment, covered by advanced work. All trees, underwood, hedges, enclosures, and houses within cannon range, should be cut down and leveled, and no stumps be allowed higher than two feet,. Trees beyond cannon range should not be felled; or, if felled they should be burnt to prevent the enemy's movements being concealed.

66. If there are approaches, such as permanent bridges, fords and roads, which may be equally serviceable to the assailed and to the enemy, they should be gurded with peculiar care; and be exposed to the enfilading fire of a work especially erected for their defence.

67. The principal artificial obstacles are *Trous-de-loup*,

or *military pits;* abattis; palisades; fraises; stockades; chevaux-de-frise; small pickets; entanglements; crows feet; inundations; and mines.

68. *Trous-de-loup.* These are pits in the form of an inverted truncated cone, or quadrilateral pyramid, and are generally made about 6 feet wide and 6 feet deep; a pointed stake is planted firmly in the bottom to prevent the enemy from using them as rifle pits. In order to form an effective obstacle, they should be disposed checkerwise in three rows, a few yards in front of the ditch with intervals of about 10 feet between them; the earth taken from them is spread over the ground between them, and is formed into hillocks to render the passage between them as difficult as possible. If brush-wood, or light hurdles, can be procured, the ditch may be made narrower, and covered with hurdle, over which a layer of earth is spread. Trous-de-loup are sometimes placed in the ditch; in this case, their upper circles touch.

69. This obstacle is principally serviceable against cavalry.

70. *Abattis.* The large limbs of trees are selected for an abattis. The smaller branches are chopped off, and the ends, pointed and interlaced with some care, are presented towards the enemy. The large end of the limb is secured to the ground by a crotchet-picket, and should be covered with earth, well rammed, to prevent its being torn up.

71. One of the best methods of forming an abattis, and which is peculiarly adapted to strengthen the skirt of a wood, occupied by light troops, is to fell the trees so that their branches will interlace, cutting the trunk in such a way that the tree will hang to the stump by a portion un-

cut. The stumps may be left high enough to cover a man in the act of firing.

72. Abattis are placed in front of the ditch; in this position, they must be covered from the enemy's fire by a small glacis, so that they may not be seen and destroyed at a distance by artillery.

73. Abattis is an excellent obstacle in a wooded country, and admits of a good defence, if a slight parapet is thrown up behind it. The parapet may be made of trunks of trees laid on each other, with a shallow ditch or trench behind them; the earth from which is thrown against the trunks. In an open position it may be relied on as a security against surprise, particularly of cavalry.

74. A detachment of 90 men can make 750 feet of abattis in a day.

75. *Palisades.* A palisade is a stake about 10 feet long, and of a triangular form, each side of the triangle being 8 inches. The trunks of straight trees should be selected for palisades. The diameter of the trunk should be from sixteen to twenty inches. The trunk is sawed into lenghts of ten and a-half feet, and is split up into rails, each length furnishing from 5 to 7 rails. The palisade is pointed at the top, the other extremity may be charred if the wood is seasoned; otherwise the charring will be of no service. A *palisading* is a row of palisades set in the ground either vertically, or slightly inclined towards the enemy. Each palisade is nailed to a strip of thick plank, termed a *riband*, placed horizontally about one foot below the ground; another riband is placed eighteen inches below the top.— To plant the palisade, a trench is dug 3 feet deep; they are then placed about 3 inches asunder, with an edge towards the enemy.

76. *Palisades* are only used in the ditches, and to close the gorges of field works, and are not as in permanent works, placed on the banquettes; when in the ditch, their best position is at the foot of the counterscarp, and slightly inclined towards it; for thus placed, they are more secure from a direct fire of artillery, and they detain the enemy at the caunterscarp under the deadly aim of the garrison; also it makes it difficult for the assailants to cut them down, there being no room between them and the counterscarp to stand and wield an axe.

77. *Fraise.* This obstacle is formed of palisades placed in juxtaposition, either horizontally or slightly inclined. The best position for a fraise is on the berme, or a little below it, so as to be covered by the counterscarp crest. The part of the fraise under the parapet is termed the *tail*, and is about 5 feet long. To make a fraise, a horizontal piece of four inch scantling, termed a *cushion*, is first laid parallel to the berme; each palisade is nailed to this, and a thick riband is nailed on the top of the fraise near the end.

78. The point of fraise should be at least 7 feet above the bottom of the ditch, and should not project beyond the foot of the scarp, so as not to shelter the enemy from logs, stones, &c., rolled from the parapet into the ditch.

79. *Stockade.* Trunks of small trees from 9 to 12 inches in diameter and 12 feet long, are selected to form a stockade. They are planted in juxtaposition, in a similar manner to a palisading, and are used for the same purposes.

80. *Chevaux-de-frise*, are beams of wood from 6 to 10 feet long, which are cut in a square or hexagonal form, and have pointed stakes or sword blades inserted in the

faces; when several are used, in one length, they are chained together to prevent the enemy from removing them; and they are made of the lengths just mentioned in order that they may be portable.

81. They are employed as temporary barriers to impede the passage of a breach, the entrance into a work, to block up a street, &c.; they are occasionally placed at the foot of the counterscarp of the ditch, and, also on the berme; in the latter situation, they must be covered from the view and fire of the enemy by a small glacis.

82. *Pointed Stakes* are frequently fixed in the ground, at any place at which the enemy might occupy at the time of an assault; as on the bermes of works, the edges of trous-de-loup, and in the spaces between them. They must be firmly planted in the ground, and if they are pointed before insertion, two mallets must be used, one of which is provided with a conical hole to receive the point of the stake, while the blows are struck with the other; these pickets may be conveniently formed of the small branches cut from the trees intended for abattis.

INUNDATIONS.

83. It frequently occurs in the field that small streams or rivulets are met with, which of themselves offer no impediment to the advance of an enemy, but which, by judicious management, may be made effectually to check his attack on certain points where the water may be collected.

84. It is done by damming back a shallow water course so as to make it overflow its valley. To be effective, an inundation should be six feet deep. When this depth can-

not be procured, trous-de-loup, or else short ditches, placed in quincunx order, are dug, and the whole is covered with a sheet of water, which, at the ditches, must be at least six feet in depth.

85. A dam may be formed in the following manner: after constructing an embankment of earth on each side of the stream, perpendicular to its length, as far as the bank, stones and gravel should be thrown into the water to diminish its depth: then two heaps of earth are prepared, one on each bank, and as many workmen being set on as can be employed without impeding each other; the earth from those heaps is thrown into the stream, over the stones and gravel, as rapidly as possible, until the embankments previously formed, are connected together across the stream.

86. It rarely occurs that sufficient means are to be found in the field to allow of a dam being made more than ten feet high; and supposing this height to be given, the difference of level between any two dams should be five feet, in order that the shallowest part of the inundation may be five feet deep, and therefore not fordable.

87. The distance at which dams should be placed from one another, will depend upon the fall of the bed of the stream, and must be determined by leveling. The thickness of the dam at the top, may be made equal to the depth of water intended to be retained, but if it is liable to be battered by artillery, it should be ten feet thick at the top. The exterior slope of the dam may be left at the natural slope, of the earth, while to that opposed to the stream, a base of not less than double its height should be given.

88. A sluice or waste weir should be provided at the height to which it is desired the water should rise, otherwise, the water being allowed to flow over every part, the dam would be destroyed. These openings, or waste weirs must be rivetted with fascines or timber, and ought to be completed before the dam is carried up to its full height.

89. Artificial inundations seldom admit of being turned to an effective use, owing to the difficulties in forming them, and the ease by which they can be drained by the enemy. But when it is practicable to procure only a shallow sheet of water, it it should not be neglected, as it will cause some apprehension to the enemy. In some cases by damming back a brook, the water may be raised to a level sufficient to be conducted into the ditches of the work, and render some parts unassailable. The ditches in such cases should be made very wide, and to hold about the depth of six feet. During freezing weather the ice should be broken in the middle of the ditch, and a channel of at least twelve feet be kept open, if practicable.— The ice taken out should be piled up irregularly on each side of the channel; and, as a farther precaution against a surprise, water should be thrown on the parapet to freeze.

MINES.

90. Attempts at applying mines to field works have seldom proved successful, owing to the rapid character of the assault, from which the mines are usually sprung too soon or too late; so that the only effect that can be counted upon for their use, is the panic they may create.

91. There is one species of mine denominated a *stone fougasse*, which it is thought might be successfully applied to the defence of the ditches and the salients of the field works. To make this mine, an inclined funnel-shaped excavation is made to the depth of five or six feet, at the bottom of the funnel, a box containing 55 lbs. of powder is placed with which a *powder-hose* communicates. A strong shield of wood, formed of battens well nailed together, is placed in front of the box; and three or four cubic yards of pebbles, or an equal weight of brick-bats, or other materials, are filled in against the shield. Earth is then well rammed around the shield on top and behind, to prevent the explosion from taking place in the wrong direction. A fougasse of this size, when sprung, will scatter the pebbles over a surface of sixty yards in length and seventy yards in breadth.

92. A good method of discharging fougasses at the moment required, is to place a loaded musket with the muzzle in the priming of the fougasse, and a wire attached to the trigger; the wire can be led in any direction, in the same manner as the hose, and being pulled at the proper moment, the explosion will take place.

THE OUTLINES OF FIELD WORKS.

93. The direction which a parapet is made to assume in order to enclose or partially enclose the ground to be fortified, is called the outline of a work.

94. The following are general principles to be observed in determining the outlines of field works:

1st. There should be a reciprocal defense between all the parts of works, so that the ground over which an enemy must pass to the attack, should, if possible, be seen both in front and in flank.

2dly. The "lines of defence" must not exceed the effective range of muskets, viz: about 160 yards.

3dly. Re-entering angles, (viz: flanking angles,) ought never to be less than 90° and seldom more than 100°; for if less than 90°, the men on the flanking parts would fire against each other; and if more than 100°, the fire of the flanking parts would diverge too far from the salient to be flanked.

4thly. The salient angles of works should be as obtuse as possible, and never less than 60°, otherwise the interior space might become too contracted; the angle would be so sharp as to be quickly worn away by the weather, and would be easily battered down; also the undefended* sectoral space in front of the salient angles (which is the supplement of the angle) would become very great; and

5thly. The outline of a field work should be proportioned in length to the number of men and guns intended for its defence. One man occupies a space of three feet.

95. The names of the works most commonly employed in field fortification, are REDANS; LUNETTES; REDOUTS; STAR-FORTS; BASTION-FORTS, &c., and works used mostly for lines of intrenchment, such as TENAILLES and CREMAILLERES.

---

*NOTE.—Undefended by direct fire. To prevent the enemy from approaching the work on these undefended sectors the salients should be directed towards some natural obstacle, such as a marsh, &c.; or if this cannot be done, then artificial obstacles should be disposed in their front.

96. The REDAN, (*Fig. 2.*) is a work consisting of two faces, which form with each other a salient angle, the rear being open. When the faces are not more than 20 yards in length, the work is sometimes called a fleche.

97. The redan is in the most advantageous position, when the ground before the salient angles and approaches to the gorge are inaccessible, or when the work can be supported by troops; for example, when with obstacles

Fig. 2.

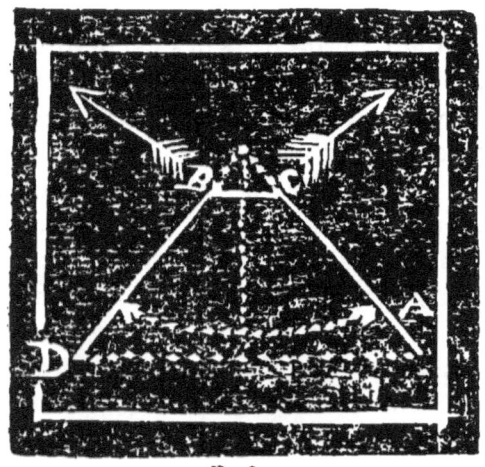

Redan.

in its front, it is employed as an advanced work to defend hollow ground which cannot be seen from the principal work—to protect a bridge, a dam, a road, a defile, or to cover a guard, an advanced post, &c.

98. The weak points of this work are: that it has an open gorge, and that its ditch, and the ground in front of the salient angle, are undefended either by direct or flanking fire.

99. On account of its having an open gorge, it is seldom advisable to construct a redan as an isolated work; its rear should be exposed to the fire of some collateral work, or have free communication with a body of troops in its rear, to whom it may form an advanced post, or outwork; or otherwise the faces should terminate on a river, a marsh or any inaccessible ground, which would prevent it from being turned.

100. The first defect, viz: that of having an open gorge, may be remedied in a slight degree by placing along the gorge, abattis, trous-de-loup, &c., (or palisades, if time and material abound); as for the second defect, a direct fire may be brought in front of the salient angle by rounding the latter, or cutting off the angle by a short face not less than 6 yards long. A flanking fire may be procured for the ditch and salients, by forming auxilliary flanks, which may be placed either towards the middle or at the extremities of the faces; such a flank ought not to be less than 12 yards long, that there may be at least 12 men firing from it.

101. DOUBLE REDANS consists of two redans joined together, their exterior faces being generally longer than the others; the French call a work of this kind a *queue d'hyronde*.

102. A TRIPLE REDAN consists of three redans joined together, the exterior faces of these are also, in general, longer than the others.

103. A LUNETTE (*Fig.* 3.) is a large redan with flanks parallel or nearly parallel to the capital; as a general rule, the flanks are traced perpendicularly to the intended

line of fire, for the purpose of bringing on certain spots a more direct fire than could be made from the faces of the work.

104. It is often desirable to secure gorges of these works against surprise; this may be done by disposing across the gorges a single or double row of palisades, or a stockade work, in the form of a front fortification or of a ten-

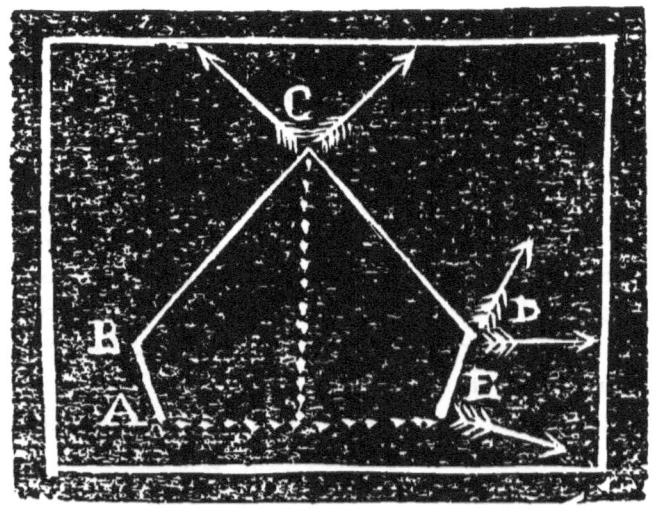

Lunette.

aille; there should be a banquette to it, that the defenders may have command over the assailants, and a ditch to prevent the enemy from getting close, and cutting, burning, or blowing down the obstacle. Trous-de-loup, abattis, and chevaux-de-frize are sometimes disposed across the gorge for the same purpose.

105. A REDOUT is a closed work, the parapet of which does not form re-entering angles; it may be quadrilateral, polygonal, or circular.

106. Circular redoubts, although they have no undefended sectors, and enclose a greater space than any other redout with an equal length of parapet, are seldom formed on account of the diffiulty of their construction, and also because their ditches are incapable of any flanking defense; the lines of fire diverging from the parapet, any one spot on the ground is very imperfectly defended.

107. A four sided figure is the best and most usual form for a redout, because it is of simple construction; the ditches are more easily flanked, and there are not so many points of attack as in a redoubt of a greater number of angles. Redouts being closed works, are better able to stand detached than redans or lunettes, and are, therefore, constructed when a small work is required without any immediate protection from the gorge—the armed party being strong enough to complete and man a four-sided redout, each side of which is not less than 15 yards long.

108. The size depends on the number of men who are to garrison it, and upon the number of guns which it is to contain; also upon the length of time during which it is to be occupied; this may be for a few hours only, (as on a field of battle) or for a period of weeks or months.

109. If wanted only for a few hours, it will be sufficient to allow 3 feet in length of parapet for every man of the detachment; or for every two men, if they are to be formed in double rank. If guns are to be placed in the work, 15 feet of parapet must be given to each, in order

that the gunners may have sufficient room on each side to work it.

110. But when the redout is destined to contain a body of men for a considerable length of time, it becomes necessary for them to have room to lie down within the banquette with their arms and packs; supposing one-third to be on guard, patrolling, &c., two square yards in addition to the slope of the banquette, are sufficient for each man, and 36 square yards for each gun and its appointments.

111. The rule, consequently, for a square redoubt is: to multiply the given number of men by 2, and number of guns by 36, for the number of square yards which the work ought to contain within the foot of its banquette, the square root of the product will be the length in yards of the side of the square forming that area; adding to this result the breadth of two interior slopes, and of two banquettes with their slopes, (about 7 yards altogether,) we shall have the side of the square formed by the crest of the parapet.

112. A square redout ought not to be traced with less extent of sides than 15 yards; for, by employing the calculation explained above, it will be found that such a work is only just sufficient to contain the number of men necessary for its defense; on the other hand, it is usual to make a square redout with a longer side than 40 yards, because it would require a garrison more suitable to a work of a stronger outline.

113. The imperfections of redoubts are, that they are entirely without a flanking fire for the defense of the ground in front of their faces, also that their ditches and

the sectoral spaces before the angles, are without any fire whatever for their defense.

114. A flanking defense for the ditches may be obtained by placing palisade or stockade caponnieres in them, either at the angles or in the middle of the faces; by tambours in a like position, or by loopholed galleries under the counterscarp at the salients of the work.

115. A ditch caponniere is an oblong structure formed with palisades, or with structure work, loop-holed, and roofed over with planks and earth to secure the men from the effects of shell, and a plunging fire from the counterscarp. It ought, if possible, to be flanked with musketry, to prevent an enemy from closing on it, and getting under cover.

116. The best position for a caponniere in the ditch of a redoubt, is at the salient angle, as then one caponniere flanks two branches of the ditch. It should be separated from the counterscarp by an enlargement of the ditch, to prevent the enemy from using it as a bridge to cross the ditch, and it ought to have a wicket to allow of sallies into the ditch.

117. To lessen the destructive effect of shell, traverses should be placed in all closed works when those missiles are likely to be employed against them.

118. The *counterscarp gallery* consists of a frame work, covered at the top with a sheeting, which is placed within the counterscarp at the salients. The front of the gallery is made of 9 or 10 inch scantling, placed upright, and arranged with loop-hole defences; these pieces are connected at the top by a cap sill. Cross pieces are notched on the cap sill about three feet apart; they are supported by

shalves placed four feet from the front piece. The cross pieces may project three feet beyond the shalves, and, if necessary, be braced from the shalves. The gallery is covered on top by one and a-half inch sheeting and behind in a similar manner, but only to the height of 5 feet above the bottom. This arrangement gives a free space behind the back sheeting for the play of the rammer in loading. The height of the gallery may be only 7 feet, its width, according to the foregoing arrangements, is 4 feet. It should be covered on top by at least 3 feet of earth. The level of the gallery should be the same as the ditch; and there should be a small ditch in front of it, to prevent the enemy from closing on the loop-holes, or obstructing their fire by filling the ditch in front of them by means of sand bags, fascines, &c. The entrance to the gallery is by a narrow door.

POWDER MAGAZINES.

119. The main objects to be attended to in a powder magazine are, to place it in a position least exposed to the enemy's fire; to make it shot proof; and to secure the powder from moisture.

120. If there are traverses, such for example, as are used in defilement, the magazines may be made in them; or they may be placed at the foot of a barbette; or, in dry soil they may be made partly under ground.

121. The magazine should be at least 6 feet high, and about the same width within; its length will depend on the quantity of ammunition. It may be constructed of fascines, gabions, or *coffer-work*, or any means found at hand may be used which will effect the end in view.

122. If fascines are used, the sides should slope out to resist the pressure of the earth; the fascines should be perfectly secured by pickets and anchoring withes. The top may be formed by a row of joists, of 6 inch scantling, placed about two and a-half feet apart; these should be covered by two layers of fascines laid side by side, and the whole covered in by at least 3 feet thickness' of earth. The bottom should be covered by a flooring of joists and boards; a shallow ditch being left under the flooring, with a pitch towards the door of the magazine, to allow any water that might leak through to be taken out. A thatch of straw might be used on the inside, but it is somewhat dangerous, owing to its combustibility; hides or tarpaulins are better and will keep out the moisture more effectually.

123. A *coffer-work* is formed by making frames of 6 inch scantling; each frame is composed of two uprights, termed *stanchions*, and a cap and ground sill, well nailed together. It is 6 feet wide, and 6 feet high in the clear. These frames are placed upright, and parallel to each other, about two and a-half feet apart; they are covered on the top and sides by one and a-half inch plank, which is termed a sheeting. The magazine otherwise is constructed as in the last case.

124. When gabions are used, a hole is usually dug in the ground to form part of the magazine; the gabions are placed in two rows, side by side around the hole, and are filled with earth. The top is formed as in the case of fascines.

125. The mouth of the magazine is covered by a *splinter proof shelter*. This is constructed by taking scantling 8 by 10 inches, cut into suitable lengths, and placing it in

an inclined position, so as to cover the mouth, and leave an easy access to it. The pieces, usually, are inclined 45° and are placed side by side; they are covered by at least two feet of earth or sods; and hides or tarpaulins are thrown over the whole.

126. Splinter proof blinds are mainly intended to afford a shelter against the fragments of hollow projectiles that explode in the work. They may be used as a kind of barrack for the troops; and to store provisions, &c.

BATTERIES.

127. The term battery is usually applied to a collection of several guns; it is also used in speaking of the arrangements made of a parapet to enable the guns to fire over it, or through openings in it; as a *barbette battery*, an *embrasure battery*, &c. Two kinds of batteries are used in the defense of intrenchments, the barbette battery and the embrasure battery.

128. The *Barbette* is a construction by means of which a piece can be fired over a parapet. It consists of a mound of earth, thrown up against the interior slope; the upper surface of which is level, and two feet nine inches below the interior crest for guns of small calibre, and four feet for heavy guns. If the barbette is raised behind a face, its length should be sufficient to allow sixteen and a half to 18 feet long the interior crest for each gun; and its *depth*, or the perpendicular distance from the foot of the interior slope to the rear, should be twenty four feet, for the service of the guns. The earth of the barbette at the rear and sides receive the natural slope. To ascend the barbette, a

construction, termed a *ramp*, is made; this is an inclined plane of earth, which connects the top of the barbette with the terre-plein. The ramp is ten feet wide at the top, and its slope is six base to one perpendicular. The earth at the sides receives the natural slope. The ramp should be at some convenient point in the rear, and take up as little room as possible.

129. The advantages of the barbette, consist in the commanding position of the guns, and in a very wide field of fire; on these accounts the salients are the best positions for them. Their defects are, that they expose the guns and men to the enemy's artillery and sharpshooters.

130. Light guns, particularly howitzers, are the best for arming barbettes; because the hollow projectile of the latter is very formidable, both to the enemy's columns and to his cavalry; and when he opens his fire against the salients, the light pieces can be readily withdrawn.

131. The *Embrasure* is an opening made in the parapet for a gun to fire through. The bottom of the embrasure, termed the *sole*, is two feet nine inches, or four feet above the ground, on which the wheels of the carriage rest, according to the size of the gun; it the interior crest. These four lines form the boundaries of the two cheeks on the superior and exterior slopes.

132. When the directrix is perpendicular to the direction of the parapet, the embrasure is termed *direct*. When the directrix makes an acute angle with it, the embrasure is termed *oblique*.

133. The manner of laying out an oblique embrasure is similar to the direct; the mouth is of a rectangular form, but is made wider in proportion to the obliquity, in order

that the part of the embrasure, which corresponds to the muzzle of the gun, is nearly of the same width in both the direct and oblique embrasures. The exterior width of the sole is made equal to one-half the length of the directrix, measured on the sole. The cheeks are laid out as in the last case.

134. The muzzle of a gun should enter at least six inches into the embrasure, to prevent the blast from injuring the cheeks; this limits the obliquity of the directrix to about 60° for long guns.

135. The height of the cheeks must not be more than four feet, for the same reason; it will, therefore, in some cases, be necessary to raise the ground on which the wheels rest.

136. The parapet of a battery is usually termed the *epaulment*. The interior face of the epaulment, and the cheeks of the slopes outward to allow the gun to be fired under an inclination, the base of this slope should never be less than six times the altitude; the interior opening, termed the *mouth*, is from eighteen inches to two feet wide, according to the calibre of the gun, and is of a rectangular form; the embrasure widens towards the exterior, which widening is termed the *splay;* the manner in which the play is regulated, is by producing the sole to the exterior slope of the parapet, and making this exterior line measured on the sole, equal to half the distance between the inner and outer lines of the sole. This construction makes the sole a trapezoidal figure, the side of the trapezoid, on the interior, being eighteen inches, or two feet; the opposite side being equal to half the perpendicular distance between the two sides. The line which bisects the

sole is termed the *directrix* of the embrasure; the sides of the embrasure, termed the *cheeks*, are laid out by setting off two points on the exterior crest of the parapet, one on the right, the other on the left of the sole, so that the horizontal distance of these points from the sole shall be equal to one-third their height above it. Lines are then drawn on the exterior slope, from these points to the exterior points of the sole; lines are in like manner drawn from the same points, on the superior slope to the upper points of the mouth, on embrasures, are riveted in the usual manner. That part of the interior face which lies below the chase of the gun is termed the *genouillere*. The mass of earth between two embrasures is termed a *merlon*.

137. The embrasures are generally cut out after the epaulment is thrown up. If their position is decided upon beforehand, they must be roughly formed at first, and be finished after the epaulment is made.

138. The advantages of embrasures are, that the men and guns are less exposed than in a barbette battery.—Their principal defects are, that they have a very limited field of fire; they weaken the parapet, and present openings through which an enemy may penetrate in an assault. Owing to their limited field of fire, they are chiefly used for the protection of particular points; as to flank a ditch, protect a salient, enfilade a road, &c. The most suitable position for them in a work is on the flanks.

139. *Platforms.* When a gun is fired often in the same direction, the ground under the wheels is soon worn into ruts; it is to prevent this, that platforms of timber are used in such cases.

140. The shape of the platform is usually a rectangle:

in some cases where a wide field of fire is to be obtained, the form is a trapezoid. The rectangular platform is 10 feet wide, and 17 feet long, for seige pieces; and 9 feet wide and 15 feet long, for the field guns. It consists of three sleepers of 6 inch scantling, either 15 or 17 feet long, which are laid perpendicular to the direction of the epaulment, and are covered with two-inch plank, twelve inches wide, and cut into lengths of 9 or 10 feet. Between the ends of the sleepers, and the foot of the genouillere, a piece of 8 inch scantling, 9 feet long, termed a *heurter*, is laid; it should project about six inches above the platform, and be bisected by the directrix. The object of the heurter is to prevent the wheels from being run against the revetment, and also to give the gun its proper direction, particularly in night firing.

141. To lay a platform, the earth on which it is to rest, should be well rammed and levelled; three trenches are then made for the sleepers, two of which should be placed ender the wheels, and the middle one under the trail. The sleepers are laid flush with the ground, and firmly secured by pickets driven at their sides and ends, and the earth is solidly packed in the trench around them; the plank is then laid and secured by nails or some other fastenings.

142. If the platform is for direct firing, with full charges, the *tail* may be made six inches higer than the front to break the recoil; in all other cases it should be horizontal.

143. A platform may be constructed simply of three pieces of timber, one under each wheel, and one under the trail, firmly secured by pickets, and connected by cross pieces, into which they are halved.

144. For barbetts, the platform may be dispensed with,

or if used, the whole surface nearly of the barbette, should be covered.

145. If the platform is made of a trapezoidal from it will require five sleepers.

LINES.

146. Lines are a series of works and trenches or of independent works, arrraged so as to defend each other, and the ground in front of and between them.

147. Lines are used to cover the front of a position, or to connect important redoubts or forts together.

148. Lines are of two kinds, such as are continuous, and such as have intervals between the works.

149. The former are principally applicable to situations where it is proposed to act on the defensive only, and when they are of such limited extent that the whole line of parapet can be occupied by troops sexclusive of reserves; as for instance, to close a pass between scarped mountains, or on the sea shore, or on the banks of large rivers; thus resting on natural obstacles which will prevent their flank being turned. They are often introduced as portions of an extended line with intervals.

150. Extensive continued lines can make but slight resistance, while the labor necessarily expended in executing them is considerable; and as the enemy may menace several points at once, it follows that as many troops would be required for the defense as for the attack, in which case the first principal of fortification is violated. Even if the defenders have a sufficient number of disposable troops, they act when within lines, under a disadvantage, for they

must watch and follow every movement of the enemy, so as to be equally prepared to resist a false and a real attack. It has often happened that while the defenders within the lines were concentrating their forces to oppose a false attack, the enemy has penetrated at a point where he was not expected; and a continued line once entered may generally be deemed lost.

151. Continuous lines of redans connected by curtains are constructed in three ways: in the first, (which is the one puincipally used,) as described by Vauban, the salients of the redans are 240 yards asunder, consequently the musketry fire of one redan does not, effectively, defend the salient of the next. To remedy this defect, it was subsequently recommended that the salients of the redans should be brought within musket range of each other, or within 160 yards.

152. In both of these constructions, the flanking angles formed by the faces of the redans and the curtains joining them must exceed 150°, and consequently the flanking defence is very imperfect.

153. Lines of *lenailles*, consists of parapets forming a series of salient and re-entering angles, and are in fact, like the improved redan lines, except that in this tracing, the redans are all of the same size, and have obtuse angles.

154. They are traced by setting off distances of about 200 yards along the front of the intended lines, to marke the position of the salient angles; these intervals are then bisected, and perpendiculars drawn towards the interior to give the places of the re-entering angles. The perpendiculars should not exceed half the distance between the salients, otherwise the re-entering angles would be less then right angles.

155. *Cremaillere lines* are composed of alternate short and long faces at right angles (or nearly so) to each other; the short faces, called *crotchets*, are made about 30 yards long, and the long faces, called *branches*, about 100 yeads long.

156. These lines possess the following advantages:

1st. The branches are little exposed to be enfiladed, owing to the small projection of the salients.

2dly. Each branch is defended not only by the fire of the adjoining crotchet, but by several others.

3dly. Their outline is very easily adapted to all varieties of the ground; and on slopes, in particular, they are very advantageous, because a small additional height given to the crotchets will defilade a long extent of earth from the fire of an enemy on the height.

157. Their defects are:

1st. The crotchets being short, very little of the ditch of each is defended by the adjacent branch.

2dly. A battery which can enfilade one branch is equally able to enfilade several.

158. Cremaillere lines may be much strengthened by placing along their front, bastions or double redans, at intervals varying from 690 to 800 yards, in order that a cross fire of artillery may be brought from them in front of the other parts of the line.

159. The crotchets should face towards the bastions, or redans, in order that the fire from the crotchets may defend the salients of these works, and that the branches may be defiladed by being directed on the bastions or double redans.

LINES WITH INTERVALS OR BROKEN LINES.

160. Broken lines should always, when practicable, be disposed in a double row, and in such a manner that the inner works may flank the outline; the advantages possessed by broken lines, are:

1st. With the same extent as continuous lines, they require less labor in the construction, and fewer troops to occupy them, consequently large reserves may be formed.

2dly. The defenders may advance in force and in a regular formation through the intervals, and attack the enemy should he have been thrown into confusion.

3dly. They oblige the enemy to overpower each separate work before he can become possessed of the whole; whereas if a continuous line be forced in one part, it is generally lost to the defenders.

4thly. If the enemy has gained one work, he will then be exposed to the flanking fire of the adjacent works, and to a fire from the works in the second line.

161. To profit fully by this advantage, when the front line consists of closed works, their rear faces ought to be of slight construction, that the artillery of the second line may easily demolish those faces, if the enemy should gain possession of the works.

162. When there are two lines of works, the heaviest artillery should be placed in the interior line, or else the enemy, obtaining possession of the exterior line, would turn the guns against the other, and have a superiority over the defenders.

163. When lines are on sloping ground descending towards the front, the slope should, if possible, be very steep, so as to form an escapement befor the works.

164. A single row of redans or redouts is comparatively weak, for the fire from them crosses at a distance in front of the intervals, and but feebly defends the salients. Lunettes are better in such a situation on account of the fire of the flanks, which may be brought to cross the capitals close to the salient angles.

165. The intervals between the works which form a broken line, should not exceed 160 yards, in order that they may be defended by an effective cross fire from those works.

166. The different works should occupy the most prominent and the highest ground; also the flanking parts ought to be perpendicular to their lines of defense.

167. The intervals between the works may be strengthened by artificial obstacles, or by a trench, for troops, with a rough parapet, (like the first parallel in a seige) having a broad interior slope to enable the men to advance over it when occasion requires.

DEFENCE OF FIELD WORKS.

168. A spot selected for a military post should not be commanded, especially on the flank or in the rear, within the ordinary range of a field piece. There should be plenty of materials on the spot to aid in strengthening the works, or in forming obstructions in front of them, the soil should be of a nature to be easily worked, and the position should be difficult of access; it should, however, offer the means of retreating in security, and with facility.

169. There is no talent more essential to an officer than that of seizing at a glance the strong and weak points of a position. This talent, known by the name of "*Military coup d' œil*" can be acquired alone by practice and study;

for whatever may be said of natural gifts, apprehension, however quick it may be, can supply the places of those indispensable requisitions in every art, and in no one are they more so than in the *Military Art.*

170. The highest ground of a position should be occupied by the salients of works, for then the adjoining faces will be, in some measure, secured from enfilade fire; it follows that the re-entering angles should be placed in the lowest spots.

171. It is very essential to create obstructions within short range of musketry in front of all works of a temporary nature, with a view of breaking the order of the assailants, and detaining them under a close and severe fire, if they persist in forcing their way through.

172. In fact, all the movements of an enemy, whether to the front, to the right or left, should be as much cramped and impeded as possible; it is important to break his order and put him into confusion when under fire, for he can seldom reform under such circumstances; and if he attacks in disorder, the chances are against his success.

173. To save time in making palisades or stockade work, the whole quantity ought to be divided into distinct portions, say 10 or 12 feet in length, to one carpenter and two laborers; and to prevent confusion in obtaining materials for constructing obstacles, it is well to divide the men into parties of 8 or 10 each, prescribing to each party the nature of the materials required, the place where they are to be obtained, and the spot at which they are to be deposited.

174. The materials are obtained by felling trees, unroofing houses, taking up floors and the like.

175. The guns of a work should not, generally, reply to the cannonade which preceds an assault, but should be placed behind traverses, or other places of shelter previously prepared by them; they should only fire at the enemy's artillery, while the latter is changing its position.

176. Round shot or shells are fired against guns; grape, canister, spherical case, and rockets against troops.

177. As soon as the enemy's light troops advance, the parapets are to be manned; sand bags, previously filled, are placed along the parapet, leaving loop holes between them; they are musket shot proof, and give the men the necessary confidence to enable them to take a steady aim. One rank of men is sufficient on the banquette, others being placed behind them to load. A reserve is to be stationed under cover, who fall upon the assailants with the bayonet, should they succed in getting into the work. For a good defence, there ought to be a file per yard to man the parapet, with a reserve of one-fourth or one-sixth of the whole, in addition.

178. As soon as the assaulting columns begin to mask the fire of their own artillery, the guns of the work will bo brought up and open their fire on them.

179. A sortie (very rarely) may be made, should the enemy be thrown into disorder; but this step requires great caution, for should the sortie be repelled, the enemy may enter the works with the retiring troops.

180. FOUGASSES, previously prepared, will be fired the instant the enemy is above them, by means of a piece of safety fuse, or a musket with its muzzle in the powder; and a wire to the trigger.

181. If the assailents at length descend into the ditch,

shells, grenades, and every sort of missile are to be thrown upon them. The shells are rolled down by being placed in troughs laid on the superior slope of the parapet.

182. If the enemy has to cross a river before he arrives at the work, the fords may be rendered impassible for artillery and cavalry, by digging pits, planting stakes, throwing in felled trees and harrows, or by driving wagons or carts full of stones into the middle, and taking off the wheels.

183. Should the ford be beyond musket range from the work, a parapet may be raised opposite to it, at such a distance from it as to permit the defenders to issue forth and charge the party crossing it, at the moment they land in disorder on the bank.

184. To prevent suprise, outposts are stationed around the work at night, and heaps of dried brushwood, or tarred fascines, should be placed along the post at intervals; at the approach of the enemy the outposts retire into the work, having set fire to the piles of brushwood; this will, in a great measure, prevent an enemy from concealing himself near the work.

LOOPHOLING WALLS.

185. Walls are made available for the purpose of defense by loopholing them, if a ditch cannot, for want of time, be dug at the foot of the wall outside. The loopholes ought to be at least 7 feet above the ground to prevent the assailants from making use of them; in the former case a temporary stage might be made of casks, ladders, &c., within 4 feet or 4 feet 6 inches of the loopholes, to enable the men to fire through them.

186. The quickest way of loopholing a wall is to break it down from the top in the form of narrow fissures about 3 feet asunder; but if the wall is very low, or there is not time to make loopholes, a piece of timber or the trunk of a tree, supported on the top of it by a couple of stones, would be a ready expedient, and the men could fire from the opening under it or sand bags, or larg stones or sods, might be placed on the wall at intervals. The roopholes made in walls or buildings can seldom be made of any regular form; The width outside should not exceed 3 inches, but inside it may be equal to the thickness of the wall. The best tools (of such as are usually found about a building) to break loopholes through a wall, are crow-bars, pick-axes, and large hammers.

187. Barricades for roads and streets, are made, if time permits, by sinking a ditch 7 or 8 feet deep, and forming the earth into a breastwork, adding palisades, &c., but if time presses, casks, boxes, or cart bodies filled with earth, stones, manure, or cinders, sacks of four, bales of merchandise, and the like, must be arranged across; paving stones may be taken up and disposed in a similar manner.

188. The mass should be raised 6 or 7 feet high, and a banquette formed for firing over it; the neighboring houses should also be loopholed so as to give a good flanking fire over the ground in front of the barricade, and stones may be collected to throw down on the assailants from the contigious houses.

FORTIFYING HOUSES.

189. The great art of converting buildings, and the outlines and wall that usually surround them, into defensible

posts, consists in selecting from the mass of objects at hand, such as will answer the purpose, and in sacrificing everything else, making use of the materials to strengthen the part which is to be fortified.

190. The building chosen should possess some of all the following requisites:

1st. It should command all that surrounds it.

2dly. It should be substantial, (not thatched,) and of a nature to furnish materials useful for ;placing it in a state of defense.

3dly. It should be of an extent not too great for the number of defenders, and should only require for the completion of the proposed object the time and means which can be spared.

4thly. It should have projections flanking the walls and angles.

5thly. It should be difficult of access on the side exposed to attack, and yet have a safe retreat for the defenders; and, of course, it must be in such a position as to answer the purpose for which the detachment is posted.

191. As a rough guide to judge of the third requisite, there ought to be a man for every 4 feet of wall round the interior of the lower story, one to every 6 feet for the second story, and one to every 8 feet for an attic, with a reserve about one-sixth of the whole.

192. Should there exist any doubt about having sufficient time to execute all that might be wished, it would be necessary to decide on the best points to be secured in order to repel an immediate attack; in such a case it might be well to employ as many men as could work without hindering each other by being too crowded, to collect materi-

als, and barricade the doors and windows on the ground floor, to make loopholes in them, and to level any obstruction outside that would give cover to the enemy, or facilitate the attack; to sink ditches opposite the doors on the outside, and arrange loopholes in the windows of the upper story; to make loopholes through the walls generally, attending first to the most exposed parts, and to break communications through all the party walls and partitions; to place abattis or any feasible obstruction on the outside, and to improve the defense of the post by the construction of tambours; to place outbuildings and garden walls in a state of defense, and establish communication between them; to make arrangements (in the lower story particularly) for defending one room after another, so that a partial possession only, could be obtained on a sudden attack being made.

193. These different works should be undertaken in the order of their relative importance, according to circumstances; and after securing the immediate object for which they are designed, they might remain to be improved on, if an opportunity should offer.

194. Houses are fortified by piercing loopholes through the walls, and if the walls are high, two or even three rows of loopholes may be made, and a temporary scaffolding of furniture, casks, &c., erected for firing from the upper ones; one row may be made close to the ground, with pits dug in the rear, or the floor may be cut through, if there is a basement, for the convenience of making use of them. The loopholes may have the dimensions before prescribed, and they ought not to be made at a less distance than three feet from each other, lest the wall should be too much weakened, or the defenders inconveniently crowded.

195. The staircases are to be cut away, the communication being kept up by ladders; and the floors, as well as the partition walls, should be loopholed.

196. Thatched roofs and all combustible materials are to be removed, and barrels of water should be placed in every room in readiness to extinguish fire.

197. A communication ought to be opened on the side farthest from the enemy, through which ammunition and reinforcements may enter.

198. The door or barrier closing this communication, may be made musket proof, by nailing strong planks to it, and if there is a basement to the house, the floor should be cut away within the door, so as to form a sort of a ditch.

199. All the doors and windows are to be barricaded and loopholed. The best barricade for a door is made by strong palisades, which are secured to a thick cross beam let into the wall on each side; a bank of earth may also be formed on the exterior.

200. All the enclosures which may afford the enemy cover, must be removed, if not included in the defense.

201. If artillery is likely to be employed against the house, it will be necessary, unless the walls are very strong, to support the timbers of the roof by means of props.

202. If there is time, the house may be formed into a block house by pulling down the upper stories, and laying the materials over the lower rooms to make the covering shell proof.

203. A ditch may be dug on the outside of the house, and the earth placed against the walls; some protection may be obtained for the doors, by placing strong beams on the wall outside in an inclined position, and heaping earth or rubbish over them.

INTRENCHING A VILLAGE.

204. In intrenching a village, the buildings, walls, and hedges on its circuit, are to be considered as part of its enclosure, and are to be made fit for the purpose of defense; all the intervals between them are to be occupied by breastworks or palisades, and strengthened by abattis.

205. The streets are to be barricaded at intervals with carts or wagons, having one or two wheels taken off, with barrels of earth, bales of merchandize, &c.; a passage should be made through the adjoining houses, which should be loopholed, and care must be taken that the barricade be not turned by an enemy passing down the neighboring streets.

206. Some strong building, such as a church, courthouse, or jail, should be selected, and fortified with particular care, to serve as a citadel or reduit, to which the defenders may retire when driven in from the exterior part of the village.

207. Advantage must be taken of any walls or outbuildings surrounding whatever has been selected as the reduit or keep; and they should be converted into outworks for strengthening it as an independent post. Should the village be of too great an extent for the force thrown into it, a portion of it only might be strengthened, and the remainder separated or destroyed; or the defence might be confined to some separate building.

208. The roads by which an enemy would advance should be cut up, and obstructed with felled trees, ploughs, harrows, &c.; bridges should be broken, and the passage disputed under cover of some simple field work placed favorably to command the road.

209. The resolute defence of villages situated on the front of an army has often decided the fate of a battle; in this position, they may be regarded as bastions connected by movable curtains.

ATTACK ON FIELD WORKS.

210. The attack on field works may be executed by surprise, or by open force; the former can only take place when the advance of the assailants is concealed by fog or darkness, or by the nature of the ground, as in mountainous countries.

211. In the attack of field works by open force, it is advisable to advance against several points at the same moment, when circumstances permit; of these some may be false attacks, and may be converted into real ones if the enemy appears weak or hesitating on the points threatened. One attack ought, generally, to be directed upon the rear of the work, (if open at the gorge,) which will always lessen the confidence of the defenders.

212. As many assaulting columns should be formed as there are points to be attacked, and before the works are stormed, pits and trenches should (when time permits, and there is no natural cover for skirmishers) be dug to conceal riflemen : these pits are about four feet wide, and, with the excavated earth raised before them, four feet in depth, in order that they may serve to cover a file of men to that height.

213. The artillery should be posted on the prolongations of the faces to enfilade them, weaken the parapets, and ruin the interior defences of the works and its ditch; for

the latter purpose howitzers are best adapted. As soon as the artillery has produced some effect, the signal for the assault should be give; light troops will gradually advance towards the counterscarp, in skirmishing order, firing at the gunners through the embrasures; they will conceal themselves in the pits and trenches prepared for them, or seek shelter in the inequalities of the ground. They should be followed by storming parties, and these should be accompanied by a detachment of sappers, (or a squad of soldiers told off for that purpose,) carrying axes, crowbars, bags of powder, &c., to force obstacles. Lastly, the reserve will follow, at some distance, to act as circumstances may require; it may repel attempts to aid the defenders, reinforce the storming parties if they succeed in entering the work, or it may afford them a rallying point, and cover their retreat if they fail.

214. The troops descend into the ditch with unfixed bayonets, in order to avoid accidents; and they fix them when on the berme.

215. Should the ditches have a great depth, it will be necessary to lessen it by means of bags with heather or grass, or by bundles of hay or straw, or fascines, &c.

216. A bridge formed of a gun limber and a ladder may be run up to the counterscarp and thrown across.

217. To avoid mistakes in marching by night to attack, each soldier should bear some visible mark by which he may be distinguished form an enemy. If a breach or any particular point is to be attacked by night, the way to it should be marked by distinguishable pickets or other objects, placed or re-marked on the ground at the time of the previous reconnoissance.

218. The columns march to the assault in the direction of the capitals; but after passing the ditch, the troops should enter the works by the faces, on each side of the salient angle, that they may present a front in the work equal or superior to that of the enemy. When it may be advisable to force an entrance at the gate of a fortified post, that gate may be destroyed by a piece of artillery brought close up to it, or by a bag of powder attached to the wood by a gimlet, or propped against it by a forked stick.

219. In assaulting a place whose scarps and counterscarps are revetted with masonry, scaling ladders must be employed. The first division of each column of assault carries the longest ladders; they descend into the ditch with them, and afterwards carry the ladders across and raise them against the scarp.

220. The next division carries other ladders, which they place and leave against the counterscarp. The ladders are carried and planted with arms slung. Ladders planted against a wall are not to slope above one-fourth of their height, lest they should break under the weight of the men.

221. A strong firing party is drawn up on the glacis to keep down the fire of the defenders, if the latter should appear on the parapets to oppose the assault.

ATTACKING HOUSES.

222. In the attack of houses, artillery should be employed to form a breach before giving the assault, and also to throw hot shot, shells, and carcasses.

223. If the detachment is unprovided with artillery, attempts must be made to force passages through doors, windows, or unflanked parts of the walls: the attack should be made on different parts of the building, to distract the attention of the defenders; in the mean time, and for the same purpose, parties of men keep up a fire on any points where there is a chance of disabling them.—Attempts may also be made to effect an entrance through the roof by means of ladders.

224. If the assailants have neither powder nor crowbars for forcing doors, a heavy beam or tree may, if at hand, be used as a battering ram; a fire of straw or brushwood may be made near the walls further to distract and alarm the defenders, and to cover the operations of the assailants.

ATTACKING BARRICADES.

225. Artillery will soon clear a passage through ordinary barricades; if not, the assaulting party must endeavor to turn the barricade, either by passing down some other street, or by forcing a passage from one house to another, until they arrive in rear of it: a few loaded muskets applied to the locks and bolts of the strongest door will force it open, and the partition walls may be destroyed by bags of powder, &c. After having taken possession of a house, troops must be left in it for the purpose of firing from it upon the barricade.

OUTPOST AND PICKET DUTY.

PART SIXTH.

ADVANCED-GUARDS AND ADVANCED-POSTS.

1. To keep an enemy in ignorance of the state of our forces and the character of our position, is one of the most indispensable duties in war. It is in this way that we oblige him to take every possible precaution in advancing; forcing him to feel his way step by step, and to avoid risking his own safety in hazarding those bold and rapid movements which, when made against a feeble or an unprepared enemy, lead to the most brilliant results.

2. This object is effected by placing between the position occupied by the main force and the presumed direction of the enemy, a body detached from the main force, but acting always with reference to it, termed an *Advanced-Guard*.

3. This term is used for any body of troops so separated from the main body, whatever its strength and composition, and whether the troops be in position or on a march.

4. For a large force, the advanced-guard is necessarily

composed of troops of all arms, its strength being proportioned to that of the main force; the more or less resistance of an independent character it may be required to make; and the greater or less extent it may be found necessary to embrace by its advanced-posts, on the front and flanks, to watch and anticipate every movement of the enemy.

5. The proportion of the advanced-guard to the main-body may vary from a third to a fifth of the total force. In armies of some strength, or large *corps-d' armee*, particularly where the nature of the country requires a wide development of advanced-posts, the larger proportion is demanded; as at least one-third or even one-half of its strength will be required for the advanced-post service. In a small force of two or three thousand men, one-fifth will usually be all that can be well spared for the same purposes.

6. Our purpose, in all cases, should be to keep the enemy in a state of uncertainty as to our actual force and movements, and this can be effected only by keeping constantly between him and our main-body a force of sufficient strength to offer an obstinate resistance, if necessary, to every attempt he may openly make to gain information, and even to act offensively against him, when occasion offers, so as to keep him in doubt as to the actual character and number of troops before him; the old military axiom being always kept in mind, that "*a sword opportunely drawn frequently keeps another back in its scabbard.*"

7. In all defensive positions, the advanced-guard and its advanced-posts should retire slowly but circumspectly, so that the main-body may have time to take all its defensive

measures. In the offensive, the attack of the advanced-guard should be decided and vigorous; pressing upon the enemy at every point, and leaving nothing undone to demoralize him, by the confusion which so often follows from an impetuous onset.

8. Whilst in position, the advanced-guard should take advantage of the natural, or other obstacles on its front and flanks which are within supporting distance, to strengthen itself, and again supports for its advanced-posts. In this way, its means of resistance, whether acting offensively, or otherwise, may be greatly augmented. Ground of this character, taken up by the troops, should not be abandoned without very cogent reasons for it; since, should circumstances bring about a forward movement, it might cost more to regain what was given up than to have maintained it obstinately at first.

9. The ground to be taken by an advanced-guard, and embraced within its advanced-posts, should be carefully chosen. To take position where the movements of the enemy can be well watched, whilst our own troops are kept concealed, and not liable to a sudden attack, either in front or flank, are the *desiderata* in such cases. If, in following this guide, it should lead to a development of advanced-posts which would be too weak at any point for a tolerable resistance, there remains but the alternative to retire slowly before the enemy,—taking care that he do not slip behind the out-posts and their supports,—upon some central point to the rear where the advanced-posts, united to the troops in reserve, may make a good stand, and from which, if the chances are favorable, they may advance upon the enemy, and make him pay dearly for his temerity.

10. In all affairs of advanced-guards great circumspection is to be shown, both by the officer in command of the advanced-guard, in throwing forward fresh troops to strengthen a point assailed, as well as on the part of the general-in-chief, in sustaining the advanced-guard by weakening his main-body. These are points that can only be decided upon the spot. The safer rule, in all cases, is not to weaken the main defense, or main attack, by detaching from it to support a feeble point. If the force engaged, under such circumstances, does not suffice for its own defence, it is best for it to fall back in time, and, taking position with the main-body, endeavor, by their combined efforts, to turn the scales of victory in their favor.

11. The duties of advanced-guards being so much more frequently to feel and occupy the enemy, preparatory to some decisive blow by the main body, than to engage him with a view to follow up any advantage gained, it follows, as a matter of course, that they should be composed of the most efficient and active light troops at the general's disposal. Such troops, in the hands of a bold, energetic, but prudent leader, will be the right arm of any army.— Prompt on all occasions, never taken at fault, they keep the enemy constantly occupied, harass him with fatiguing precautions to secure his flanks and rear, whilst their own face is kept relieved from these annoyances, and always fresh for any great emergency.

ADVANCED POSTS.

12. The duties of the advanced posts are the same whether the troops are stationary, or in movement: they are,
1. To keep a good lookout for the enemy, and when in his

immediate presence to take all means to be accurately informed of his strength, position and movements; 2. Should the enemy advance, to hold him in check long enough to give the main body ample time to be prepared for his attack.

13. By a faithful discharge of these duties, the whole army can, at all times, and under all circumstances, be kept in a state of readiness for action, without subjecting the soldier to any fatigue beyond the ordinary physical endurance of a well-developed manhood, as but a small portion, comparatively, of the forces present is required to watch over the safety of the rest, and can therefore be frequently relieved, so that every one may have time sufficient for the repose demanded after extraordinary exertions.

14. The object being to secure the front and flanks of the position occupied by the main body, from any attempt either to reconnoitre or attack it, the detachments which form the advance posts must be so distributed as to embrace all the avenues by which the enemy can approach the position. The system adoped, in most services, to effect this object, consists of two or three concentric lines of posts, disposed in a *fan-shaped* order. The exterior line, which forms the *Out-Posts*, embraces a wide circumference, and by means of a chain of *Sentinels*, posted in advance, prevents any one from penetrating to the rear between the posts, without being seen.

15. The second line, which is one of *Grand-Guards*, embraces a narrower circumference than the line of outposts, occupying the more important avenues from the outposts to the interior, so as to be in position to support the

out-posts in case of necessity, and to receive them if driven in.

16. The interior line consists of several strong detachments, termed *Pickets*, posted upon the main avenues to the position. They serve as supports to the two exterior lines, upon which they rally if forced to retire before the enemy.

17. Besides these dispositions for security, *Patrols* are kept up between the line of posts, to keep the one informed of the state of the other; and also between the outposts and chain of sentinels, to see that the duties of the latter are well performed, and to search any ground not brought well under the eyes of the sentinels. The whole, in this way, forms a connected system, for observing the enemy and for mutual support in case of attack.

18. The duties of the out-posts, and of the grand-guards which form their supports, are strictly those of observation. If attacked, they offer no resistance farther than to enable them to feel the enemy perfectly, and never lose sight of him. The task of holding the enemy in check by a vigorous resistance, so as to procure sufficient time for the main body to make its dispositions for battle, is consigned to the pickets.

19. The ground taken up by the advanced-posts will depend on the capabilities which its natural features offer for defence, on the number and character of the approaches it presents to an enemy for attacking the front or flanks of the position occupied by the main body, and upon the facilities it may afford for communication between the posts.

OUT-POSTS.

20. The position of the out-posts, with respect to the main body, will be regulated by the more or less broken character of the country. As a general rule, the mean distance may be taken at about two miles. The line occupied by these posts should take in all the approaches to the front and flanks of the main position. When a position is to be held for some time, or is taken up after a battle, the out-posts may be thrown farther in advance, to procure greater repose and security for the main body.

21. The ground on which the line of out-posts is established, should be carefully examined, with a view both to observation and defence. As far as practicable, those points should be selected for posts which present some natural advantages for the defence; will screen the troops from the enemy's view, and enable them to watch all his movements. Whenever the features of the ground do not offer natural obstacles to cover the posts, artificial means of a slight character should be resorted to. The flanks of the line should rest upon strong natural obstacles; when such cannot be found, without giving the line too great an extent, these points must be secured by strong pickets of cavalry or infantry, thrown back to form crotchets, from which patrols must be constantly kept up on the flanks, in the presumed direction of the enemy.

22. The strength of each out-post, and the distance from one to the other, will be regulated by the features of the ground, and the number of sentinels or vedettes that each post must throw out. The posts should, as far as practicable, be within sight of the grand-guards to which they

belong, and the sentinels of their respective posts. When the ground does not permit this arrangement, sentinels should be placed at intermediate points, to communicate promptly whatever may happen at the line of posts, or of sentinels, to the rear. Posts of infantry should not, as a general rule, be placed farther apart than 600 paces, nor their sentinels more than 300 paces in advance of the posts. Those of cavalry may be some 1500 paces apart, and their vedettes from 600 to 800 paces in advance. The strength of each post should be calculated at the rate of four men for each sentinel, or vedette.

SENTINELS.

23. The sentinels and vedettes form a chain in advance, and are posted on points from which they can best watch the enemy without being seen by, or exposed to him, in any way. As one of their main duties is to prevent any one from passing their chain, they should be so placed, with respect to each other, that they can see all the ground between their respective posts, and be able to stop any one who may attempt to pass between them. At night and in misty weather, the sentinels should be doubled and be drawn in nearer to the out-posts.

24. Whenever it may be deemed necessasy to post sentinels on points beyond the line of out-posts, they should be furnished by posts detached in advance of the line.

GRAND-GUARDS.

25. As the grand guards furnish the out-posts, and serve as their supports, not more than one-third of their force

should be taken for the out-posts. The grand-guards are posted on the principal avenues leading to the detachments on which they are to fall back, if driven in; and when of infantry, about 200 paces, and of cavalry, 600 to 800 paces, in the rear of the out-posts. The points which they occupy should be selected, both to secure them from the enemy's view, and to give a ready communication between them and their respective out-posts. No difficult or broken ground should lie between the grand-guards and their out-posts; if any such occur, particularly if it be of a nature to offer facilities to an enemy to penetrate to the rear, the whole should be posted on the farther, or either side of it, and in preference in the latter position, if by it the chain of post can be preserved unbroken.

PICKETS.

26. The main detachments or pickets, which form the supports to the grand-guards and out-posts, occupy the principal avenues to the position of the main body. As their duty is to hold the enemy in check, the points which they take up should be susceptible of a good defence; such, for example, as villages, defiles, &c. Whenever these advantages are not found at hand, resort should be had to any temporary obstacles, as abattis, &c., which can be readily procured, to place the troops under shelter. The points thus occupied should, as a general rule, be about midway between the line of out-posts and the position of the main body.

27. Small posts should be thrown forward by the pickets, between their position and the line of grand-guards;

both for the greater security of the detachments, and as supports to the grand-guards. In like manner, when the line of pickets is of considerable extent, intermediate posts must be established, to keep open a communication between them.

28. No pains should be spared to obstruct the approaches of the enemy to the points occupied by the pickets, particularly those which lead to the flanks, leaving open such only as will oblige the enemy to attack under the most unfavorable circumstances, and if, between the advanced posts and the main body, a defile, or other unfavorable pass should occur, which the enemy, by turning the line of the advanced posts, might seize upon, and thus cut off their retreat, it should be occupied by a strong detachment, both to prevent such a manœuvre, and to favor the retreat on the main body.

STRENGTH OF THE ADVANCED-POSTS.

29. The entire strength of the advanced posts, as well as the relative strength of the pickets, grand-guards, and out-posts, will depend upon the character of the ground covered by them, as being more or less open, and presenting more or less facilities for circumscribing the approaches of the enemy to the main position. It rarely occurs that sufficient troops can be detached to cover all the accessible ground, and perform the duties in a thorough manner.

30. The strength of each picket, and the kind of troops of which it is composed, will depend on the degree of resistance to be offered to the enemy's attack, and the character of the position occupied. In most cases where a vig-

orous defence is called for, they will consist of troops of all arms, and an aggregate of several hundred men. The grand-guards, out-posts, and patrols, should not exceed one-third the strength of the pickets to which they belong. They will be composed of cavalry, or infantry, according to the more or less broken features of the ground.

31. It rarely occurs that artillery is placed at the out-posts. Whenever it happens that a piece or two may be deemed necessary, to sweep some passage, or defile, in advance of the line of out-posts, the guns must be protected by a strong post, to insure their safety in a retreat.

32. If, from the character of the ground, the out-posts are mainly of infantry, some cavalry should always be attached to them, to patrol in advance of the position, and to convey intelligence to the rear, of what may be passing in the neighborhood of the out-posts.

33. When the advanced posts cover an advanced-guard, the commanding officer of the whole should take a position, with his artillery and the main body of his command, at some central point, in the rear of the pickets, in order to be ready to support them if hard pressed by the enemy. The choice of this position is an object of the greatest importance, as the safety of the advanced-posts, as well as that of the main body, may depend upon the degree of judgment shown in this selection.

34. So soon as the advanced-posts have taken up their stations. instructions should be given to the officers of the different posts, with respect to the points upon which they are to fall back, in case of being forced in, the lines of communication they must retire by, and the position they must take up, in joining the supports to which they respectively belong.

DUTIES OF OFFICER COMMANDING AN OUT-POST.

35. An officer in command of any of the out-posts must be capable of untiring vigilance and activity, to perform the various duties which devolve upon him. He should be provided with a good map of the country, a telescope, and writing materials.

36. He will thoroughly reconnoitre the ground upon which he is to dispose his command, and also as far in advance as circumstances will admit, questioning closely any inhabitant he may find. After taking up his position, he should go forward, with the half of his command, and post each sentinel himself. If, however, he relieves another in the command, and deems it advisable to make any changes in the dispositions of his predecessors, he should promptly report the facts to the commanding officer in his rear.

37. When the officer finds that the enemy is not in his immediate neighborhood, he should endeavor to feel his way cautiously towards him by patrols; and when in immediate presence, he should omit no means to watch the enemy's movements, and from the occurrences of the moment, such as noises, the motion of clouds of dust, camp fires, conflagrations, &c., endeavor to divine what is passing in his camp, and his probable intentions.

38. Accurate written reports should be promptly sent to the officer in command, in the rear, on all these points. The reports should be *legibly* written, and should clearly but *concisely* state what has fallen under the officer's eye, what he has learned from others, and the character of the sources from which his information is drawn.

39. He will particularly see that no communication with the enemy be allowed, and that no flag be permitted to pass the line of post, without orders from the rear.

40. The post under the officer's command, whether horse or foot, should not all be allowed to sleep or eat at once. The horses, when watered, should be taken singly or by pairs, and always mounted. At night, one half of the command should be under arms, prepared for an attack, the other seated, their arms and the bridles of their horses in hand. The men should never be permitted to occupy a house; and if the weather is such that a fire out of doors is indispensable, it should be as much concealed as practicable; one-half only being allowed to sit near it, the other posted, at a convenient spot at hand, to fall on the enemy should he attempt a stroke.

41. When the position taken up is to be held for some time, it will be well to change the locality of the posts occasionally; this should be done, particularly at night, in a hilly district, changing the post from the brow of the hill, where the men can best keep a look-out by day, to the low ground at night, as more favorable to detect any movement above.

42. The out-posts are usually relieved at day break, as being the most favorable moment for the enemy to attempt a surprise; the new guard will serve to reinforce the old. For the same reason, the old guard should not be suffered to retire before the patrols come in, and report all safe.

43. As a general rule, no post should ever retire before an inferior force; and, if attacked by one superior to it, resistance should be cautiously made with a view solely to give time to the graud-guard to be in readiness to receive

the enemy. When it is seen that the movement of the enemy is serious, the officer should draw in his sentinels as skirmishers, and retire upon the grand guard; the latter will usually be divided into two divisions, one of which will be sent to take up a position to the rear, to cover the retreat; the other will act as a support to the line of skirmishers, so as to feel the enemy. In all cases of retiring, whether of sentinels upon their posts, or of posts upon their supports, care should be taken to assume a direction towards the flank of the force in rear, so as to unmask its front and not impede any forward movement it may make, if necessary.

44. The degree of resistance to be offered by the pickets will depend on the object to be obtained, and the importance of the point occupied. They should not retire until they have received the whole of their grand-guards, out-posts and patrols.

45. At night the precautions should be necessarily redoubled, and every movement be made with extreme caution. Whenever any noise is heard in the direction of a sentinel's post, the officer should proceed, with a part of his command, in its direction, to ascertain the cause of it. If he finds that it arises from an onward movement of the enemy, he should only fall back upon his grand-guard when he sees that resistance would be unavailing; retiring slowly and cautiously, and taking every advantage, which the ground offers, to check the enemy's advance. Should the enemy fall suddenly upon his commmand, he must endeavor to cut his way through, and reach his position in the rear by the best circuit he can find.

ADVANCED-GUARDS.

46. Measures of precaution, for a force in position, are far more easily arranged than for one in motion. At a halt of some days, but slight changes in the first dispositions, arising from a more thorough knowledge of the ground taken up, will be requisite; on a march the scene is continually shifting, and the enemy may fall on just at that point or under those circumstances in which we are least prepared to meet him. Hence a necessity for doubling the ordinary precautions on a march, and keeping the troops more in hand, so as to be, at all moments, prepared for any emergency.

47. The spirit of the dispositions is the same in both cases: changes in the details, so as to adopt our force to the changing features of the ground passed over, present the real difficulty. On a march, we may have to guard against an attack on the head of the column, on either flank, or both, and in the rear. Hence a necessary disposition of movable advanced-posts, in each of these directions, keeping pace with the progress of the main body, and far enough from it to give it timely warning of a threatened attack.

RECONNOISSANCES.

48. There are no more important duties which an officer may be called upon to perform than those of collecting and arranging the information upon which either the general or daily operations of a campaign must be based. For the proper performance of the former, acquirements of a very high order, in the departments of geography and statistics, are indispensable requisites, to which must be added a minute acquaintance with topography, and a good *coup d'œil militaire* for that of the latter.

49. However detailed and perfect may be a map, it can never convey all the information that will enable an officer to plan even an ordinary march with safety, still less operations that necessarily depend for their success upon a far greater number of contingencies. To supply these deficiencies of maps, an examination of the ground must be made by the eye, and verbal information be gained, on all the points connected with the operation over this ground. This examination and collection of facts is termed a *Reconnoissance*.

50. From the services demanded of a reconnoitering officer, it is, in the first place, evident that he should possess acquirements of no ordinary character, but in addition to these, he should be gifted by nature with certain traits,

without which his acquisitions would be of little account in the discharge of the responsible duty in question.

51. With clear and specific information before him, one-half of a general's difficulties in planning his measures, are dissipated. In a letter from Gen. Washington to Major Tallmadge, now to be seen framed in the office of the Commissary-General of New York, he remarks, in relation to reports made to him on a certain occasion: "But these things not being delivered with certainty, rather perplex than form the judgment." It is in truth this feeling of certainty that constitutes all the difference; having it, the general makes his dispositions with confidence; without it, he acts hesitatingly, and thus communicates to others that want of confidence felt in his own mind.

52. An officer then, selected for the duty in question, should be known to be cool-headed and *truthful*—one who sees things as they are, and tells clearly and precisely what he has seen. In making his report, whether verbally or in writing, the officer should study conciseness and precision of language. He must carefully separate what he knows from his own observation, from that which he has learned from others, and add all the circumstances of place and time with accuracy.

DUTIES OF RECONNOITERING OFFICER.

53. The first thing to be done by an officer selected for a reconnoissance, is to ascertain *precisely* the duty required of him; and what further should be done in case of certain contingencies that may, from the nature of the duty, be naturally looked for. In the performance of the duty,

assigned him, and in making his report, the officer should keep always in mind the specific character of his mission, as his guide in both points.

54. As the need of a reconnoissance supposes a deficiency in information upon the features of the country, the officer detailed to make one should provide himself with maps, a good telescope, such simple aids for judging of distances, and ascertaining the relative positions of objects, as he can himself readily make; writing materials; one or more good guides; and gain all the knowledge he can, from the inhabitants at hand, bearing upon his mission.

55. The talent of judging of distances, and of the connection between the various features of a country within the field of vision, is partly a natural and partly an acquired one. Some individuals can never be brought to have any confidence in their own judgment on these points; others have a natural aptitude for them, which requires but little practice for their perfect development. The powers of the eye vary so greatly among civilized persons, that no general rules can be laid down as a guide for the matter in question. Among uncivilized hordes, used to a roaming life, there are found standards which are well understood by all; the Arab, for instance, calling that distance a mile, at which a man is no longer distinguishable from a woman—growing out of their habits.

56. The first thing, then, to be done by an officer in acquiring the *coup d'œil militaire*, is to learn, both from books and on the field, what space is taken up by a battalion and its intervals, by a squadron and by a battery when in order of battle; how much when in column of march; and the average time required for certain movements, un-

der given circumstances of the ground. This acquirement he may make by adopting some standard of his own, his ordinary pace, and that of a horse, serving for computing time and distance reciprocally. The next step is to acquire the habit of estimating, by the appearances of these different objects, from various points of view, how far off they are. This must be done practically. A very simple aid to it is the following : Upon the stem of a lead pencil, cut square, and held out at a uniform arm's length from the eye, by means of a thread attached to it and fastened to the top button-hole, let the officer mark off, on one of the edges, the length seen on it by holding the pencil upright between the eye and a man placed successively at different distances from it, as 100, 150—1000 yards. This will give one rough standard for practice. Another may be made by first ascertaining the average height of certain cultivated trees, as the apple, &c.

57. For getting relative positions, a contrivance for measuring angles roughly must be used. This is done by first folding a leaf of paper across, and then doubling it along the folded edge, as if to divide it into four equal parts. The angle between the edge of the first fold and that of the second, will be a tolerably accurate right-angle. Now, by cutting off carefully along the fold one of the pieces, we obtain a quadrant, or 90°; then folding this at the angle, so that the two edges will exactly coincide, we get the half of a quadrant, or 45°; and so on, by successive bisections we can mark off smaller angles. Then making a pen or pencil-mark along each of the folds, and numbering the angles successively from 0 to 90°, we have a rough *protractor*, that can be used both for measuring

angles and setting them off on a sketch. To measure vertical angles, a thread with a light plummet, must be attached to the angular point. If the object is above the horizon of the eye, we hold the protractor *with the angular point from the eye*, so that the plumb-line will fall along the face of the paper, just touching it; then directing the top edge of the protractor on the object, so that it is just seen by the eye, sighting along the edge, the angle formed between the plumb-line and the other edge, will be the same as the angle between the line of sight and the horizon of the eye.

58. If the object is below the horizon of the eye, the angular point *is placed towards the eye*; the same series of operations will give the angle below the eye's horizon.

GUIDES.

59. Trustworthy guides are invaluable, but most rare, in an enemy's country. The best, from the information they acquire by their habits of life, are to be found among those classes whose avocations keep them much abroad, going from place to place within a certain sphere constantly—such as common carriers, hunters, smugglers, &c. Among the first things to be attended to by an officer, in taking post at any point, is to find out persons of this class, and to ascertain their whereabout when wanted. Kind treatment, *douceurs*, and promises, should not be spared, to enlist either their good will or their interests; and, if policy requires it, they may openly be treated with apparent harshness, to screen them from odium among their neighbors.

60. If none of this class can be found, then resort must be had to a higher—local authorities being in preference selected—and if necessary, forced to act. Here very careful treatment is requisite. When the necessity of the case is admitted by them, much may be gleaned by kindness, courtesy, and a certain deference, from such persons, that cannot be looked for from their inferiors.

61. Before starting on his mission, the officer should question his guide thoroughly; and if he has several, question each apart; like precautions should be taken with respect to other inhabitants. Care must be had to find out the usual beats of one taken as a guide, so as not to take him out of his own neighborhood. In all cases, the guide must be well watched, however trustworthy he may seem. If unwilling or sulky, he must if needs be, be tied, and attached to a strong man, with a rope round his middle; being first strictly searched for any cutting instrument about him.

62. Should there be but one guide, he must necessarily be placed with the most advanced portion of the detachment accompanying the officer. If there are several, one must be there also; the one apparently the most intelligent with the officer, who should ply him with questions, and the others in the rear strictly guarded.

63. It may be well to remark, that guides are useful even in a country of easy communications; as in case of a rencontre, they may point out bye-ways convenient for retreat, if necessary.

RECONNOISSANCE.

64. To designate all the objects to be embraced in a reconnoisance, would lead farther than the limits of this little work will allow; some general heads, which will serve as guides in all cases, will therefore be alone noticed.

65. A general view of the ground to be examined must first be taken in, so as to obtain some notion of the forms of the parts, their connection and relations to each other, before going into a detailed examination. To one possessed of some topographical knowledge, this study of what is before him will not demand much time. A level country for example, he knows is usually well cultivated, and therefore has plenty of hedges, ditches, &c., which lend themselves well to affairs of light troops, may be not a little inconvenient to manœuvres of artillery, and frequently bring up cavalry very unexpectedly in full career. In a mountainous one, dangerous passes, narrow roads, torrents with rough beds, ugly sudden turns, &c., will necessarily be met with. Each and all these demand a particular examination, and in his report their advantages and disadvantages should be clearly pointed out by the officer.

66. If the reconnoissance is for an onward movement, the distances from halt to halt, as well as all others, should be estimated in *hours of march*; the nature of the roads, and the obstacles along them be carefully detailed; the means that may be gathered along the line to facilitate the movement, as vehicles, men and materials for removing obstacles, &c. The points where cross-roads are found,

must be specified; the direction of these roads, their uses, &c.

67. All local objects along the line, as villages, farm-houses, &c., should be carefully designated, both as to their position on the line, or on either side of it; and also as to their form, and color, &c., as "square white house on the right," "round gray stone tower on hill to left."

68. The names of localities, in the way in which the inhabitants pronounce them, should be carefully written, and called over several times, so as to be sure to get them as nearly as practicable right in sound; then the names, as written by an intelligent inhabitant, should be added.

69. All halting points must be well looked to; their military capabilities in case of attack, as well as their resources for accommodating the troops, be thoroughly gone into.

70. If the halt is to take position for some time, to await or watch the enemy, then more care must be taken, the whole site be well studied as to its fulfilling the proposed end; the points of support on the flanks be designated, as well as others in front and rear, that may require to be occupied; the suitable localities to be chosen for parks, hospital, &c; the communications to be opened or repaired, pointed out; and all the facilities either for an advance or a retrograde movement to be laid down.

ARMED RECONNOISSANCE.

71. Reconnoissances, made in the neighborhood of an enemy, require to be done under the protection of a proper detachment, the strength and composition of which will depend on the object to be attained.

72. If the object be to gain secretly a knowledge of the enemy's whereabout and strength, then a detachment of light cavalry, conducted by a trusty guide, through circuitous bye-ways, and moving with celerity, but with proper precautions against falling into an ambush, or having his retreat cut off, is usually resorted to. The details for this will be found under the head of Patrols.

73. When an enemy's position is to be reconnoitered, with a view to force him to show his hand, by causing him to call out all his troops, then a large detachment of all arms, adequate to the task of pressing the enemy vigorously, and also of withdrawing with safety when pressed in turn, must be thrown forward.

74. Under the shelter of either of these forces, the officer charged with the reconnoissance, takes the best moment, and best point of view, for carefully ascertaining the dispositions made by the enemy. A good time will be at early dawn, when troops, in most services, are all made to stand to their arms. The points which the officer must exhibit most attention in finding out, are those occupied by the batteries, and all those in any way intrenched.

PATROLS.

76. Patrols are of two classes, from the different objects had in view. The first are those made with a view of insuring greater security from the enemy's attempts to pass, or force the line of out-posts, and may therefore be termed *defensive patrols*. They consist usually of three or four men, who go the rounds, along the chain of sentinels

and between the posts; seldom venturing farther than a few hundred paces beyond the sentinel's chain; the object being to search points which might present a cover to the enemy's scouts, and to keep the sentinels on the alert.

76. The second class are those made exterior to the line of out-posts, with a view of gaining intelligence of the enemy's whereabout, and may therefore be termed *offensive patrols*. They are composed of larger bodies of men than the first class, the number being proportioned both to the distance to be gone over, and the extent of front to be examined. In a position, presenting but few cross-roads, and sparsely settled, a patrol of ten or twenty horsemen, may be found ample, to search with all desirable thoroughness, from twenty to forty miles in advance of the position, along the principal avenues to it; whereas, with a more extended front, presenting many lateral avenues, double this number might be required for the same duty. From the information obtained, through the ordinary channels of maps, and by questioning the inhabitants at hand, the commanding officer can usually settle, with sufficient accuracy, the strength of a patrol.

77. From the duties to be performed by patrols, cavalry are usually employed alone; in cases of very broken country, infantry may be necessary, but they should always be accompanied by some horse, if for no other purpose than to transmit intelligence promptly to the rear.

78. The main duties of a patrol are to find the enemy if in the neighborhood, gain a good idea of his position and strength, to make out his movements, and to bring in an accurate account of his distance from the out-posts of their own force, and the character of the ground between the position occupied by the respective forces.

79. From the nature of these duties, it is evident that both officers and men, for a patrol, should be selected with especial reference to their activity, intelligence, and the aptitude they may possess, from previous habits of life, for a service requiring a union of courage, prudence, and discriminating observation—usually to be met with only in individuals who have been thrown very much upon their own resources. When the character of the country admits of it, the employment of such individuals, singly, or in very small bodies, as scouts, is one of the most available means of gaining intelligence of an enemy, without betraying the secret of our own whereabout.

DUTIES OF OFFICER IN COMMAND OF A PATROL.

80. In conducting a patrol, the commanding officer should provide himself with a good map, telescope, and guides, and gain all the information he can before starting, by questioning persons in the neighborhood. Nothing should escape his eye along his line of search, and he should particularly note points which might be favorable to his defence, if driven back by the enemy, or by which his retreat might be endangered.

81. The order of march of the patrol will be regulated by the circumstances of its strength, kind of troops employed, the character of the country passed over, the hour of the day, and the particular object in view. The intelligence and judgment of the officer in command will have sufficient exercise on these points, as he will be continually called upon to vary his dispositions. The general and obvious rule of keeping a look-out on all sides, will prompt

the general disposition of an advanced-guard, rear-guard, and flankers, according to the circumstances of the case, however small his command. The sole object being to carry back intelligence of the enemy, no precaution should be omitted to cover and secure his line of march, without making, however, too great a subdivision of his force.

82. Too much circumspection cannot be shown in approaching points favorable to ambuscades, as woods, ravines, defiles, inclosures, farm-houses, villages, &c. The main body should always be halted, in a good position beyond musket-shot, or where cover can be obtained, whilst a few men proceed cautiously forward, following at some distance in the rear of, but never losing sight of each other, to examine the suspected spot. If the officer deem it necessary, at any point, to detach from his command smaller patrols, to examine points at some distance on his flanks, he should halt the rest at the point where they separate, until the detachments come in and report; or if he decides to move forward, he should leave three or four men at the spot, to convey intelligence promptly to the rear, if anything is discovered, as well as to himself.

83. It may frequently be found that some eminence on the flanks may present a good view of the surrounding country, in which case, if it be decided to use it, two or three men ought to be detached for the purpose, with orders to keep in sight of each other, but far enough apart to guard against a surprise of the whole.

84. When the officer finds himself in the presence of the enemy, he should halt his command at a convenient spot, where they will be screened from the enemy's view,

and having made his dispositions against a surprise, he will proceed with a few picked men to the most favorable point from which he can obtain a good look-out, to reconnoitre the position occupied, and the other points of interest. If he deem it advisable to keep his position, or change it for some other point more favorable, he will first transmit a report to the rear of what he has observed.

85. When the patrol moves by night, the ordinary precautions must be redoubled. Signals must be agreed upon to avoid danger, should any of the party become separated from the main body. Careful attention must be given to every thing passing around, as the barking of dogs, noises, fires, &c. On approaching any inhabited spot, the command should be brought to a halt, whilst a few picked men move noiselessly forward, and if practicable, by stealing up to the windows, learn the character of the inmates.

86. It cannot be too strongly impressed upon the mind of the officer in command of a patrol, that he must be all ears and eyes; that he will be called upon in turn, to exercise great boldness, caution, presence of mind and good judgment, in accomplishing a mission where the enemy must be seen but not encountered; and such roads and halting points be selected, both in moving forward and returning, as shall be most favorable to his movements, and least liable to expose him to surprise, or a disadvantageous collision with the enemy.

SURPRISES AND AMBUSCADES.

87. These two classes of operations depend for their success upon the same point—that of being able to attack the enemy suddenly when he is not prepared to resist. The term *surprise* is applied to unexpected attacks upon an enemy's position; that of *ambuscade*, where a position is taken for the purpose of falling suddenly upon the enemy when he reaches it. Secrecy, good troops, and a thorough knowledge of the localities, are indispensable to the success of either of these operations.

SURPRISE.

88. In planning a surprise, the officer must spare no pains in ascertaining the fact of the country leading to, and in the immediate vicinity of the enemy's position, the character and disposition of his troops, and the state of preparation of the defenses of the position. Information may be obtained on the points from the spies, deserters, inhabitants of the locality occupied by the enemy, good maps, &c.

89. The troops to be employed in the expedition, as well as the other necessary arrangements, will depend upon the information gained on these points. If the position be an intrenched one, infantry will constitute the main force;

cavalry and artillery can be of little other use than to cover the retreat of the infantry, and to make prisoners of those who may escape from the position.— A body of engineer troops or of picked men used to handling tools, will accompany the infantry, carrying with them such implements as may be requisite from the character of the defenses, as axes, saws, crowbars, small scaling ladders, &c.

90. If the position be not intrenched, as an open village, &c., cavalry may perform a very important part, by a sudden dash among the enemy, in creating confusion and alarm.

91. As the success of the affair will greatly depend upon the secrecy with which these preparations are made, and the celerity with which it is conducted, all orders for collecting the necessary implements and assembling the troops, should be given at the shortest notice; no more troops should be taken than are indispensably necessary, and they should cary nothing with them but their arms, and the requisite amount of ammunition.

92. Midnight is the best hour for small bodies of troops to carry out such enterprise, as they must effect all they desire to do and be off before day break. A few hours before daylight is the best time for large expeditions, as the dawn of day will be favorable to their retreat by which time they will have been able to effect their purposes. The season of the year and the state of the weather should be taken advantage of. Winter and bad weather are most favorable, as the enemy's sentinels and out-posts will then, in all probability, be less on the alert, and more disposed to keep under such shelter as they can procure.

93. As our purpose may be divined by the enemy, measures should be taken against such a contingency. These will mainly consist in securing by detachments all defiles and roads by which our retreat might be cut off, and by designating a rallying point, on which our force will fall back, if repulsed, which should be strongly occupied by cavalry and artillery, if they constitute a part of the force.

94. In conducting the march, the troops will be kept well together; the greatest order and silence be observed. Instead of the ordinary precautions of an advanced-guard and flankers, reliance should rather be placed upon a few active and intelligent scouts, to gain timely notice of any movement on the part of the enemy.

95. Concerted attacks upon several points are good means of creating confusion and paralyzing the enemy's efforts, when they can be successfully carried out; but, as they may require some of the detachments to make considerable circuits to reach their points, much will depend upon chance as to their success. In such cases, some signal must be agreed upon, to let the detachments, already in position, know when those which are likeliest to reach theirs latest, are ready; but this may have the inconvenience of giving the alarm to the enemy. Rockets may be used for this purpose, and also to give notice to the troops to retire together.

96. The retreat after a successful issue, should be conducted with the same promptitude as the advance. Time must not be lost in waiting too long for all the detachments to come in at the rallying point, as the safety of the whole command might be compromised.

AMBUSCADE.

97. In planning an ambuscade, we should be well acquainted with the enemy's force, and the state of discipline shown by it. The position chosen for the attempt, must be favorable to the concealment of troops, and if practicable, it should be reached by night, every precaution being taken to insure secrecy. The best positions are those where the enemy is inclosed by a defile, or village and has not taken the proper precautions to secure himself from an attack. By seizing the outlets of the defile by infantry, in such cases, and making an impetuous charge of cavalry into it, the enemy may be completely routed.

98. Ambuscades may frequently be attempted with success in the affairs of the advanced and rear-guards, by pushing the enemy vigorously and then falling back, if he offers a strong resistance, so as to draw him upon a point where troops are posted in force to receive him.

99. To trace anything more than a mere outline, as a guide in operations of this kind, which depend upon so many fortuitous circumstances, would serve but little useful purpose. An active, intelligent officer, with an imagination fertile in the expedients of his profession, will seldom be at a loss as to his best course when the occasion offers; to one without these qualities, opportunities present themselves in vain.

REGULATIONS AS TO INSPECTIONS, PARADE, ETC., ETC.

PART SEVENTH.

FORM OF INSPECTION.

1. The inspection of troops, not less than a company, will generally be preceded by a review. The present example embraces a battalion.

2. The inspecting officer and the field and staff officers will be on foot. The battalion being in the order of battle the colonel will cause it to break into open column of companies, right in front. He will next order the ranks to be opened; when the color-rank and color-guard, under the direction of the adjutant, will take post ten paces in front, and the band ten paces in rear of the column. The colonel seeing the ranks aligned, will then command:

1. *Officers and Sergeants to the front of your Companies.*
2. MARCH.

3. The officers will form themselve in one rank, eight paces, and the non-commissioned officers in one rank, paces in advance, along the whole fronts of their r

tive companies, from right to left in the order of seniority; the pioneers and music of each company, in one rank, two paces behind the non-commissioned officers. The colonel will then command:

1. *Field and Staff to the front.* 2. MARCH.

4. The commissioned officers thus designated, will form themselves in one rank, on a line equal to the front of the column, six paces in front of the colors from righ to left in the order of seniority: and the non-commissioned staff, in a similar manner, two paces in rear of the preceding rank. The colonel seeing the movement executed, will take post on the right of the lieutenant colonel, and wait the approach of the inspecting officer. But such of the field officers as may be superior in rank to the inspector, will not take post in front of the battalion.

5. The inspector will commence in front. After inspecting the dress and general appearance of the field and commissioned staff under arms, the inspector, accompanied by these officers, will pass down the open column, looking at every rank in front and rear.

6. The colonel will now command. 1. *Order*—ARMS. 2. REST; when the inspector will proceed to make a minute inspection of the several ranks or divisions, commencing in front.

7. As the inspector approaches the non-commissioned staff, color-rank, the color-guard and the band, the adjutant will give the necessary orders for the inspection of arms, boxes and knapsacks. The colors will be planted firm in the ground to enable the color-bearers to display the contents of their knapsacks. The non-commissioned

staff may be dismissed as soon as inspected, but the color-rank and color-guard will remain until the colors are to be escorted to the place from which they were taken. As the inspector successively approaches the companies, the captains will command:

1. *Attention.* 2. *Company.* 3. *Inspection*—ARMS.

8. The inspecting officers will then go through the whole company, and minutely inspect the arms, accoutrements and dress of each soldier. After this is done the captain will command: *Open*—BOXES; when the ammunition and boxes will be examined. He will then command:

1. *Shoulder*—ARMS. 2. *Close-Order.* 3. MARCH. 4. *Order*—ARMS. 5. *Stack*—ARMS. 6. *To the rear open order.* 7. MARCH. 8. *Front rank, About*—FACE. 9. *Unsling Knapsacks.* 10. *Open Knapsacks.*

9. The sergeants will face inward at the second command, and close upon the centre at the 3rd, and at the 5th command stack their arms; at the 6th they will face outward, and at the 7th resume their position. When the ranks are closed, preparatory to *take arms*, the sergeants will also close upon the centre, and at the word, take their arms and resume their position.

10. The knapsacks will be placed at the feet of the men, the flaps from them, with the great coats on the flaps, and knapsacks leaning on the great coats. In this position the inspector will examine their contents or so many of them as he may think necessary, commencing with the non commissioned officers, the men standing at attention. When

the inspector has passed through the company, the captain will command: *Repack Knapsacks*, when each soldier will repack and buckle up his knapsack, leaving it on the ground, the number upwards turned from him, and then stand at rest. The captain will then command:

1. *Attention*. 2. *Company*. 3. *Sling Knapsacks*. 4. *Front rank*, ABOUT FACE. 5. *Close Order*. 6. MARCH. 7. *Take*—ARMS. 8. *Shoulder*—ARMS. 9. *Officers and Sergeants to your posts*. 10. MARCH.

11. At the work *sling* of the 3rd command, each soldier will take his knapsack, holding it by the inner straps, and stand erect; at the last word, he will replace it on his back. At the 10th command, the company will file off to their tents or quarters, except the company that is to re-escort the colors, which will await the further orders of the colonel.

FORMS OF PARADE.

12. The examples here given embrace a battalion of infantry. A single company will parade as if it were with the battalion.

I. DRESS PARADE.

13. At the hour appointed, on the signal of the adjutant the captains will march their companies to the parade-ground, where they take their positions in the order of battle. When the line is formed, the captain of the first company, on notice from the adjutant, steps one pace to the front and gives to his company the command: *Order*—ARMS; *Parade*—REST: which is repeated by each cap-

tain in succession to the left. The adjutant takes post two paces on the right of the line; the sergeant-major two paces on the left. The music will be formed in two ranks on the right of the adjutant. The senior officer present will take the command of the parade, and will take post at a suitable distance in front, opposite the centre, facing the line.

14. When the companies have ordered arms, the adjutant will order the music to *beat off*, when it will commence on the right, beat in front of the line to the left, and back to its place on the right. The adjutant will then step two paces to the front, face to the left, and command:

1. *Attention.* 2. *Battalion.* 3. *Shoulder*—ARMS. 4. *Prepare to open ranks.* 5. *To the rear open order.* 6. MARCH.

15. At the sixth command, the ranks will be opened, the commissioned officers (field and staff dismounting) will march to the front, field officers six paces, the company officers four paces, opposite to their position in line of battle, halt and dress. The adjutant seeing the ranks aligned, will command: FRONT, and march along the front to the centre, face to the right, and pass the line of company officers, eight or ten paces, face to the right about and command:

Present—ARMS.

16. Seeing this executed, he will face about to the commanding officer, salute and report, *"Sir, the parade is formed."* The adjutant will then, on intimation to that effect, take his station three paces on the left of the commanding officer, one pace retired, passing around his rear.

17. The commanding officer, having acknowledged the salute of the line by touching his hat, will, after the adjutant has taken his post, draw his sword and command:

1. *Battalion.* 2. *Shoulder*—ARMS,

and add such exercises as he may think proper, concluding with *Order*—ARMS. He will then return his sword, and direct the adjutant to receive the reports.

18. The adjutant will now pass around the right of the commanding officer, advance upon the line, halt midway between him and the line of company officers, and command:

1. *First Sergeants to the front and centre.* 2. MARCH.

19. At the first command, the first sergeants will *shoulder arms*, march two paces to the front, and face inward. At the second command, they will march to the centre, and halt. The adjutant will then order:

1. *Front*—FACE. 2. *Report.*

20. At the last word, each in succession, beginning on the right, will salute by bringing the left hand smartly across the breast to the right shoulder, and report the result of the roll-call previously made on the company parade. The adjutant then commands:

1. *First Sergeants, outward*—FACE. 2. *To your posts*—MARCH,

when they will resume their places and order arms. The adjutant will then face to the commanding officer, salute, report absent officers, and give the result of the first sergeants' reports. The commanding officer will then direct the orders to be read, when the adjutant will face about and announce:

ATTENTION TO ORDERS.

21. Having read the orders, the adjutant will face to the commanding officer, salute and report; when, on an intimation from the commander, he will face again to the line and announce:

PARADE IS DISMISSED.

22. All the officers will now return their swords, face inward, and close on the adjutant, he having taken position in their line, the field officers on the flanks. The adjutant commands:

1. *Front*—FACE. 2. *Forward*—MARCH.

When they will march forward, dressing on the centre, the music playing, and when within six paces of the commander, the adjutant will give the command: HALT. The officers will then salute the commanding officer by raising the hand to the cap, and there remain until he shall have communicated to them such instructions as he may have to give, or intimates that the ceremony is finished. As the officers disperse, the first sergeants will close the ranks of their respective companies, and march them off, the band continuing to play until the companies clear the regimental parade ground.

II. REVIEW.

23. Preparatory to a review, the adjutant will cause a camp-color to be placed 80 or 100 paces, or more, in front of, and opposite to, where the centre of the battalion will rest, where the reviewing officer is supposed to take his station; and although he may choose to quit that position, still the color is to be considered as the point to which all the movements and formations are relative. The adjutant will also cause points to be marked, at suitable distances, for the wheelings of the divisions, so that their right flanks, in marching past, shall only be about four paces from the camp-color, or position of the reviewing officer.

24. The battalion being formed in the order of battle at *shouldered arms*, the colonel will command:

1. *Battalion, prepare for review.* 2. *To the rear, open order.* 3. MARCH.

25. At the word *march*, the field and staff officers dismount, the company officers and the color-rank advance four paces in front of the first rank, and place themselves opposite to their respective places in the order of battle; the color-guard replace the color-rank; the staff officers place themselves, according to rank, three paces on the right of the rank of the company officers, and one pace from each other; the music takes post as at dress parade; the non-commissioned staff takes post one pace from each other, and three paces on the right of the front rank of the battalion.

26. When the ranks are aligned, the colonel will command: FRONT: and place himself eight paces, and the

lieutenant-colonel and major will place themselves two paces, in front of the rank of company officers, and opposite to their respective places in the order of battle, all facing to the front.

27. When the reviewing officer presents himself before the centre, and is fifty or sixty paces distant, the colonel will face about and command :

Present—ARMS ;

and resume his front. The men present arms, and the officers salute, so as to drop their swords with the last motion of the firelock. The non-commissioned staff salute by bringing the sword to a *poise*, the hilt resting on the breast, the blade in front of the face, inclining a little outwards. The music will play, and all the drums beat, according to the rank of the reviewing officer.*

28. The reviewing officer having halted and acknowledged the salute by touching or raising his cap or hat, the colonel will face about and command : *Shoulder*—ARMS ! when the men shoulder their pieces ; the officers and non-commissioned staff recover their swords with the last motion, and the colonel faces to the front.

29. The reviewing officer will then go towards the right, the whole remaining perfectly steady, without paying any further compliment, while he passes along the front of the battalion and proceeds around the left flank, and along

---

* If the reviewing officer be junior in rank to the commandant of the parade, no compliment will be paid to him, but he will be received with arms carried, and the officers will not salute as the column passes in review. The colors salute such persons only as from their rank, and by regulation, are entitled to that honor.

the rear of the file closers, to the right. While the reviewing officer is going round the battalion the band will play, and will cease when he has returned to the right flank.

30. When the reviewing officer turns off to place himself by the camp-color in front, the colonel will face the line and command:

1. *Close order.* 2. MARCH.

31. At the first command the field and company officers will face to the *right-about;* and at the second command, all persons, except the colonel, will resume their places in the order of battle; the field and staff officers mount.

32. The reviewing officer having taken his position near the camp-color, the colonel will command:

1. *By Company, right wheel.* 2. *Quick*—MARCH. 3. *Pass in review.* 4. *Column, forward.* 5. *Guide right.* 6. MARCH.

33. The battalion, in column of companies, right in front, will then in common time, and at *shoulder arms,* be put in motion; the colonel four paces in front of the captain of the leading company;. the lieutenant-colonel on a line with the leading company; the major on a line with the rear company; the adjutant on a line with the second company; the sergeant-major on a line with the company next preceeding the rear—each six paces from the flank (left) opposite to the reviewing officer; the staff officers in one rank, according to order of precedency, from the right, four paces in rear of the column; the music preceded by the principal musician, six paces befor the colonel,

the pioneers preceded by a corporal, four paces before the principal musician; and the quartermaster-sergeant two paces from the side opposite to the guides, and in line with the pioneers. The guides and soldiers will keep their heads steady to the front in passing in review.

34. The music will begin to play at the command to march, and after passing the reviewing officer, wheel to the left out of the column, and take a position opposite and facing him, and will continue to play until the rear of the column shall have passed him, when it will cease, and follow in the rear of the battalion.* The officers will salute the reviewing officer when they arrive within six paces of him, and recover their swords when six paces past him. All officers, in saluting, will cast their eyes towards the reviewing officer. The colonel, when he has saluted at the head of the battalion, will place himself near the reviewing officer, and will remain there until the rear has passed, when he will rejoin the battalion. The colors will salute the reviewing officer, if entitled to it, when within six paces to him, and be raised when they have passed by him an equal distance. The color-bearer will remain in ranks while passing and saluting.

35. The reviewing officer, or personage, will acknowledge the salute by raising or taking off his cap, or hat, when the commander of the troops salutes him; and also when the colors pass. The rest of the time, occupied by the passage of the troops, he will be covered.

36. When the column has passed the reviewing officer, the colonel will direct it to the ground it marched from,

---

* That is, unless the battalion is to pass in *quick time* also, in which case it will keep its position.

and command *Guide left*, in time for the guides to cover. The column having arrived on its ground, the colonel will command: 1. Column. 2. Halt; from it in order of battle, and cause the ranks to be opened as above directed. The review will terminate by the whole saluting as at the beginning.*

37. The colonel will afterward cause the troops to perform such exercises and manœuvres as the reviewing officer may direct.

38. A number of companies, less than a battalion, will be reviewed as a battalion, and a single company as if it were with the battalion. In the latter case the company may pass in column of platoons.

III. GUARD-MOUNTING.

39. At the first call for guard-mounting, the men warned for duty turn out on their company parades for inspection by the first sergeants. Each detachment, as it arrives, will, under the direction of the adjutant, take post on the left of the one that preceded it, in open order, arms shouldered and bayonets fixed; the supernumeraries five paces in the rear of the men of their respective companies;

---

* If, however, instructions have been given to march the troops past in *quick time* also, the column will, instead of changing the guide, halting the column, and wheeling it into line, as above directed, give the command: 1. *Quick time*. 2. March. In passing the reviewing officer again, no salute will be offered by either officers or men. As the column approaches, the music, having commenced playing at the command *march*, will place itsef in front of, and march off with the column, and continue to play until the battalion is halted on its original ground. The review will terminate in the same manner as above directed.

the first sergeants in rear of them. The sergeant-major will dress the ranks, count the files, verify the details, and when the guard is formed, report to the adjutant, and take post two paces on the left of the front rank.

40. The adjutant then commands: *Front*, when the officer of the guard takes post twelve paces in front of the centre, the sergeants in one rank, four paces in rear of the officers; and the corporals in one rank, four paces in rear of the sergeants—all facing to the front. The adjutant then assigns their places in the guard.

41. The adjutant then command:

1. *Officer and non-commissioned Officers.* 2. *About face.* 3. *Inspect your guards*—MARCH.

42. The non-commissioned officers then take their posts. The commander of the guards then commands:

1. *Order*—ARMS. 2. *Inspection*—ARMS.

and inspects his guard. When there is no commissioned officer on the guard, the adjutant will inspect it. During inspection the band will play.

43. The inspection ended, the officer of the guard takes post as though the guard were a company of a battalion in open order, under review; at the same time, also, the officers of the day will take post in front of the centre of guard; the old officer of the day three paces on the right of the new officer of the day, one pace retired. The adjutant will then command:

1. *Parade*—REST. 2. *Troop*—BEAT OFF.

when the music, beginning on the right, will beat down

the line in front of the officer of the guard to the left, and back to its place on the right, it will cease to play.

44. The adjutant will command:

1. *Attention.*   2. *Shoulder*—ARMS.   3. *Close Order.*—MARCH.

45. At the word "close order," the officer will face about; at "march," resume his post in line. The adjutant then commands: *Present*—ARMS: at which he will face to the new officer of the day, salute and report, *"Sir, the guard is formed."* The new officer of the day, after acknowledging the salute, will direct the adjutant to march the guard in review, or by flank to its post. But if the adjutant be senior to the officer of the day, he will report without saluting with the sword then, or when marching in review.

46. In review, the guard march past the officer of the day, according to the order of review, conducted by the adjutant, marching on the left of the first division; the sergeant-major on the left of the last division. When the column has passed the officer of the day, the officer of the guard marches it to its post, the adjutant and sergeant-major retiring. The music, which has wheeled out of the column and take post opposite the officer of the day, will cease, and the old officer of the day salute, and give the old or standing orders to the new officer of the day. The supernumeraries, at the same time, will be marched to their respective company parades and dismissed.

47. On the approach of the new guard, the officer of the old guard having his guard paraded, will command:— *Present*—ARMS. The new guard will march in quick

time, past the old guard, at *shoulder arms*, officers saluting, and take post four paces on its right, when, being aligned with it, its commander will order: *Present*—ARMS. The two officers will then approach each other and salute. They will then return to their respective guards, and command:

   1. *Shoulder*—ARMS. 2. *Order*—ARMS.

48. The officer of the new guard will now direct the detail for the advance guard to be formed and marched to its post, the list of the guard made and divided into three reliefs, and perform all the other duties incident to his post and necessary at this time to be done.

49. The first relief having been designated and ordered two paces to the front, the corporal of the new guard will take charge of it, and go to relieve the sentinels, accompanied by the corporal of the old guard, who will take command of the old sentinels, when the whole are relieved. The relief, with arms at a support, in two ranks, will march by a flank, conducted by the corporal on the side of the leading front rank man; and then men will be numbered alternately in the front and rear rank, the man on the right of the front rank being No. 1. Should an officer approach, the corporal will command: *Carry arms*, and resume the support arms when the officer is passed.

50. When the sentinel sees the relief approaching, he will halt and face to it, with his arms at a shoulder. At six paces the corporal will command: 1. *Relief*, 2. HALT; when the relief will halt and carry arms. The corporal will then add, "No. 1," or "No. 2," or "No. 3," according to the number of the post, *Arms*—PORT. The two

sentinels will, with arms at *port* then approach each other, when the old sentinel, under the correction of the corporal, will whisper the instructions to the new sentinel. This done, the two sentinels will shoulder arms, and the old sentinel will pass, in quick time, to his place in rear of the relief. The corporal will then command: 1. *Support—Arms*. 2. *Forward*. 3. MARCH. And the relief proceeds in the same manner until the whole are relieved.

51. The detachments and sentinels from the old guard having come in, it will be marched, at *shoulder arms*, along the front of the new guard, in quick time, the new guard standing at *presented arms*; officers saluting and the music of both guards beating, except at the out-posts.

52. On arriving at the regimental or garrison parade, the commander of the old guard will send the detachments composing it to their respective regiments or companies.

53. When the old guard has marched off fifty paces, the officer of the new guard will order his men to stack their arms, or place them in the arm-racks.

GUARDS AND SENTINELS.

54. Camp and garrison guards will be relieved every twenty-four hours. Sentinels will be relieved every two hours. The officers are to remain constantly at their guards, except while visiting the sentinels or necessarily engaged elsewhere on their proper duty. Neither officers nor soldiers are to take off their clothing or accoutrements while they are on guard. When a fire breaks out, or any alarm is raised in a garrison, all guards are to be immediately under arms. Sentinels will not take order or allow themselves to be relieved, except by an officer or non-

commissioned officer of their guard or party, the officer of the day, or the commanding officer. Sentinels will report every breach of orders or regulations they are entrusted to enforce. They must keep themselves on the alert, observing everything that takes place within sight and hearing of their post. They will carry their arms habitually at support or on either shoulder, but will never quit them. In wet weather they will secure arms. No sentinel will quit his post or hold conversation not necessary to the proper discharge of his duty.

55. Sentinels will be respected by all persons of whatever rank. They will present arms to general and field officers, to the officer of the day, and to the commanding officer of the post. To all other officers they will carry arms. The sentinel at any post of the guard, when he sees any body of troops, or an officer entitled to compliment, approach, must call *"Turn out the guard;* and announce who approaches. Guards do not turn out as a matter of compliment after sunset, but sentinels will, when officers in uniform approach, pay them proper attention, by facing to the proper front and standing steady at *shoulder arms.* This will be observed until the evening is so far advanced that the sentinels begin challenging.

CHALLENGING.

56. After *retreat* (or the hour appointed by the commanding officer) until broad daylight, a sentinel challenges every person who approaches him, taking at the same time the position of *arms port*. He will suffer no person to come nearer than within the reach of his bayont, until

the person has given the *countersign*. A sentinel in challenging, will call out: "*Who comes there?*" If answered—"*Friend, with the countersign,*" and he be instructed to pass persons with the countersign, he will reply—"*Advance, friend, with the countersign.*" If answered—"*Friends*" he will reply—"*Halt friends. Advance one with the countersign.*" If answered—"*Relief,*" "*Patrol,*" or "*Grand rounds,*" he will reply—"*Halt; advance sergeant (or corporal) with the countersign,*" and satisfy himself that the party is what it represents itself to be. If he have no authority to pass persons with the countersign, if the wrong countersign be given, or if the persons have not the countersign, he will cause them to stand, and call—"*Corporal of the guard.*"

GRAND ROUNDS.

57. The officer wishing to make the rounds, will take an escort of a non-commissioned officer and two men. When the rounds are challenged by a sentinel, the sergeant will answer—"*Grand rounds;*" and the sentinel will reply—"*Halt, grand rounds. Advance, sergeant with the countersign.*" Upon which the sergeant advances and gives the countersign. The sentinel will then cry—"*Advance rounds;* and stand at a shoulder till they have passed.

58. When the sentinel before the guard challenges, and is answered—"*Grand rounds,*" he will reply "*Halt, grand rounds. Turn out the guard, grand rounds.*" Upon which the guard will be drawn up at shouldered arms. The officer commanding the guard will then order a sergeant and two men to advance; when within ten paces, the sergeant

challenges. The sergeant of the grand rounds answers—
"*Grand rounds.*" The sergeant of the guard replies—
"*Advance, sergeant, with the countersign.*"

59. The sergeant of the rounds advances alone, gives the countersign, and returns to his round. The sergeant of the guard calls to his officer—"*The countersign is right*"; on which the officer of the guard calls—"*Advance rounds.*" The officer of the rounds then advances alone, the guard standing at shouldered arms. The officer of the rounds passes along the front of the guard to the officer, who keeps his post on the right, and gives him the *parole*. He then examines the guard, orders back his escort, and taking a new one, proceeds in the same manner to other guards.

ESCORTS OF HONOR.

60. The escort will be drawn up in line, the centre opposite to the place where the person to be escorted presents himself, with an interval between the wings to receive him and his retinue. On his appearance he will be received with the honors due to his rank. When he has taken his place in the line, the whole will be wheeled into platoons or companies, as the case may be, and take up the march. The same ceremony will be observed, and the same honors paid, on his leaving the escort.

61. When the position of the escort is at a considerable distance from the point where he is expected to be received, a double line of sentinels will be posted from that point to the escort, facing inward, and the sentinels will successively salute as he passes. An officer will be appointed to attend him, to bear such communications as he may have to make to the commander of the escort.

COLOR ESCORT.

62. When a battalion turns out under arms, and the color is wanted, a company, other than that of the color, will be put in march to receive and escort the color, in the following order, in quick time and without music: the drum-major and field music followed by the band; the escort in column by platoon, right in front, with arms shifted to the right shoulder, and the color-bearer between the platoons.

63. Arrived in front of the tent or quarters of the colonel, the escort will form into line, the field music and band on the right, and arms will be carried. The color-bearer, preceded by the first lieutenant, and followed by a sergeant of the escort, will then go to receive the color.

64. When the color-bearer shall come out, followed by the lieutenant and sergeant, he will halt before the entrance; the captain will cause the escort to *present arms*, and the drums will beat to the color for half a minute, when arms will be shouldered, and the escort will be broken into column by platoon. The color bearer will place himself between the platoons. The lieutenant and sergeant will resume their posts, and the escort will march back to the battalion to the sound of music, in quick time and in the same order as above.

65. Arrived at the distance of twenty paces from the battalion the escort will be halted, and the music will cease; the colonel will place himself six paces before the centre of the battalion, the color-bearer will approach the colonel, by the front, in quick time; when at the distance

of ten paces, he will halt; the colonel will cause arms to be presented, and *to the color* to be played, which being executed, the color-bearer will take his place in the front rank of the color-guard, and the battalion, by command, will shoulder arms. The escort, field music and band will return in quick time to their several places in the line of battle, marching by the rear of the battalion.

66. The color will be escorted back to the colonel's tent or quarters with like ceremony and in the same order.

FUNERAL HONORS.

67. The funeral escort will be formed in two ranks, opposite to the quarters or tent of the deceased, with shouldered arms and bayonets unfixed; the artillery and cavalry on the right of the infantry.* On the appearance of the corpse, the officer commanding the escort will command:

Present—ARMS.

68. When the honors due to the deceased will be paid by the drums and trumpets. The music will then play an appropriate air, and the coffin will be taken to the right, when it will be halted. The commander will then order:

1. *Shoulder*—ARMS. 2. *By company (or platoon) left wheel.* 3. MARCH. 4. *Reverse*—ARMS. 5. *Column, forward.* 6. *Guide right.* 7. MARCH.

69. The column will be marched in slow time to solemn

---

* The usual badge of military mourning is a piece of black crape around the left arm, above the elbow, and also upon the sword hilt, and will be worn when in full or undress uniform. The drums of a funeral escort will be covered with black crape, or thin black serge.

music, and on reaching the grave, will take a direction so as that the guides shall be next to the grave. When the centre of the column is opposite the grave, the commander will order:

1. *Column.* 2. HALT. 3. *Right into line wheel.* 4. MARCH.

70. The coffin is then brought along the front, to the opposite side of the grave, and the commander then orders:

1. *Shoulder.*—ARMS. 2. *Present*—ARMS.

71. And when the coffin reaches the grave, he adds:

3. *Shoulder*—ARMS. 4. *Rest on*—ARMS.

72. After the funeral service is performed, and the coffin is lowered into the grave, the commander will order:

1. *Attention.* 2. *Shoulder*—ARMS. 3. *Load at will.* 4. LOAD.

73. And cause three rounds of small arms to be fired by the escort. He will then command:

1. *By company (or platoon) right-wheel.* 2. MARCH. 3. *Column forward.* 4. *Guide left.* 5. *Quick*—MARCH.

74. The music will not begin to play until the escort is clear of the enclosure.

AMMUNITION.

Troops in the field should not only be supplied with a sufficient quantity of ammunition, but the men of the command should be taught how to prepare it. Cartridges for small arms are made of paper in the following manner: Having prepared the paper, which should be strong, but not too thick, by cutting it first into strips eight and a half inches wide, then cutting these strips crosswise to smaller strips four and a half inches in width, and then cutting these last diagonally, so that the pieces will be three inches on one side and five and a half on the other; the pieces are then rolled on a small cylindrical stick of the same diameter as the ball to be used, about six inches long, having a spherical cavity at one end and rounded at the other. The paper is laid on a table with the side perpendicular to the bases next the workman, the broad end to the left; the stick laid on it with the concave end half an inch from the broad edge of the paper, and enveloped in it once. The right hand is then laid flat on the stick, and all the paper rolled on it. The projecting end of the paper is now neatly folded down into the concavity of the stick, pasted, and pressed on a ball imbedded in the table for the purpose.

Instead of being pasted, these cylinders may be closed by choking with a string, tied to the table, and having at the other end a stick by which to hold it. The convex end of the *former* is placed to the left, and after the paper is rolled on, the *former* is taken in the left hand, and a turn made around it with the choking string half an inch from the end of the paper. Whilst the string is drawn tight with the right hand, the former is held in the left with the forfinger resting on the end of the cylinder, folding it neatly down upon the end of the former. The choke is then firmly tied with twine.

For ball cartridges, make the cylinders and choke them as above described, and the choke tied without cutting the twine. The former is then withdrawn, the ball put in, and the concave end of the former put in after it. The half hitches are made a little above the ball, and twine cut off.

For ball and buckshot cartridges, make the cylinder as before, insert three buckshot, fasten them with a half-hitch and insert and secure the ball as before.

For buckshot cartridges, make the cylinder as before, insert four tiers of three buckshot each, as at first, making a half hitch between the tiers, and ending with a double hitch.

To fill the cartridges, the cylinders are placed upright in a box, and the charge poured into each from a connical charger of the appropriate size; the mouths of the cylinders are now folded down on the powder by two rectangular folds, and the cartridges bundled in packages of ten. For this a folding box is necessary; it is made with two vertical sides at a distance from each other equal to five diameters of the ball, and two diameters high.

FORMS.

Form No. 1.
FORM OF FURLOUGH.
FURLOUGHS TO ENLISTED MEN.

Furloughs will be granted only by the commanding officer of the post or the commanding officer of the regiment actually quartered with it. Furloughs may be prohibited at the discretion of the officer in command.

Soldiers on furlough shall not take with them their arms or accoutrements.

Form of furlough:

TO ALL WHOM IT MAY CONCERN.

The bearer hereof, ———— ————, a Sergeant [corporal, or private, as the case may be] of Captain ———— ———— company — regiment of ————, aged — years, — feet, — inches high, ———— complexion, ———— eyes, ———— hair, and by profession a ————; born in the ———— of ————, and enlisted at ————, in the ———— of ————, on the — day of ———— eighteen hundred and ————, to serve for the period of ———— is hereby permitted to go to ———— in the county of ————State of ———— he having received a Furlough from the — day of ————, to the — day of ————, at which period he will rejoin his company or regiment at ————, or wherever it then may be, or be considered a deserter.

Subsistence has been furnished to said ———— ————, to the — day of ————, and pay to the — day of ————, both inclusive.

Given under my hand, at ————, this — day of ————, 18—,

Signature of the officer } \
giving the furlough } ———— ————

FORM NO. 2.—OFFICERS' PAY ACCOUNT.

The Confederate States to ——————.   Dr.

On what account	Commencement and expiration.		Term of service charged.		Pay per month.		Amount.		Remarks.
	From—	To—	M'nths	Days.	Dolls.	Cts.	Dolls.	Cts.	
Pay— For myself......									
For myself for —— y'rs service									
Forage— For horse......									

OFFICERS' PAY ACCOUNT.—Concluded.

I hereby certify that the foregoing account is accurate and just; that I have not been absent without leave during any part of the time charged for; that I have not received pay, forage, or received money in lieu of any part thereof, for any part of the time therein charged; that the horses were actually kept in service and were mustered for the whole of the time charged; that for the whole of the time charged for my staff appointment, I actually and legally held the appointment and did duty in the department; that I have been a commissioned officer for the number of years stated in the charge for every additional five years service; that I am not in arrears with the Confederate States, on any account whatsoever; and that the last payment I received was from ——, and to the —— day of ——, 186 .

I at the same time acknowledge that I have received of ——, this —— day of ——, 18 , the sum of — dollars, being the amount in full of said account.

[Signed Duplicate.]

, Pay..................
To — years service...
Forage..............
                        ——
Amount............ $

NO. 3.—SUBSISTENCE FORM.

Provision Return for Captain   , Company   , Regiment of   , for   days; commencing   , and ending   .

POST OR STATION.	No. of men.	No. women.	Total.	No. of days.	No. rations.	Fr. beef	Pork.	Flour.	Beans.	Rice.	Coffee.	Sugar.	Vinegar.	Candles	Soap.	Salt.	REMARKS.

RATIONS OF

—————, Commanding Company.

The A. C. S. will issue agreeably to the above return.

—————, Commanding Post.

NO. 4.—SPECIAL REQUISITION.

For

I certify that the above requisition is correct, and that the articles specified are absolutely requisite for the public service, rendered so by the following circumstances: [here the officer will insert such reasons as he may think fit to give, tending to show the necessity for the supplies.]

Captain J. B. Assistant Quartermaster Confederate States Army, will issue the articles specified in the above requisition.

C. D. *Commanding.*

Received at ...., the ..... of ...., 186 , of ...., Assistant Quartermaster Confederate States Army, [hereinsert the articles] in full of the above requisition.
(Signed duplicates.)

NOTE.—The cost of articles issued on special requisitions, and orders of commanding officers, will be entered on the requisition and on the list er invoice furnished the receiving officer.

APPENDIX.

1. The following movements are designed principally for the use of volunteer companies on public occasions, for parade and show, and when properly executed, greatly enhance the looks of a corps of citizen soldiery.

2. In the execution of these movements, the company is supposed to be in one rank, facing to the front; the captain then counts off the strength of the company from right to left, and divides them into four equal parts, termed "Sections." To execute movement No. 1., he will command:

1. *Break into column by sections.* 2. *By sections right wheel.* 3. MARCH.

(*Fig.* 1.)

_____

_____

....

_____

3. At the command *march*, the sections wheel as is pre-

scribed in company drill for *breaking into column by platoon*, being halted and dressed in the same manner, and each officer and non-commissioned officer taking the position prescribed for them, that is, the captain takes command of the first section, the first lieutenant the fourth, &c., and the first sergeant acting as guide of the first section, and the second of the fourth. At the command, *Forward*—March, they will step off promptly.

(*Fig. 2.*)

———— ————
———— ————
———— ————
———— ————

4. To execute Fig. 2., the company is supposed to be marching in the position of Fig. 1.; the captain will give the cautionary command, *Subdivision of sections*, at which each chief of sections will, with his sword, divide his sections in two parts, and at the command: 1. *Subdivisions of sections, right and left oblique*, 2. March, each subdivision will oblique two paces, the right going to the right and the left subdivision to the left, and when at that distance the captain will command: 1. *Forward*, 2. March. The captain may sometimes command: *Officers, centre*, when each chief will take his place in the interval formed in the centre of his section.

5. To cause the position of Fig. 1., to be resumed, the command will be. 1. *Subdivisions of sections, right and left*

oblique to place, 2. MARCH; at the command *march*, each subdivision will oblique to its place, and as soon as the connexion is made they will continue the march to the front without further command.

(*Fig.* 3)

———
———
———
———
———
———
———
———

6. Fig. 3. is formed by giving the command :

1. *Subdivisions of sections to rear.* 2. MARCH.

7. At the first command the guide of each section will go immediately to the right, if not already there, and at the command *march*, each left subdivision will mark time until each right subdivision gets about 3 paces in front, the left subdivisions will then oblique right until exactly behind and in a line with their right subdivisions when the command will be given 1. *Forward.* 2. MARCH.

8. To cause a resumption of Fig. 1, the command will be, 1. *Form sections.* 2. MARCH. At the command *march*,

the right subdivisions mark time until the left shall have obliqued left to their places, when the command will be given, *forward, march.*

(*Fig.* 4.)

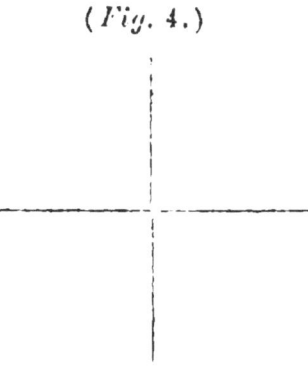

9. To form Fig. 4, the campany is supposed marching to the front in position of Fig. 1.; the captain will command :

1. *Form cross.* 2. MARCH.

10. At the first command the guide of each section will place himself promptly on the right, and at the command *march*, the first section will come by the *right flank, file left*, and mark time, forming the first wing of the cross: the second section will march straight to the front and form the left wing of the cross; the third will oblique to the right and connecting its left flank to the rearmost file of the first section, will form the right wing; the fourth will come by the *right flank, by file left*, and the front man of this section will connect himself with the rearmost man of the first, forming the fourth wing; the wole move- ent will be done simultaneously, and as soon as it is

executed the captain will command, 1. *Forward*, 2. MARCH; at which command the company will move off promptly.

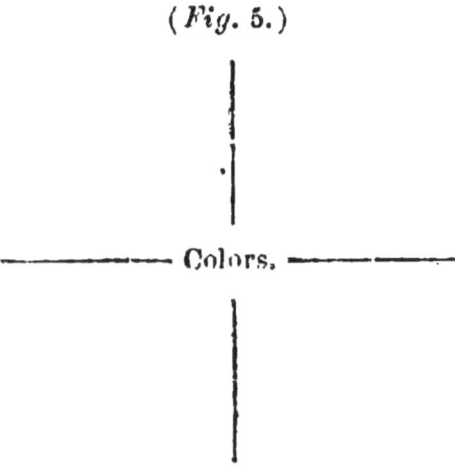

(*Fig.* 5.)

Colors.

11. The company marching in the position of Fig. 4., and the captain wishing it to execute the movement of Fig. 5, will command:

    1. *Open order by sections.* 2. MARCH.

12. At the command *march*, the fourth section will mark time until the first has gotten to the distance of four paces to the front, at the same time the second and third sections will oblique to the right each two paces, the captain will then command: 1. *Forward*, 2. MARCH, when the company will move off.

13. In both these movements the flag will take position in the centre of the cross.

14. The captain wishing to change the movement, will command: 1. *Close orders*, 2. MARCH: at the second com-

APPENDIX.   307

mand the first section will mark time and the others will close on it, assuming the position of Fig. 4. The command will then be given:

 1. *Form column by sections.*   2. MARCH.

15. At the command *march*, the men of the first section will form rapidly on the left of the front rank man in the manner prescribed in the movement, *by platoon in line*, the front rank man (who is the first sergeant), marching straight to the front; the second section continues to march straight to the front at its proper distance; the third obliquing to its place in rear of the second and the fourth, going through the movement prescribed for the first; the company will then be in the position of Fig. 1.

(*Fig.* 6.)

16. The company marching in the position of Fig. 1, the captain wishing to cause it to assume the position of Fig. 6, will command:

 1. *Form square.*   2. MARCH.

17. At the command *march*, the first and fourth sections will mark time, the second will come *by the right flank, by*

file left, and form the right side of the cross, the third will come *by the left flank, file right,* and form the left wing of the cross; as soon as executed the captain will command: 1. *Forward*, 2. MARCH, at which command the company will step off.

18. To execute this movement well, it is exceedingly necessary that it be done all together; the captain should dwell sometime between the command of *caution* and that of *execution*, to enable the men to think how the movement is to be executed.

19. The captain may add to this command by halting the company, and putting them through the different firings, to do this he will command:

1. *Company.* 2. HALT.

20. At the second command the company will halt promptly, closing up any interval that may have been made; the captain will then command: *Outward face,* at which the 2nd, 3rd and 4th sections will face outwards, they will then be put through the firings as the captain may see proper; when he wishes them to march forward again he will cause them to *cease firing,* and command:— 1. *To first position.* 2. FACE. At this command they will face promptly to their places.

21. To cause them to resume their position of Fig. 1, the captain will command:

1. *Form sections.* 2. MARCH.

22. At the command *march,* the first section will continue to march straight forward, the second section, which is the right side of of the square, will form promptly on its

right guide and follow in the rear of the first; the third will form in like manner, and the fourth will march straight forward; but marking time a little at first, to allow the second and third to finish the execution of their movement.

(*Fig.* 7.)

23. The company marching in the position of Fig. 1, and the captain wishing it to assume the position of Fig. 7, he will command:

1. *Echelon by sections to the right.* 2. MARCH.

24. At the command *march*, the first section will continue to march straight forward, the 2nd, 3rd and 4th, will commence obliquing to the right, and as soon as the left file of the second section is in a line with the right file of the first, the chief of the section will command: *Forward March*; as soon as the left file of the third has gotten in line with the right file of the second, the same command will be given; the same thing is applicable to the fourth section.

25. This movement may be varied by commanding *Echelon, to the left—March*, which will be done in the same manner, except in this case the sections oblique to the left.

26. To cause the position of Fig. 1, to be resumed, the captain will command:

    1. *Form column.* 2. MARCH..

27. At the command *march*, the sections will oblique to their places, keeping the regular distances from each other.

    (Fig. 8.)

28. The company marching in the position of Fig. 1, and the captain wishing it to assuume that of Fig. 8, will command:

    1. *Echelon by sections, right and left.* 2. MARCH.

29. At the command *march*, the first section marches straight forward; the second obliques right until it gets into the position as indicated in Fig. 7.; the third obliques left in the same manner, the fourth continuing to march forward. The second and third must be exactly opposite each other.

30. To cause the position of Fig. 1 to be resumed, the command will be: 1. *Form column.*—2. MARCH, at which the sections oblique to their proper places.

(*Fig.* 9.)

31. To assume the position of Fig. 9, the company is supposed to be marching in the position of Fig. 3, when the captain will command:

1. *Echelon by subdivision of sections to the right (or left)*
2. MARCH.

32. At the command *march*, each subdivision will oblique right (or left) as has been indicated in No. 24, Fig. 7, except that as soon as the left flank man of each subdivision is in line and covers the right flank man of the preceding section, they will forward without further command.

33. To resume the position of Fig. 3, the captain will command:

1. *Form column by subdivision of sections.* 2. MARCH.

34. At the command *march*, each subdivision will oblique to its proper place, keeping the required distance from each other.

APPENDIX.

(*Fig.* 10.)

―――

――   ――

――   ――

――   ――

―――

35. The company being in march, in the position of Fig. 3, and the captain wishing it to assume the position of Fig. 10, will command:

1. *Echelon by subdivision of sections to front and rear.* 2. MARCH.

36. At the command *march*, the first subdivision will continue to march forward, the 2nd and 3rd will oblique to the right and left, and place themselves opposite each other, the 4th and 5th execute the same movement; the 6th and 7th oblique right and left until they get opposite each other and in an exact line with the 2nd and 3rd; the 8th continues to march forward, and the whole keeping the proper interval between them.

37. To resume the position of Fig. 3, the captain will command:

1. *Form column by subdivision of section.* 2. MARCH.

38. At the command *march*, the subdivisions will oblique right and left until they get in their proper positions.

APPENDIX. 313

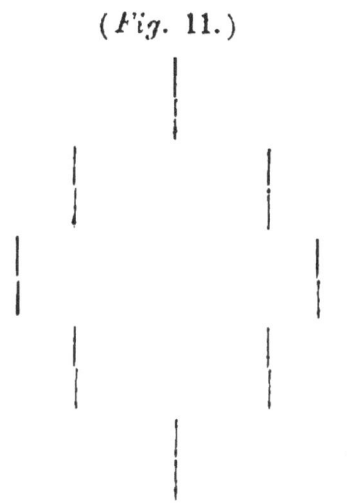

(*Fig. 11.*)

39. The company marching in the position of Fig. 10, and the captain wishing it to assume that of Fig. 11, will command:

1. *Subdivisions of sections.* 2. *By the right flank, file left.* 3. MARCH.

40. At the command *march*, each subdivision will promptly and simultaneously execute the movement of *flanking to the right and filing to the left.*

41. To resume the position of Fig. 10, the captain will command: *Subdivisions of sections, file right—March,* and as soon as they shall have filed, he will command:

1. *By the left flank.* 2. MARCH.

(*Fig.* 12.)

41. To execute the movement of Fig. 12, the company is supposed to be marching in the position of Fig. 3, when the captain will command:

1. *Echelon by subdivisions of sections, right and left.* 2. MARCH.

42. At the command *march*, the first subdivision of section continues to march forward, the second obliques right, the third left, the fourth right, the fifth left, and so on forming the movement as indicated in Fig. 12.

43. The captain wishing them to assume the position of Fig. 3, will command:

1. *Form column by subdivision of sections.* 2. MARCH.

44. At the command *march*, each subdivision will oblique right and left to its proper place, taking care not to lose the distance between them.

(Fig. 13.)

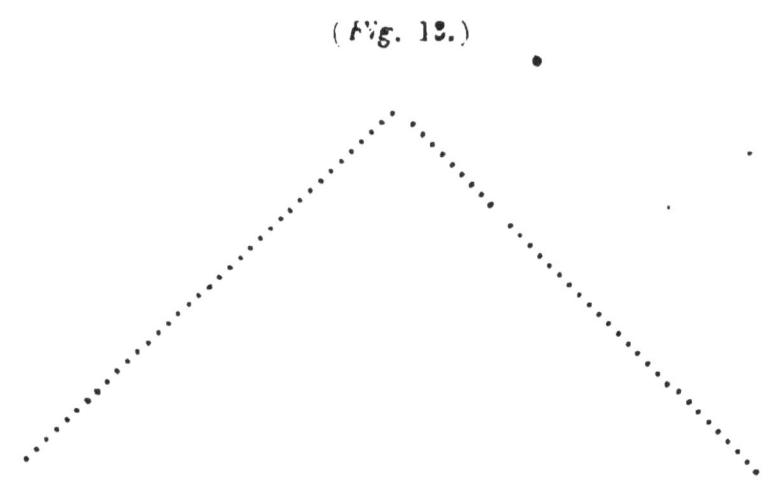

45. In the execution of Fig. 13, the company should be marching in one rank, (single file), and when the captain shall wish to cause the movement to be executed, he will command:

    1. *Echelon by file right and left.* 2. MARCH.

46. At the command *march*, the first sergeant continues to march forward, the man next in his rear will oblique to the right until his left shoulder is in a line and thirteen inches in rear of the sergeant's right shoulder; thus the movement will continue alternately from right to left, each man obliqueing in the opposite direction from the one in front of him. In the execution of this movement the first sergeant will shorten his steps to enable the men to execute it without confusion. Should the company be a large one, t movement had better be done in double quick time.

47. The captain may vary this movement by commanding: *Right about—March*, when in the position of Fig. 13. He may also put the company through the different firings in this position.

48. The captain may vary these movements as he sees proper.

49. He may also greatly add to the appearance of the company when marching by section, to give the cautionary command, *subdivisions of sections, right and left wheel*, and then command:

1. *First section, right and left wheel*. 2. MARCH,

at which command, each subdivision of section will begin wheeling, the right subdivision wheeling *right* and the left wheeling *left*, they will continue the wheel and go to the rear, passing to the right and left of the other three sections, who continue to march straight to the front; as soon as it has arrived to the rear, its chief will command: 1. *First section right and left wheel—March*; both subdivisions will wheel at the same time and form the section again, which will march on after the other three; the second will go through the same movement and by the same commands from its chief, as soon as it has arrived at section distance in front of the ground where the first section wheeled; the third and fourth will execute the same movement, thus keeping up a succession of wheels as the column moves on.

50. In the execution of Figures 4, 5, 6. 8, 10 and 11, the color-bearer takes his place in the centre.

Adjutant and Inspector-General's Office,
Richmond, Va., June 6, 1861.
General Orders, No. 9.]

UNIFORM AND DRESS OF THE ARMY.

TUNIC.

For Commissioned Officers.

1. All officers shall wear a tunic of gray cloth, known as cadet gray; the skirt to extend half-way between the hip and the knee; double breasted for all grades.

2. For a *Brigadier-General*—Two rows of buttons on the breast, eight in each row, placed in pairs; the distance between the rows four inches at top and three inches at bottom; stand up collar, to rise no higher than to permit the chin to turn freely over it; to hook in front at the bottom, and slope thence up and backward, at an angle of thirty degrees, on each side; cuffs two and a half inches deep on the under side, there to be buttoned with three small buttons, and sloped upwards to a point, at a distance of four inches from the end of the sleeves; pockets in the folds of the skirt, with one button at the hip and

one at the end of each pocket, making four buttons on the back and skirt of the tunic, the hip buttons to range with the lowest breast buttons.

3. For a *Colonel*—the same as for a Brigadier-General, except that there will be only seven buttons in each row on the breast, placed at equal distances.

4. For a *Lieutenant-Colonel, Major, Captain* and *Lieutenant*—the same as for a Colonel.

For Enlisted Men.

5. The uniform coat for enlisted men shall be a double breasted tunic of gray cloth, known as cadet gray, with the skirt exending half-way between the hip and the knee; two rows of buttons on the breast, seven in each row; the distance between the rows four inches at top and three inches at bottom : stand-up collar, to rise no higher than to permit the chin to turn freely over it ; to hook in front at the bottom, and slope thence backwards at an angle of thirty degrees on each side; cuffs too and a half inches deep at the under seam, to button with two small buttons, and to be slightly pointed on the upper part of the arm; pockets in the folds of the skirts. The collars and cuffs to be of the color prescribed for facings for the respective arms of service, and the edges of the tunic to be trimmed throughout with the same colored cloth. Narrow lining in the skirts of the tunic of gray material.

Facings.

6. The facings for General Officers, and for Officers of the Adjutant-General's Department, the Quartermaster-General's Department, the Commissary-General's Depart-

ment, and the Engineers—buff. The tunic for all officers to be edged throughout with the facings designated.

7. For the Medical department—black.
8. For the Artillery—red.
9. For the Cavalry—yellow.
10. For the Infantry—light blue.
11. For fatigue purposes, a light gray blouse, doubled breasted, with two rows of small buttons, seven in each row; small turn over collar—may be issued to the troops.
12. On all occasions of duty, except fatigue, and when out of quarters, the coat will be buttoned and hooked at the collar. Officers on bureau duty may wear the tunic open.

Buttons.

13. For General Officers and Officers of the General Staff—bright guilt, rounded at the edge, convex, raised eagle in the centre, with stars surrounding it; large size, one inch in exterior diameter; small size, half an inch.
14. For Officers of the Corps of Engineers, the same as for the General Staff, except that, in place of the eagle and stars, there will be a raised E in German text.
15. For Officers of Artillery, Infantry, Riflemen, and Cavalry—guilt, convex, plain, with large raised letter in the centre: A, for Artillery; I, for Infantry; R, for the Riflemen; C, for the Cavalry; large size, seven-eights of an inch in exterior diameter; small size half an inch.
16. Aids-de-Camp may wear the button of the General Staff, or of their regiments or corps, at their option.
17. For enlisted men of Artillery—yellow, convex, large raised letter A in the centre; three-quarters of an inch in exterior diameter.

18. For all other enlisted men, the same as for the Artillery, except that the number of the regiment, in large figures, will be subtsituted for the letter A.

Trowsers.

19. The uniform trowsers for both officers and enlisted men will be of cloth throughout the year; made loose, and to spread well over the foot; of light (or sky) blue color, for regimental officers and enlisted men; and of dark blue cloth for all other officers; reinforced for the cavalry.

20. For General Offiers—two stripes of gold lace on the outer seam, one-eighth of an inch apart, and each five-eighths of an inch in width.

21. For Officers of the Adjutant-General's Department, the Quartermaster-General's Department, the Commissary General's Department, and the Corps of Engineers—one stripe of gold lace on the outer seam, an inch and a quarter in width.

22. For the Medical Department—a black velvet stripe; one inch and a quarter in width, with a gold cord on each edge of the stripe.

23. For Regimental Officers—a stripe of cloth on the outer seam, one inch and a quarter in width; color according to corps; for Artillery, red; Cavalry, yellow; Infantry, dark blue.

24. For the non-commissioned staff of regiments and for all sergeants, a stripe of cotton webbing or braid on the outer seam, one and a quarter inch in width; color according to arm of service.

25. For all other enlisted men—plain.

Chapeau, or Cocked Hat.

26. A chapeau, or cocked hat, will be worn by General officers and officers of the General Staff and Corps of Engineers, of what is called the French patern; the model to be deposited in the office of the Quartermaster-General.

27. Forage cap for officers—a cap similar in form to that known as the French kepi, according to pattern to be deposited in the office of the Quartermaster-General.

28. Uniform cap—according to pattern to be deposited in the office of the Quartermaster-General,

Pompon.

29. For the Artillery—red.
30. For the Infantry—light blue.
31. For the Cavalry—yellow.

Cravat or Stock.

32. For all officers—black. When a cravat is worn, the tie not to be visible at the opening of the collar.

33. For enlisted men—black leather, according to pattern.

Boots.

34. For all officers—ankle or Jefferson.
35. For enlisted men of Cavalry—ankle and Jefferson, according to pattern.
36. For other enlisted men—Jefferson, according to pattern.

Spurs.

37. For all mounted officers—yellow metal or guilt.

38. For enlisted mounted men—yellow metal, according to pattern.

Gloves.

39. For General Officers, and officers of the General Staff Corps—buff or white.

40. For officers of Artillery, Infantry and Cavalry—white.

Sash.

41. For General Officers—buff silk net, with silk bullion fringe ends; sash to go twice round the waist, and to tie behind the left hip; pendent part not to extend more than eighteen inches below the tie.

42. For officers of the General Staff and Engineers, and of the Artillery and Infantry—red silk net. For officers of the Cavalry—yellow silk net. For medical officers—green silk net. All, with silk bullion fringe ends; to go around the waist, and to tie as for General Officers.

43. For sergeants—of worsted, with worsted bullion fringe ends; red for Artillery and Infantry, and yellow for Cavalry. To go twice around the waist, and to tie as above specified.

Sword Belt.

44. For all officers—a waist belt, not less than one and one-half inches, not more than two inches wide; to be worn over the sash; the sword to be suspended from it by slings of the same material as the belt, with a hook attached to the belt upon which the sword may be hung.

45. For General Officers—Russian leather, with three stripes of gold embroidery; the slings embroidered on both sides.

46. For all other officers—black leather, plain.

47. For all non-commissioned officers—black leather, plain.

Sword Belt Plate.

48. For all officers and enlisted men—gilt, rectangular; two inches wide, with a raised bright rim ; a silver wreath of laurel encircling the "arms of the Confederate States."

Sword and Scabbard.

49. For all officers—according to patterns to be deposited in the Ordinance Bureau.

Sword Knot.

50. For all officers—of plaited leather, with tassels.

Badges to distinguish Rank.

51. On the sleeve of the tunic, rank will be distinguished by an ornament of gold braid, (in form as represented in the drawing deposited in the Quartermaster-General's office,) extending around the seam of the cuff, and up the outside of the arm to the bend of the elbow. To be of one braid for lieutenants; two, for captains; three for field officers; and four, for general officers. The braid to be one-eighth of an inch in width.

52. On the front part of the collar of the tunic, the rank of the officer will be distinguished, as follows :

53. *General Officers*—A wreath with three stars enclosed, embroidered in gold. The edge of the wreath to be three-fourths of an inch from the front edge of the collar ; the stars to be arranged horizontally ; the centre one to be one and one-fourth inches in exterior diameter, and the others three-fourths of an inch.

54. *Colonel*—Three stars, embroidered in gold, arranged horizontally, and dividing equally the vertical space of the collar. Each star to be one and one-fourth inches in exterior diameter; the front star to be three-fourths of an inch from the edge of the collar.

55. *Lieutenant-Colonel*—Two stars of same material, size and arrangement, as for a colonel.

56. *Major*—One star, of same material and size as for a colonel; to be placed three-fourths of an inch from edge of collar, and dividing equally the vertical space.

57. *Captain*—Three horizontal bars, embroidered in gold; each one-half inch in width; the upper bar to be three inches in length; the front edge of the bars to incline to correspond with the angle of the collar, and to be three-fourths of an inch from the edge; the line of the back edges to be vertical.

58. *First-Lieutenant*—Two horizontal bars of the same material and size as for captains, and dividing equally the vertical space of collar.

59. *Second-Lieutenant*—One horizontal bar of the same material and size as for the centre bar of captain, and dividing equally the vertical space of collar.

Overcoats for enlisted Men.

60. For mounted men—of cadet gray cloth; stand-up collar; double breasted; cape to reach to the cuff of the coat, when the arm is extended, and to button all the way up, (buttons, eighteen.)

61. For footman—of cadet gray cloth; stand-up collar; double breasted; cape to reach to the elbows, when the arm is extended, and to button all the way up, (buttons,

eighteen.) For the present to be a talma, with sleeves, of water-proof material; black.

Chevrons.

62. The rank of non-commissioned officers will be marked by chevrons on both sleeves of the uniform tunic and the overcoat, above the elbow, of silk or worsted binding, half an inch wide; color the same as the edging of the tunic; points down, as follows:

63. For a *Sergeant-Major*—three bars and an arc in silk.

64. For a *Quartermaster-Sergeant*—three bars and a tie in silk

65. For an *Ordnance-Sergeant*—three bars and a star in silk.

66. For a *First* (or *Orderly*) *Sergeant*—three bars and a lozenge in worsted.

67. For a *Sergeant*—three bars in worsted.

68. For a *Corporal*—two bars in worsted.

Hair and Beard.

69. The hair to be short; the beard to be worn at the pleasure of the individual; but, when worn, to be kept short and neatly trimmed.

BY COMMAND OF THE SECRETARY OF WAR:

S. COOPER,
Adjutant and Inspector-General.

TABLE OF CONTENTS.

	PAGE.
INTRODUCTION	ix

PART FIRST.

Position of the Soldier	1
Facings	3
The Direct Step	4
The Quick Step	5
The Double Quick Step	5
The Run	7
Alignments	7
To March to the Front	9
To Mark Time	11
To Change Step	11
To March by the Flank	13
Wheelings	16
Wheeling from a Halt, or on a Fixed Pivot	16
Wheeling in Marching or on a Moveable Pivot	18
Turning	19
Manual of Arms for Heavy Infantry	20
Principles of Shoulder Arms	21
Position of Order Arms	23
To Ground Arms	32
Inspection of Arms	36

	PAGE
Loading and Firing	38
Load in Four Times	41
Load at Will	42
The Firings	45
The Oblique Fire	46
Position of Ranks in the Oblique Fire to Right	46
" " " " " " " Left	47
To Fire by File	47
To Fire by Flank	48

PART SECOND.—THE COMPANY.

Formation of Company	64
To Open Ranks	66
Alignment in Open Ranks	67
Manual of Arms	67
To Fire by Rear Rank	69
To Advance in Line of Battle	70
To March in Retreat	71
Oblique March in Line of Battle	72
To March by Flank	73
To Change Direction by File	75
Movements in Column	78
Post of Officers in Column	83
To March in Column	84
To Change Direction	85
To Halt the Column, and to form to the right (or left) into line either at a Halt or on the March	87
To Break the Company into Platoons	91
To Re-form the Company	92
Being in Column, to Break Files to the Rear, and to	

TABLE OF CONTENTS.   III

	PAGE.
cause them to Re-enter into Line	93
The Column in Route	95
Countermarch	98
Formation of Company from Two Ranks into Single Rank, and Reciprocally	103
Formation of a Company from Two Ranks into Four, and Reciprocally, at a Halt and in March	103

PART THIRD.

Manual of Arms for Riflemen or Light Infantry	107
The Position of Order Arms	110
To Stack Arms	123
To Resume Arms	124
Formation of a Regiment in Line of Battle or in Line	124
Position of Field Officers and Regimental Staff	126
Posts of Field Music and Band	127
Color Guard	127
General Guides	128

PART FOURTH.

Instruction for Skirmishers	129
Deployments	132
Bayonet Exercise	169
Position of the Guard	170
Develop and Volts	171
Develop	172
Combinations of the Movements	174
Parries and Thrusts	176
Guard against Infantry	179

	PAGE:
Guard against Cavalry	180
Manual of Sword or Sabre for Officers	182
Manual for Relieving Sentinels	183
Color Salute	182
Instruction for Chief Bugler	184
General Calls	185
Calls for Skirmishers	186

PART FIFTH.—FIELD FORTIFICATION.

Nomenclature and General Principles of Field Fortification	187
Manner of Throwing up a Work	193
Distribution of the Working Party	194
Revetments	196
Obstacles	201
Inundations	205
Mines	207
The Outlines of Field Works	208
Powder Magazines	216
Lines	223
Lines with Intervals or Broken Lines	226
Defence of Field Works	227
Loopholing Walls	230
Fortifying Houses	231
Intrenching a Village	235
Attack on Field Works	236
Attacking Houses	238
" Barricades	236

PART SIXTH.—OUTPOST AND PICKET DUTY.

	PAGE.
Instructions for Picket Duty	240
Advanced Posts	243
Out Posts	246
Sentinels	247
Grand Guards	247
Pickets	248
Strength of the Advance Posts	249
Duties of Officer Commanding Out Posts	251
Advanced Guards	254
Reconnoissances	255
Duties of Reconnoitering Officer	256
Guides	259
Reconnoissance	262
Armed Reconnoissance	262
Patrols	233
Duties of Officer in Command of Patrol	265

SURPRISES AND AMBUSCADES.

Surprise	268
Ambuscade	271

REGULATIONS AS TO INSPECTIONS, PARADE, &c.

Form of Inspection	272
Forms of Parade	275
Dress Parade	275
Review	279
Guard Mounting	283
Guides and Sentinels	287

	PAGE.
Challenging	288
Grand Rounds	289
Escort of Honor	290
Color Escort	291
Funeral Honors	292

AMMUNITION.

Preparation of Ammunition	294

FORMS.

Form of Furlough	297
Officers' Pay Account	298
Subsistence Form	300
Requisition Form	301

APPENDIX.

The Movements of Volunteer Corps for Public Occacasions	302—316

UNIFORM AND DRESS OF THE ARMY.

For Commissioned Officers, &c.	317—324

ERRATA.

By neglect of the Proof-reader several mistakes have occurred in *numbering the pages* of the foregoing work. The errors, however, are confined to the figures on the upper corners of the pages. The text is in its proper order and the whole number of pages contained in the work is correctly given in the concluding pages. In other respects it is believed the work is generally accurate.

www.ingramcontent.com/pod-product-compliance
Lightning Source LLC
Chambersburg PA
CBHW021159230426
43667CB00006B/464